Resource Radicals

Radical Américas

A series edited by Bruno Bosteels
and George Ciccariello-Maher

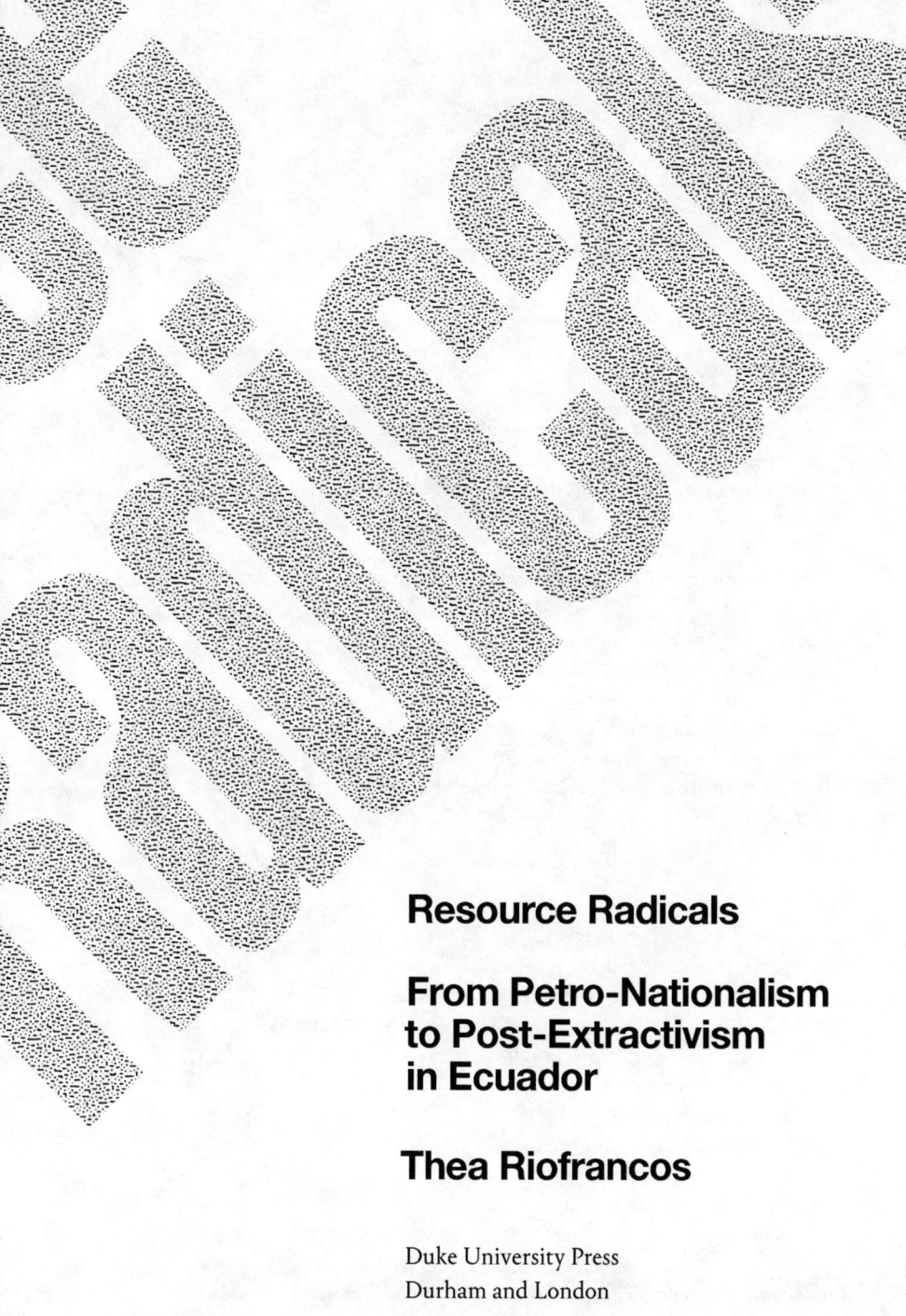

Resource Radicals

From Petro-Nationalism to Post-Extractivism in Ecuador

Thea Riofrancos

Duke University Press
Durham and London
2020

Printed in the United States of America on acid-free paper ∞
Designed by Drew Sisk
Typeset in Portrait Text and Helvetica Neue by Westchester
Publishing Services.

Library of Congress Cataloging-in-Publication Data

Names: Riofrancos, Thea N., author.
Title: Resource radicals : from petro-nationalism to post-extractivism
    in Ecuador / Thea Riofrancos.
Other titles: Radical Américas.
Description: Durham : Duke University Press, 2020. | Series:
    Radical Américas | Includes bibliographical references and
    index.
Identifiers: LCCN 2019046729 (print)
LCCN 2019046730 (ebook)
ISBN 9781478007968 (hardcover)
ISBN 9781478008484 (paperback)
ISBN 9781478012122 (ebook)
Subjects: LCSH: Mineral industries—Political aspects—Ecuador. |
    Mineral industries—Government policy—Ecuador. | Economic
    development—Environmental aspects—Ecuador. | Natural
    resources—Political aspects—Ecuador. | Energy policy—Ecuador. |
    Environmental policy—Ecuador.
Classification: LCC HD9506.E22 R56 2020 (print) | LCC HD9506.E22
    (ebook) | DDC 333.809866—dc23
LC record available at https://lccn.loc.gov/2019046729
LC ebook record available at https://lccn.loc.gov/2019046730

Cover art: Elisa Levy, *El agua baila en la Wiphala*, 2012. Courtesy of
the artist.

CONTENTS

ACKNOWLEDGMENTS

This book began before I knew it would be a book, before I knew I would be admitted into a PhD program, and before I knew I was conducting what would in hindsight constitute the preliminary fieldwork for my dissertation. It was born in late 2007 with a decision that was equal parts spontaneous and deliberate to move to Ecuador with Daniel Denvir, my partner and co-adventurer then and since. We were drawn by the country's natural landscapes, rebellious uprisings, and by what we understood was the beginning of a momentous political transformation: after decades of social mobilization, the country's first democratically elected leftist president had been inaugurated, and had promised a constituent assembly to rewrite the constitution, an end to the long night of neoliberalism, and sovereignty from US hegemony. Over the three years prior to this decision, Daniel and I had been active in PCASC, a Portland-based Latin American solidarity organization, and had lived and traveled elsewhere in the region where the Left had already come to power. We knew that the Left's electoral ascent was marked by both heady optimism and fraught relationships with the wide array of movements that had long struggled for social justice and popular power. We wanted to see how this process would unfold in Ecuador. Right away, we learned that resource extraction and indigenous rights would form the intertwined sites of contestation between the leftist government and the social movements that were still, at that moment but not for much longer, its allies. I knew that these two issues had long been central to radical politics in the region, but had never before witnessed a Left so internally riven by disagreements over the model of development, the relationship between society and nature, and the territorial self-determination of indigenous nations and peoples. It was an immersive educational experience, and I found myself challenged by political questions I had never thought to pose. It was in this moment that this book was born.

As is already apparent from this brief autobiographical narrative, I am in no sense the sole author of the pages that follow. My arguments and observations were articulated in constant conversation with Daniel and with the many people we met and formed long relationships with in Ecuador. They drew on a prior set of analyses developed in my undergraduate thesis on social movements and economic policy in Bolivia, written under the guidance of my adviser Casiano Hacker-Cordón at Reed College. I am forever indebted to Casiano's intellectual mentorship. He encouraged me to unsettle the boundaries between academic subfields and disciplines, and between political commitments and scholarly research. His criticism—of my work and of the world— was always equal parts ruthless and generous; I aspire to emulate his example in my relationships with my own students.

From before I even officially matriculated at the University of Pennsylvania, Tulia Falleti was a constant source of support, encouragement, and intellectual rigor. She was a model of a dissertation adviser: with the knowledge that an ethnographic study of conflict over mining in Ecuador represented a triply marginalized topic in the discipline (on methodological, substantive topic, and case selection grounds), she simultaneously pushed me to articulate my ideas in terms intelligible to other scholars, believed that I could do it, and valued my work as a necessary challenge to hegemonic approaches in political science. She read and carefully commented on every chapter of my dissertation more than once. She also taught me how to structure my writing on a demanding but achievable timeline, and how to graciously receive critique while always giving me the space to push back against her own authority. And she inspired my interest in the fundamental territoriality of politics and in the myriad institutional arrangements for linking geographic scale and democratic governance.

The other members of my dissertation committee also went beyond the call of duty. Anne Norton helped me draw out the deeper questions at stake in my work: What is a community, and what practices and identities bind it together or tear it apart? What is the content of sovereignty? How do the seemingly neutral realms of the law and science become politicized? What are the complex subjectivities and temporalities at play in a fight against an extractive sector still in its early stages? Who speaks for the land, the water, and the resources we hold in common? I still wrestle with these questions, and to the extent that this book sketches the outlines of how one might answer them, I am indebted to her. Robert Vitalis taught me to distrust just about everything already written on resource politics and the rentier state, to dispense with prepackaged concepts, to listen to the actors on the ground, and to trace the history that emerged from my encounters with people, events, and archives. He encouraged me to search out the fissures within the state and to pay close attention to the everyday practices of bureaucracy. And he always brought his expansive insight on oil politics in the Middle East to bear on my research in Ecuador, helping me specify both what was shared across contexts and what was unique to my fieldwork sites. From Erica Simmons, I learned both how to work against the grain of political science and still participate in and enrich the debates within the field. Her work on social movements and the politics of subsistence broadened my conceptual horizons: disputes over the management or ownership of natural resources are always disputes over the meanings we ascribe to them, and the contested ways that political communities are built through and around extraction, production, and consumption.

In addition to my committee, I want to note the support and intellectual influence of other members of the department, especially Jeffrey Green, Ian Lustick, Julia Lynch, Rudra Sil, and Rogers Smith. And lastly, outside political science, my fieldwork experience, dissertation, and book benefited immeasurably from the courses I took and the mentorship I received from Asif Agha, professor of linguistic anthropology and social theory polymath. It is not an overstatement to say that Asif taught me how language works, how—through the words we speak, write, and read—we reflexively constitute social life, linking, in webs of interaction, a casual conversation to the assembly of macropolitical orders. My analysis of *extractivismo* discourse is unthinkable without the lessons I learned in his seminars.

Throughout graduate school, I participated in intellectual communities both on and off campus, and made what would be deep and lasting friendships. I survived intimidating seminars, impossible reading loads, comprehensive exams, dissertation proposals, and fieldwork with the companionship of Begüm Adalet, Osman Balkan, Laura Finch, Kathryn Hardy, Ian Hartshorn, Adam Leeds, Shy Oakes, and, from a distance, Isabel Gabel. I would never, ever have written a dissertation without the camaraderie of my writing crew (Adam, Laura, Kathryn, and Shy). These four and many more were also involved in a rotating series of off-campus social theory reading groups, held in the living rooms and finished late in the night on the front porches of West Philly, and which included undergrads, grad students, and unaffiliated scholars. They are the closest thing I have experienced to something like a salon, unencumbered by the sometimes stifling norms of the classroom.

My year and a half of fieldwork was enabled by yet another community of generous individuals and groups. I am grateful for the institutional home FLACSO provided (coordinated by Santiago Basabe), and for the opportunity to present my research and work with graduate students. I appreciate the many conversations I had with Veronica Albuja, Abel Arpi, Juan Auz, Chela Calle, Kléver Calle, David Chavez, Paúl Cisneros, Luis Corral, Pablo Iturralde, Carlos Larrea, Patricio Matute, Nayana Román, and William Sacher—several of whom also invited me into their political and intellectual worlds, resulting in bonds of friendship and solidarity that I hope this book reflects and honors. I also benefited from the fieldwork companionship of Nicholas Limerick, Taylor Nelms, and Karolien van Teijlingen, as well as that of Elisa Levy and Sander Otten, with whom I experienced the 2012 march and 2011 *consulta*, respectively, and who were generous enough to give me permission to use their photographs of these processes. My life in Ecuador was enriched tremendously by Robin Fink, with whom I shared an apartment and many formative life experiences. And, finally, Marcelo Torres (Lino): dear friend, confidante, and wise beyond his years. Together we explored the many marvelous worlds of Quito and beyond—both more deeply understanding and transforming ourselves in the process.

The chapters that comprise this book went through countless revisions and reframings. My first attempts to think through converting my dissertation to a book occurred during my year as a Visiting Fellow at the Kellogg Institute of Notre Dame. Robert Fishman, Evan Harris, Sandra Ley Gutiérrez, Jamie Loxton, Ann Mische, and Antina von Schnitzler all provided invaluable feedback on the project as it developed. Over the past few years, Santiago Anria, Hannah Appel, Osman Balkan, Alyssa Battistoni, Guzman Castro, Daniel Aldana Cohen, Daniel Denvir, Gabriel Fonseca, Janice Gallagher, Kathryn Hardy, Evan Harris, Adam Leeds, Ian Hartshorn, Jeffrey Isaac, Joshua Simon, Dawn Teele, and Sarah Thomas all read drafts of one or more chapters, and provided rigorous commentary. Of all of these, Adam Leeds read the most drafts. I am deeply indebted to him, not only for his editorial genius, but for our decade-long close friendship, stimulating conversations, and shared intellectual development; it is hard to imagine writing this book without all I have learned from—and with—him. From book prospectus to final manuscript and all the late-night anxious queries in between, George Ciccariello-Maher has been much more than a series editor: a wise mentor and a dear friend, he believed in my work and in its relevance to the vibrant field of radical politics in the Americas. Courtney Berger was an exemplary editor, providing patient and constructive guidance throughout the entire process. And I benefited from the feedback of two anonymous reviewers, whose comments pushed me to broaden the manuscript's analytic scope and zoom out to the dilemmas marking the Pink Tide writ large.

In Providence, I have had the fortune of the friendship and near constant companionship of Sarah Thomas. At Providence College, I have had the unusual luck of an extremely supportive and convivial department. In particular, I would like to thank Chairs Bill Hudson and Joseph Cammarano for doing all in their power to give me time to devote to research and writing, the college's

CAFR grant for funding follow-up fieldwork and archival research, and two indispensable research assistants, Christian Balasco and Taylor Gibson.

I want to acknowledge Alyssa Battistoni and Daniel Aldana Cohen again, for helping me draw the connections between conflict over extraction in Ecuador, and the urgent and intertwined challenges of climate change and socio-economic inequality. Both pushed me to elucidate the planetary stakes of local struggles over oil and mining, and have encouraged me to intervene in debates well beyond the confines of academia.

I now return to where I started these acknowledgments. Daniel Denvir, you are the love of my life, a bedrock of support, and a constant inspiration. I can only aspire to match your discipline and your unwavering commitment to justice. You have accompanied me, whether physically or in spirit, on every single moment of the journey along which this book was conceived, written, rewritten, and submitted.

And, finally: Maro Riofrancos and Joyce Ilson—critical thinkers, nonconformers, and loving parents—you always encouraged me to take risks and question authority in all its forms, read to me and taught me to love reading, and opened my eyes to the joys of travel, the value of curiosity, and the beauty of New York City in its infinite diversity. Thank you.

Earlier versions of portions of Chapters 1 and 2 appeared, in a different form, in *Cultural Studies*, while an earlier version of Chapter 4 appeared in *Perspectives on Politics*. Sections of the Conclusion contain revised text and ideas that were first published in essays in *Dissent*, *n+1*, and *Jacobin* magazines.

Resource Radicalisms

To legitimate a supposed image of the left, the government uses a discourse that makes it appear radical, but it is a double discourse . . . The rights of nature and indigenous territories are recognized in name only, the extractivist model that the government advocates contradicts them and brutally attacks them . . . But the other reality is that of the [indigenous] peoples, the social movements and organizations that today resist this model, just as yesterday we resisted neoliberalism.
　　—"The Manifesto of the Meeting of Social Movements for
　　　Democracy and Life," Quito, 2011

It is madness to say no to natural resources, which is what part of the left is proposing—no to oil, no to mining, no to gas, no to hydroelectric power, no to roads. This is an absurd novelty, but it's as if it has become a fundamental part of left discourse. It is all the more dangerous for coming from people who supposedly speak the same language. With so many restrictions, the left will not be able to offer any viable political projects . . . We cannot lose sight of the fact that the main objective of a country such as Ecuador is to eliminate poverty. And for that we need our natural resources.
　　—Rafael Correa, "Ecuador's Path," 2012

In 2011, the fourth year of the administration of Ecuadorian leftist president Rafael Correa, more than a hundred social movement organizations and leftist political parties gathered for the "Meeting of Social Movements for Democracy and Life." According to the manifesto written at this meeting, these organizations and parties were rooted in diverse experiences of social mobilization, including anti-mining, environmentalist, public transit worker, feminist, and sexual diversity struggles, and "the indigenous and peasant uprising for water and land."[1] They condemned Correa's government for "represent[ing] an authoritarian and corrupt model of capitalist modernization."

Popular movements had rebuked prior governments for being antidemocratic and neoliberal. But this document also deployed a new critical category: "the extractivist model," defined as a political-economic order based on the intensive extraction and export of natural resources.[2] The manifesto stated that this model, with its blatant disregard for nature and indigenous communities, was all the more pernicious for being shrouded in a "supposed image of the left" and "a double discourse"—and must be as militantly resisted as neoliberalism had been in the recent past.

A year later, in an interview in the Chilean leftist magazine *Punto Final*, and during protracted political conflict with many of these same social movements, President Correa charged that rejecting the extractive model was a "colossal error" that was particularly "lethal because it utilizes our same language, proposes the same objectives and even invokes our same principles."[3] Correa grounded his arguments in appeals to the leftist canon, asking, "Where in *The Communist Manifesto* does it say no to mining?" and "What socialist theory says no to mining?" A few months later, in an interview in *New Left Review*, he expressed exasperation with what he saw as activists' "absurd" and "dangerous" opposition to resource extraction.[4]

While Correa and the organizations that signed the manifesto vehemently disagreed over the model of development, they did agree on one thing: to each, the other represented a perversion of leftism, a perversion particularly insidious for being cloaked in the language of radical transformation. Each side accused the other of betraying the principles of socioeconomic equality, popular empowerment, and anti-imperialism that have defined the Latin American Left for over a century. Correa identified himself with a regional movement of "socialism for the twenty-first century," named neoliberalism as the cause of myriad social, economic, and political ills, rejected US hegemony, and presided over a state that had dramatically increased social spending and that enjoyed widespread political support among the poor. His discourse resonated with a long history of popular calls for the expropriation and nationalization of natural resources. The anti-extractive social movements that opposed him traced their organizational lineage to worker, campesino, and indigenous struggles, and their critique of the extractive model was indebted to the systematic analysis of imperialism and dependency that characterizes Latin American critical thought. But they also voiced a more recent radical demand: an end to the extractive model of development.

Why did activists who had for decades resisted neoliberalism now protest against a leftist government? More generally, what accounts for the emergence of radical anti-extractive movements? And how might they reshape resource politics across the globe?

This book explores the conditions and consequences of the radical politicization of resource extraction. Dominant approaches to the study of oil or mineral-dependent states focus on how resource dependency shapes regime type or economic development.[5] They conclude that such states tend to be authoritarian and corrupt, and rule over societies that are alternately portrayed as politically quiescent or prone to violent resource-related conflicts. Completing this picture of pathology is economic underdevelopment. Some combination of Dutch disease, boom-and-bust price cycles, profligate state spending, and a pervasive "rentier mentality" is seen to divert investment away from productive sectors—thus reproducing resource dependency and all its perverse effects.[6]

In contrast, my approach rejects such pessimistic determinism and expands the study of resource politics well beyond the halls of the petro-state.[7] In Ecuador, grassroots activists were key protagonists in the contentious politics of oil and mining. In dynamic conflict with state and corporate elites, popular mobilization shaped the political and economic consequences of resource extraction. And the stakes of these conflicts were high. Constitutional authority, democratic sovereignty, and the possibility of a post-neoliberal state hung in the balance.

In the heat of political struggle, social movement activists craft critiques of extraction and enact processes of resistance. I call these *resource radicalisms*, and show how they shape the strategies, identities, and interests of state and movement actors alike. The concept of resource radicalism brings into relief how intellectual production is intertwined with political mobilization. From rallying cries to animated debates to everyday reflection, activists analyze the prevailing order and articulate visions of a world otherwise.

Drawing on an archival and ethnographic study of three decades of dramatic resource politics in Ecuador, I identify two such resource radicalisms, *radical resource nationalism* and *anti-extractivism*, each of which transformed the political terrain of extraction. The former demands collective ownership of oil and minerals; the latter rejects extraction entirely and envisions a post-extractive society. In the chapters that follow, I demonstrate that resource radicals forced state and corporate elites to respond—whether by accommodation, co-optation, or criminalization—and, in some cases, affected the fate of extractive projects.

Around the globe, conflict in relation to extraction, energy, and infrastructure has escalated—and it will only continue to do so in a rapidly warming and politically unstable world.[8] Situated at the frontiers of capitalism's relentless expansion, mining and oil projects are sites of dispossession and contamination. They are structured by local, national, and global scales of political economy and ecology.[9] As a result, they afford multiple venues of conflict. Due to their uneven geographic distribution, and that of their environmental and social impacts, natural resources are "intensely local."[10] At the same time, they are commodities in international supply chains shaped by the investment decisions of multinational firms and volatile global prices. Dangerous labor conditions and relative worker autonomy have historically made sites of extraction focal sites of class conflict. And these local conflicts also have national significance: governments around the world have taken an acute interest in regulating oil and mineral sectors since the early twentieth century, including via direct ownership of extractive firms.[11] As a key source of fiscal revenue, these sectors are considered "strategic"—a status justifying the deployment of physical force to protect extractive projects from protest or other disruptions. More fundamentally, in such national contexts, the processes of extraction and state-formation have reinforced each other.[12] Meanwhile, potent resource imaginaries, developed by movements and institutions, have shaped their political consequences.[13]

In Latin America, the politics of resource extraction are particularly charged. Across the region's diverse histories, resource extraction traces a long arc: colonial plunder, independence-era "enclave economies," midcentury nationalist projects of oil-fueled modernization, subsequent privatization and deregulation of hydrocarbon and mineral sectors, and, most recently, attempts at oil-funded equitable development. Over the course of four centuries, the extraction (or harvesting) and export of primary commodities has relegated the region to "peripheral" status in the global division of labor.[14] This status, rooted in colonial domination, places it on the losing end of an unequal exchange of raw goods for refined or manufactured imports. Dependency only intensified after independence, with the proliferation of mines and plantations that functioned as economic enclaves, often foreign-owned and with weak linkages to the rest of the national economy. Although the history of extraction is a history of underdevelopment, natural resource sectors have long inspired developmentalist ambitions on the part of state officials— and hopes of radical sovereignty on the part of popular movements.[15] Inspired by such visions, in the mid-twentieth century, several resource-dependent

Latin American countries underwent forms of "endogenous development," investing rents in industrial sectors. Their goal was to ultimately diversify economies and export revenues. But ensuing neoliberal reforms of deregulation and market integration reinforced the reliance on primary sectors—a trend only exacerbated by the commodity boom (between 2000 and 2014), and trade and financial dependency on the United States, Canada, Europe, and China.

Recent leftist administrations in Latin America are ideal sites to explore resource conflict because of this history, and because both policymakers and social movements have explicitly politicized—and radicalized—the relationship between development and extraction. In the process, they have raised deeper questions about the state, democracy, and the ecological foundations of global capitalism. Ecuador in particular is an especially revealing window into regional, and global, resource radicalisms. It is among the most commodity-dependent economies on the continent, and has seen intense conflict between a leftist government committed to an extraction-fueled, broad-based development model and an array of movements militantly opposed to resource extraction in all forms.

The Ecuadorian dispute over resource extraction between a self-described socialist leader and the social movement activists who helped bring him to power testifies to a unique historical moment. In Latin America, the turn of the millennium was marked by the proliferation of "counter-hegemonic processes" in the halls of state power and in the streets.[16] At the height of the Pink Tide in 2009, leftist administrations governed almost two-thirds of the region's population.[17] But this moment was also marked by the intensification of an export-oriented, resource-intensive model of accumulation, highly dependent on foreign capital. In Ecuador, activists who had protested decades of neoliberal policies in tandem with the region's leftist, critical, and decolonial intellectuals now resisted a leftist government and what they called "the extractive model" of development.[18]

The region is home to a variety of resource radicalisms. Depending on the context, activists' grievances and demands center on indigenous rights, environmental contamination, labor exploitation, foreign ownership, territorial autonomy, and local self-determination—or, often, some combination thereof. In some cases, disputes over extraction pit leftists with histories of common political struggle against one another. Leftist governments in Bolivia, Ecuador, and Venezuela espoused a state-centric resource nationalism, while indigenous and popular environmental movements (*ecológismo popular*) struggling against the expanding extractive frontier envisioned a post-extractive future.[19] These movements articulated a novel critical discourse centered on the concept of extractivism that called into question the unity of state, nation, territory, and resources. Although this discourse has circulated transnationally in both activist and academic circles, in Ecuador the radicalization of resource politics was both particularly acute and historically dynamic.[20] It was acute because, during the presidential administration of Rafael Correa, the dispute over extraction became *the* primary source of discord between state actors and social movements—and among bureaucrats themselves. And it was historically dynamic because in the space of less than a decade, many popular sector organizations dramatically changed their position on resource extraction.[21] In response to the social and environmental impacts of extractive projects, they abandoned their historic calls for expropriation, nationalization, and the collective ownership of the means and products of extraction—what I call *radical resource nationalism*—and embraced *anti-extractivism*: the militant opposition to all forms of resource extraction. In the streets and in the courts, in popular assemblies in affected communities and on nature walks to the sites of planned extraction, they identified and resisted the disparate nodes of extractivism. From their perspective, each of these nodes reproduced the extractive model—and furnished an opportunity to disrupt its ubiquitous development.

Resource Governance

A central aim of this book is to identify models of *resource governance* and show how they structure and are structured by popular mobilization. Resource governance refers to "the political and economic coordination of socio-natural relations" on the part of state and corporate elites.[22] The prevailing paradigm of resource governance shapes the political consequences of, and conflicts around, dramatic shifts in commodity prices.

Such governance paradigms vary over time and across national contexts, are inflected with specific ideological commitments, and supported by distinct constituencies. From 1972 through the end of Correa's third administration in 2017, Ecuador saw three approaches to resource governance: oil-based developmentalism, neoliberalism, and post-neoliberal resource nationalism.[23] Continuities cut across these periods: each model of governance bequeathed institutional and ideological legacies that shaped subsequent moments of policymaking and protest.

My analysis attends to these continuities as well as the conflictual junctures at which resource governance is transformed. As the two epigraphs that open this chapter highlight, during Correa's tenure in office (2007–2017), competing visions of resource extraction split the Ecuadorian Left, and opened up a debate over the means and ends of radical transformation. These competing visions emerged in a regional context characterized by two processes: the electoral success of leftist governments, and a sustained commodity boom. The causes of each were distinct, but once set in motion they together transformed political and economic horizons.

The electoral success of leftist politicians and parties in Latin America had causes both distant and proximate.[24] In any given case, the timing and character of successful leftist presidential campaigns can only be understood in light of the domestic balance of forces, the history of leftist, labor, urban barrio, campesino, and indigenous organizing, and the severity and consequences of neoliberal reforms. However, shared political and economic circumstances across the region help explain the simultaneous success of leftist electoral bids. Democratization was one such factor: although the risk of repression on the part of the domestic elite, and intervention by the US, has by no means disappeared, the wave of formal re-democratizations across the region in the late 1970s and 1980s opened up more political space for leftist parties to mobilize and compete. Second, decades of austerity had deepened poverty and inequality—and created a large constituency for leftist policies of economic redistribution, social welfare, and more substantive democratization of the state. Finally, and as crucial as re-democratization and economic devastation, was the role of sustained anti-neoliberal protest in politicizing neoliberal policies and challenging the hegemony of free markets and limited formal democracy.

Overlapping with the electoral ascendancy of the Left, between 2000 and 2014, demand from China (due to rapid industrialization and related growth in domestic consumer markets) drove historically high global commodity prices.[25] The trend was reinforced by disruptions to Middle Eastern and North African oil supplies (and associated investor panics) during the Arab Spring. In Latin America, the boom resulted in a substantial economic reorientation, and deepening fiscal dependency on the extraction and export of oil, metals, and agricultural commodities.[26] Commodity booms and busts, however, do not directly determine resource policy or the broader politics surrounding resource extraction. The prior decades of neoliberal deregulation across the region had enabled this rapid expansion of oil and mining development. As a result of global market integration, the activity of resource governance increasingly encompasses both public policymakers and private corporate actors, often in explicit partnership with one another.[27]

From Oil-Based Developmentalism
to Neoliberalism

Soon after the discovery of oil in the northern Amazon in 1967 by Texaco-Gulf, oil policy in Ecuador took a nationalist and developmentalist turn. The first step toward resource nationalism began under the populist Velasco Ibarra government's fifth and final administration (1968–1972) with the 1971 Hydrocarbons Law, which declared oil the "inalienable property of the state," eliminated the concession model, and replaced it with a contract model that stipulated taxation and royalty rates, and required investments.[28] However, the law was not retroactive and the new contract model was voluntary. In February 1972, a military coup deposed the Ibarra administration. One motive was the prospect of asserting firmer state control over oil and using oil rents as a basis for national development. The historical moment was auspicious for nationalist oil policies. In the early 1970s, a wave of oil sector nationalizations swept the Middle East.[29] At the same time, the Group of 77—the UN caucus of Third World countries—increasingly advocated the shared interests of commodity exporters and the need for national control over these sectors.[30] Prices were on the rise as global demand grew, and several major producers were reaching their peak production levels.[31] In this context, the Rodríguez Lara government (1972–1976) made oil policy its central focus, and it explicitly framed its policies in terms of nationalism, developmentalism, and decolonization. Between June 1972 and March 1973, the military junta reestablished the national oil company, Corporación Estatal Petrolera Ecuatoriana (CEPE), reviewed all existing concessions and limited their size (resulting in the return of over 5 million hectares to the state), forced the renegotiation of all contracts, and, most controversially, mandated that CEPE hold 25 percent of the rights to any contract.[32] In November 1973, Ecuador joined the Organization of the Petroleum Exporting Countries (OPEC). With an eye to promoting broader socioeconomic development, the government reinvested oil revenues in a variety of industrial and petrochemical sectors, implemented land reform in the highlands, and promoted agricultural settlement ("colonization") in the Amazon.[33]

The nationalist policy of resource extraction and associated developmentalism was short-lived. The ensuing backlash from the domestic business class and foreign oil companies ended this brief but transformative experiment in resource nationalism and helped introduce neoliberal oil governance in 1980, which remained in place until 2006.[34] As I detail in Chapter 1, neoliberalism was marked by privatization and deregulation, with the aim of courting foreign investment. The proceeds from oil extraction were primarily realized as corporate profits and foreign debt payments. Despite this radical shift in resource governance, however, the policies of the Rodríguez Lara government left an enduring ideological legacy of resource nationalism, which would later be reappropriated and radicalized by popular movements. It also bequeathed an institutional and organizational infrastructure (most importantly, the state-owned oil company) that would form the foundation of resource nationalist policies under the Correa administration.

Renewed Resource Nationalism

During the commodity boom, Ecuador became one of the most primary resource dependent economies in the region. Between 2000 and 2010, its five most important primary resources accounted for on average three-quarters of total exports, with oil alone accounting for almost half.[35] From Correa's inauguration in 2007 up until 2014 (and the precipitous drop in oil prices), oil revenues financed on average over one-third of the state budget.[36] Yet even when oil prices were high, social spending still outpaced revenues. Chinese loans, secured by future oil revenues, covered a substantial percentage of the budget shortfall.[37] By 2017, the government and the state-owned oil company, Petroecuador were over $17 billion in debt to the Chinese Development and Export-Import Banks.[38] Searching for a broader revenue base, Correa increasingly prioritized mining Ecuador's untapped gold and copper reserves, and drilling for oil in the southeastern Amazon. His administration was not the first to attempt to develop a large-scale mining sector in Ecuador. But, unlike previous governments, it made mining a national policy priority.[39] Out of five strategic projects, the administration's efforts resulted in contracts for two large-scale, open-pit copper mines (the Mirador mine in Zamora Chinchipe, and San Carlos-Panantza Project in Morona Santiago) and offers from foreign firms for four out of thirteen new oil concessions. Other mining projects are now in various stages of exploration, and some are stalled due to social conflict and investors' perceptions that the contract model overly favors the state.

In Ecuador and other South American countries governed by leftist administrations, the renewed ascendancy of resource nationalism shaped the social, economic, and political effects of the commodity boom.[40] In Argentina, Bolivia, Ecuador, and Venezuela, legislative reforms and executive decrees stipulated contract models that increased state revenue from extractive projects (though often less dramatically than claimed by conservative opposition, and the US media) and/or increased the share of state ownership ("forced divestments").[41] In Ecuador, there were no expropriations or nationalizations of foreign oil firms, but the oil contract model was reformed to increase the tax rate on extraordinary profits and to channel profits to the state in the event of production above forecasted levels, thus increasing state revenues when oil prices rose.[42] Similarly, the 2009 Mining Law increased royalty rates, and channeled a portion of revenues for investment in directly affected communities.

The combination of the commodity boom, the new contract models, and significantly increased state spending on basic needs began to chip away at what Correa called the "social debt" that had accumulated during hundreds of years of inequality and had intensified during the "lost decade" of debt crises and neoliberal policies. As a result, poverty and inequality declined significantly, and access to education, sanitation, housing, and healthcare increased.[43] Among Latin American countries, under the Correa administration, Ecuador spent the highest percentage of GDP on its monthly cash transfer program (*bono de desarrollo humano*).[44] And, compared to similar programs across the region, the *bono* accounted for the highest decrease in poverty and had the greatest redistributive effect.[45]

However, when it came to transforming historically unequal and dependent economies, commodity-dependent leftist populism was a double-edge sword. In Ecuador, the price of improving millions of citizens' socioeconomic well-being was further fiscal dependency on the extraction and export of natural resources, and the subjection of indigenous communities to sometimes violent displacement and of fragile ecosystems to contamination. Although during the boom years this model provided revenue for social spending, the truly "popular and solidary" economy officially promoted by the state proved elusive. In the context of an economy still dominated by oligopolistic consumer markets, state revenues were a boon to private sector firms. Substantial reductions in poverty and income inequality, and improvements across an array of health, sanitation, education, and housing indicators, coexisted with the persistent informality of work, inequality in land tenure, and, in some sectors, increasing concentration of capital.[46] In addition, the economy as a whole was vulnerable to commodity price volatility, as evidenced by the 2015 recession, which was triggered by a sharp decline in oil prices, and led to ensuing cuts in social spending. To wit, the budget for the aforementioned monthly *bono* was slashed by almost half in 2015.[47]

What ties together these seemingly contradictory outcomes is the availability of historically high resource rents, which enabled the Correa government to attend to social needs without deeper transformations in class relations. So long as there was an influx of oil rents, the income of the poor could be increased without expropriating the wealth of the rich. Juan Ponce and Rob Vos refer to this dynamic as "redistribution without structural change."[48] Ultimately, it was the continued reliance on a primary-export model of accumulation that generated these persistent forms of precarity, inequality, and the concentration of wealth—and in part accounts for the subsequent political "retreat" of leftist governments.[49]

Thus, during the Pink Tide, in Ecuador and other South American countries, the transition from neoliberalism to a new, post-neoliberal version of resource nationalism was not a total rupture with prevailing power structures. The legacy of market reforms continued to shape the parameters of state intervention and corporate investment in resource sectors. Decades of the deregulation of resource markets had encouraged the sale of vast tracts of land for exploration and extraction, often to foreign oil and mining companies, for low prices, and with scant legal, environmental, or labor oversight. In addition, the years of austerity and privatization had weakened state regulatory capacity and hollowed out formerly state-owned oil, mining, and gas companies, forcing states to partner with foreign firms in order to realize extractive projects—and sharply limiting resource sovereignty.[50] Lastly, insofar as these states still courted foreign investment, they were forced to take "business confidence" into account, bowing to the demands of large companies to avoid capital strikes or capital flight.[51] In Ecuador, the power of investor leverage became apparent in June 2014, when under pressure from the mining multinational Kinross, the legislature approved reforms to the 2009 Mining Law that delayed the payment of the windfall profit tax until investment had been recouped and established a ceiling for royalty payments.[52] Despite these reforms, contract negotiations with Kinross fell through, and the perception that Ecuadorian mining law was overly "statist" continued to circulate in trade publications.[53] As a result, although there have been important changes in natural resource governance, the institutional legacy of neoliberal policymaking and the power of foreign investors exercises significant constraints on leftist governments.[54]

Continuities between the neoliberal and Pink Tide administrations are particularly salient at the immediate sites of extraction. Bureaucrats in the Correa administration developed a range of strategies to mitigate protest and promote resource extraction at the community level. One way to convince affected communities is with concrete economic benefits. In September 2011, Correa signed Executive Decree 870, which established state-owned enterprise Ecuador Estratégico for the purpose of "the redistribution of national wealth and to bring development to citizens through the execution of programs and projects to provide infrastructure, equipment and services to the areas in whose territory nonrenewable natural resources are located" in order to "make these [directly affected] communities the first beneficiaries of oil, mining and natural wealth in general."[55] Another policy to fast-forward the local economic benefits of mining is "anticipated royalties." Royalties are usually paid once extraction begins, but the contract for the Mirador mine stipulates that Chinese mining conglomerate Ecuacorrientes S.A. (ECSA) pay a total of $100 million in royalties in advance of generating income. And, as per the 2009 Mining Law, 60 percent of royalties must be channeled to "productive projects and sustainable local development" via local governments."[56]

Although public regulation and investment can reduce and compensate for socio-environmental impacts, from the perspective of the communities directly affected by extractive projects, the increased involvement of state officials did not fundamentally alter the experience of an extractive model of accumulation and the forms of dispossession it entails.[57] Moreover, according to environmentalist and indigenous critics, such state interventions mimic the dissembling practices of "corporate social responsibility," designed by multinational firms in order to improve their corporate image (in the eyes of shareholders and consumers) and buffer their operations from local political resistance. In this sense, anticipated royalties and investment in affected communities represent more continuity than departure from the neoliberal era.[58]

Resource Radicalisms

While the ascendancy of new leftist governments may have unevenly transformed resource *policy*, it has fundamentally transformed the *politics* of extractive economies.[59]

Indigenous, campesino, environmental, and labor movements, among others that had protested against neoliberalism, paved the way for the electoral success of leftist parties. In the wake of electoral victories, these movements demanded a range of deeper initiatives to reorganize the relationship between state, society, economy, and nature—from wholesale nationalization to the construction of a post-extractive economy—that leftist governments have not implemented. From the perspective of these movements' activists, such reorganizations are vital to the project of decolonizing a continent in which the history of resource extraction is intimately tied to that of conquest and subjugation. In response to such demands, leftist governments in countries such as Argentina, Bolivia, Brazil, Ecuador, and Venezuela have often reprimanded indigenous and environmental groups, framing them as obstacles to the national good of resource-funded development. Meanwhile, as the Ecuadorian case reveals, these groups have struggled to organize an anti-extractive mass movement with the size and capacity of the earlier anti-neoliberal popular bloc—a point to which I return in the Conclusion.

What is the relationship between resource governance and the radical critique of it? In Ecuador, both neoliberal and nationalist policies have been unevenly implemented. But as ideologically inflected policy paradigms, they oriented state and corporate actors vis-à-vis resource sectors. They formed part of the political terrain that structured (and was structured by) the interactions between state actors and social movements. And these governance models were imbued with social meaning via the emic categories through which they were apprehended and analyzed—including those articulated by social movements.[60]

Much scholarship on protest around resource extraction sees social movements as responding either to state policies and ideologies, or to corporate strategies. But state policy, corporate strategy, and social movement resistance cannot be studied in isolation from one another. My analysis decenters state resource policy and the official ideologies that undergird it, and locates both in a field of political struggle populated by actors with contending visions of resource extraction. Among those visions are those I have called resource radicalisms, which are articulated by popular organizations and social movements, whether oil and mine workers' unions, urban neighborhood associations, environmental groups, or indigenous federations. Their members, militants, and activists are the architects of these radical critiques of prevailing models of extraction, critiques which not only guide social movement strategy—and, in moments of confrontation, elicit repressive responses from the state—but shape the terms and stakes of political conflict. As will be seen in the chapters that follow, state actors responded to new critiques of resource extraction by redeploying the terms of critique as justifications for extraction.[61]

Popular movements articulated the two resource radicalisms analyzed in this book—radical resource nationalism and anti-extractivism—in the course of struggles over economic development, resource extraction, territorial rights, and democratic sovereignty. These radicalisms map onto two different political periods (1990 to 2006, and 2007 to 2017, respectively), but not neatly or discretely: prior to their bifurcation as two distinct discourses, a nascent rejection of oil-led development coexisted alongside calls to nationalize oil resources. Popular movements consolidated and deployed these resource radicalisms in opposition to the prevailing paradigm of resource governance (neoliberalism and post-neoliberal resource nationalism). And in each period, activists' critiques and processes of resistance also shaped state practices. They forced state actors to adopt new ideological justifications for their promotion of extraction, incited ideological disputes among bureaucrats, and slowed down the development of large-scale mining as well as new oil exploration.[62]

As a pair, the two epigraphs to this introduction reveal a historically dynamic field of debate over the governance of resource extraction, understood broadly as not only models of development but as forms of political rule. Both epigraphs bear the traces of prior conflicts, even as they adjust past radical visions and evince the unpredictable futures of political projects.

During what the social movement manifesto refers to as the "yesterday" of neoliberalism, the same organizations that now fought against extractivism had instead demanded the nationalization of resource extraction. They saw the nationalization of ownership as vital to the recuperation of national sovereignty and the redistribution of national wealth. This was a regional pattern: in Argentina, Bolivia, Brazil, Chile, Venezuela, and elsewhere, indigenous, campesino, trade union, and environmental organizations resisted the deregulation and privatization of resources such as oil, minerals, water, and natural gas.[63] These groups demanded various forms of popular control over resource extraction, ranging from nationalization to worker control to local management by the indigenous peoples whose territory overlapped with hydrocarbon reserves. The hegemony of neoliberal policies allowed for this provisional alignment of social movement organizations with such distinct political trajectories and positions on extraction. I call this formation *radical resource nationalism*. As Benjamin Kohl and Linda Farthing discuss in regard to the case of Bolivia, this popular resource imaginary is firmly "anti-imperialist and proto-nationalist."[64] It is also an emotionally charged appeal that is often "formed around grievances rather than potentialities and focus[ed] on demands to recoup what has been lost and continues to be lost through foreign-controlled extraction."[65]

In Ecuador, during that same period and alongside the crystallization of radical resource nationalism, another radical position on extraction was beginning to emerge. In the course of conflictual and sometimes violent encounters between oil companies and indigenous peoples of the Amazon, the latter articulated a militant defense of territory against oil exploration. The demands voiced by Sarayaku, Achuar, and Shuar leaders provided the discourses and shaped the political strategies that would be subsequently unified under the banner of anti-extractivism.

These intertwined critiques of extraction coexisted until the new political conjuncture of the late 2000s converted them into mutually opposed positions. In this new context—marked by Correa's inauguration (in 2007), a Constituent Assembly (2007–2008) that rewrote the constitution, and the Correa government's avid promotion of large-scale mining (2009–2017)—the first position, radical resource nationalism, became an ideological resource for an administration seeking to take political and economic advantage of soaring global demand for primary commodities. But state actors reinterpreted nationalism as the *redistribution* of resource rents, rather than *expropriation* and national ownership. This was a nationalism amenable to courting foreign capital and deepening global market integration. In response, social movement activists and critical intellectuals abandoned their previous demands for nationalization, and reoriented their resistance to target what they now called the extractive model, amplifying the history of localized opposition to oil extraction in the Amazon into wholesale anti-extractivism. This model, they argued, pollutes the environment, violates collective rights, reinforces dependency on foreign capital, and undermines democracy. The gravity of the extractive model's political, economic, and environmental consequences is matched by the *longue durée* timescale of its domination: for anti-extractive activists, extractivism originated with European conquest and was only reproduced by the recent turn to post-neoliberal resource nationalism.

Although its elements had existed in inchoate form prior to Correa's rise to power, the reign of an avowedly post-neoliberal administration was the key historical condition for a mode of critique and resistance that zeroed in on resource extraction itself. Correa spoke of the nation, sovereignty, democracy, a "solidary" economy, equality, citizenship, participation, and, most importantly and poetically, of an end to the "long night of neoliberalism." He emphasized paying off the social debt accumulated under decades of austerity and economic crisis. Drawing on a long-established discursive repertoire of social resistance, he identified a cast of political and economic enemies: the international financial system, foreign corporations, domestic oligarchs, and corrupt political parties. In direct response to resounding popular demands, he called for a constituent assembly to refound the state. But in part because of these clear ideological signals, Correa found himself in heated political conflict with indigenous, campesino, environmental, labor, and feminist social movements. If even a self-identified leftist government could reproduce or, worse, intensify the rapacious exploitation of nature and the subordination of indigenous communities to a homogenously defined nation, in the process violating collective rights and centralizing power, then, social movement activists concluded, the root of the problem was not the ideological stripe of elected officials but the "civilizational" model that encompassed socialism and capitalism alike. The crystallization of this discourse in turn fomented a dispute among the Left over whether emancipation lies in an alternative form *of* economic development, or in alternatives *to* the very concept of development, seen as historically rooted in relations of coloniality.[66]

The Material Practice of Situated Critique

This book traces a genealogy of the critique of extractivism, and analyzes how its crystallization inflected resource-related contention, constitutional interpretation, radical democracy, claims to knowledge and expertise, and the fraught construction of a post-neoliberal state. In doing so, I take an approach distinct from that of extant scholarship on extractivism—and, as I detail below, from the study of resource politics more broadly. Most scholarship on extractivism employs it as a descriptive or analytical term to refer to extractive activities, the policies and ideologies that promote them, their socio-environmental effects, and the forms of resistance that they provoke.[67] In contrast, this book analyzes extractivism as the central term that unifies an emic discourse articulated by situated actors reflecting on and critiquing historically specific models of resource governance. In other words, my analysis centers on the collective agency of grassroots activists who, through their intertwined activities of critique and mobilization, shape the terms and stakes of resource politics. For this reason, when referring to this discourse as a whole, I use the Spanish *extractivismo*.[68]

I take methodological inspiration from Michel Foucault's archaeological and genealogical approaches: "I do not question discourses about their silently intended meanings, but about the fact and the conditions of their manifest appearance; not about the contents which they may conceal, but about the transformations which they have effected; not about the sense preserved within them like a perpetual origin, but about the field where they coexist, reside and disappear."[69]

Here, I identify the conditions of appearance of *extractivismo* discourse.[70] Under what conditions did social movement activists and intellectuals begin to critique "the extractive model"? What were the political and intellectual sources of this critique, and what were the historic conditions of its crystallization? What were its regularities, its variations, and its pragmatic political effects? My analytic perspective historicizes this critical discourse, and regards social movement activists and intellectuals as protagonists in crafting its conceptual architecture. This mode of analysis does not regard discourse as ontologically distinct from or epiphenomenal of "reality," but rather takes discourse to be the linguistic mediation of social relations and the concrete medium through which we reflect upon, make, and remake our social worlds.

Critique is a genre of discourse that endeavors to reveal the root causes and systemic nature of its object. In the case of the movements analyzed in this book, and radical politics more broadly, the practice of critique also opens up the possibility of—and the demand for—a world otherwise. Radical resource nationalism imagines a world of popular and democratic control over oil and minerals. Anti-extractivism, in contrast, aspires to a post-extractive future characterized by a harmonious relationship between humans and nature.

Critique is a form of creativity facilitated by the reflexive capacity of semiosis. As Andreas Glaeser writes, semiotic activity, and language particularly, "enable[s] human beings to escape the strictures of the immediate context of action."[71] Through symbols, "the world can be differentiated and integrated in the lofty modality of the 'as-if.'"[72]

The creative capacity of discourse is to an extent bounded: in order to take hold in and potentially transform a particular social context, critiques must resonate with the existing understandings of the world relevant to that social domain. For this reason, creativity often takes the form of the recombination of existing elements or the redeployment of available repertoires to ends not previously envisioned.[73] Radical resource nationalism echoed the developmentalist resource nationalism associated with the Rodríguez Lara military government. Anti-extractive movements, meanwhile, drew on the grievances and demands of southeastern Amazonian indigenous communities, which formed the basis for a wholesale rejection of extraction in all forms.

Critiques exist in complex relations with broader processes of resistance. They present grievances and demands, define shared identities, select targets, inform tactics, mediate alliances, and constitute a key element of the rich symbolism that accompanies acts of protest. They are in turn shaped by the exigencies and events of mobilization. As I show in the chapters that follow, under the rubric of anti-extractivism, a multi-scalar alliance of indigenous and environmental movements enacted new forms of democratic participation, organized outings to the territories slated for extraction, produced their own knowledge regarding socio-environmental impacts, brought cases to the Constitutional Court, and physically blockaded attempts to develop mining or oil projects. The systemic object of their critique was immanent in the spatial contours of their resistance. Traversing mountains, wetlands, and rainforest, they mobilized a network of directly affected communities along the frontiers of extraction, confronting the extractive model at the roots of what they saw as its expansionary imperative.

The conditions of critique are *historically specific* and *sociologically asymmetric*: specific historical junctures and social resources facilitate the emergence and consolidation of critique.[74] In Ecuador, the proximate historical conditions of new resource radicalisms were transformations in the ideological orientation of resource policy coinciding with broader disputes over the political-economic model.[75] In response to state actors' embrace of neoliberalism, social movements coalesced around a radical resource nationalism; a decade later, with the rise of a leftist populist administration that sought to channel the economic benefits of extraction to the majority, these movements rallied under the banner of anti-extractivism.

Battling state institutions and domestic and foreign firms, those involved in labor unions, indigenous, campesino, and urban neighborhood organizations, and environmental groups found themselves on an uneven field of engagement, marked by an unequal distribution of institutional and financial resources. In the neoliberal era, state and economic elites crafted a shared vision of a "multicultural market democracy" that formally incorporated indigenous peoples and other marginalized groups while excluding more radical demands from the political agenda.[76] Subsequently, in post-neoliberal Ecuador, the diffusion of technocratic discourses through networks that encompassed both state and corporate actors facilitated elite coordination, resulting in shared strategies for responding to, and repressing, anti-extractive resistance.

Yet despite the unequal distribution of the means of discursive production and dissemination, activists did have access to their own communicational infrastructure.[77] This infrastructure was comprised of social movement organizations' physical headquarters and e-mail listservs, social media and blogs, event spaces at universities and cultural centers, informal venues for gathering and conversation, and—especially during public demonstrations—streets, highways, and plazas. During the two-week long March for Water, Life, and the Dignity of Peoples, discussed in several of the following chapters, the daily output of the blog maintained by the highland indigenous federation Ecuarunari contributed to the production of a shared narrative about the march among both participants and supporters. The production and dissemination of the blog exemplified the imbrication of online and offline political activity, as well as the materiality of discursive production. Blog posts were produced in the heat of political practice, whenever the communications team could find an internet café or a Wi-Fi connection. It was a collaborative effort. The Ecuarunari communications team was part of the march and built their reports via face-to-face communication with march participants, as well as by attending press conferences. The posts were then collectively authored by the blog team, with others (including myself) providing editorial or translation assistance. Once posted and disseminated via e-mail and social media, at the next opportunity to access the internet, we marchers would subsequently read them and incorporate them into the ongoing, reflexive construction of a shared narrative about our own political activity. This process strengthened marchers' political resolve and provided a counter-narrative to the claims of state actors (for example, that the march was ineffective, a result of political manipulation, or an attempt to overthrow the government).

In contrast to political scientists' tendency to regard discourse as ideational or as disembodied meanings floating in the ether, the discursively mediated interactions I observed in closed meetings, public events, and protests, elicited in interviews, read in texts, or heard on radio or television broadcast were material acts. They consisted of "vibrating columns of air, ink on paper, pixels in electronic media."[78] It is the very materiality of linguistic communication (and of semiosis more broadly) that allows discourse to function as a mediator of social relations. The materiality of individual discursive artifacts spatiotemporally limits them, circumscribing their circulation and reception. But materiality is also what enables the reinterpretation, reanimation, and reappropriation of discursive artifacts: "burning documents turns on paper's combustibility, using paper as a toy airplane turns on its foldability, storing it turns on its perdurability."[79] Materiality can thus be conceived as "a *relationship* across events of semiosis."[80]

The understandings of the world communicated through language therefore exist in determinate relations with the material conditions of social life.[81] Although ideas are only thinkable and speakable within historically specific regimes of discourse or ideological problematics, they are not epiphenomenal or symptomatic reflections of an underlying reality.[82] Language shapes the world, whether through its performative function or as a medium of political justification and critique, governance, and resistance.[83]

The ongoing communicative acts that comprise radical critiques of prevailing economic models unfold on the plane of material relations and they can only be understood as articulated and deployed in concrete political struggles with adversaries. As the epigraphs suggest, in Ecuador the conflict over resource extraction took place on a terrain shaped by past struggles over resources and territory, and in the midst of a dispute over the content of leftism. The conflict over resource extraction was structured by the unequal relations between actors and unified by the problematic of *extractivismo*.[84] This problematic was the shared ground against which distinct positions were brought into relief and without which they would be mutually unintelligible.[85] At the same time, the conflict was also characterized by innovation, unexpected outcomes, and reversals of position. Although from the perspective of any given actor the terrain was given or "objective" in the sense that it was "largely not of their own choosing," the dynamics of conflict kept the terrain in motion.[86] Conceiving of this conflict as a field of social action—a relationally defined terrain of struggle—captures this dual nature.[87]

The Double-Edge of Critique

The dynamic, conflictual, and asymmetric nature of this social field, combined with the material infrastructure of communicative activity, results in the unexpected redeployment and resignification of the discourses of one's opponents.[88] The very same communicational infrastructure that enables discourse to travel beyond its initial moments of production and generate macropolitical effects also makes it available for subsequent reanimation—as well as more strategic reappropriation by those with competing political projects.[89] Because discourses can potentially travel beyond their intended audiences, they can be redeployed for purposes other than those imagined by their authors.[90] Discourses have unpredictable and unexpected futures ahead of them. Reanimations and reappropriations of discourse are key to understanding the dynamics of conflict.

In Chapter 3, I show that indigenous activists reanimated arguments made by allied delegates during the Constituent Assembly that drafted the constitutional text. After the Constitution was ratified, they drew on those arguments to advocate for more radical provisions than the text itself contained. They reanimated proposals that had failed on the plenary floor—for example, a proposal to require the consent of affected communities prior to extractive projects—to craft an interpretation of the Constitution that exceeded its literal content. More politically strategic reappropriations by one's opponents can elicit frustration on the part of situated actors.[91] As suggested by the epigraph, for social movement activists, state actors' use of terms like *buen vivir* and post-extractivism is a form of "double discourse," proclaiming a commitment to a different model of development while, from the perspective of those activists, perpetuating extractivism.

Such instances of reanimation and reappropriation underline the fact that political discourse is always already collectively authored. Any attempt to stabilize social meanings comes up against the others who have spoken and will speak those same words, but to different ends and with different consequences: "That is what reclaimed words do—they retain, they insist on retaining, a sense of the fugitive."[92] Or, as Mikhail Bakhtin put it, "The word in language is half someone else's . . . Language is not a neutral medium that passes freely and easily into the private property of the speaker's intentions; it is populated—overpopulated—with the intentions of others."[93]

Words arrive already overpopulated with meanings. No actor can control in advance what meanings will be crowded into their words or what political projects their words will be used to support.

The Temporality of Critique

The potential for reanimation and reappropriation of discourse is in turn grounded in the complex temporality of critique. Although activists articulated and deployed resource radicalisms in a mutually constitutive relationship with the model of resource governance that they critiqued, these critical discourses evinced a historicity distinct from the chronology of governance. First, there was a lag between the shift in governance and the mobilization against it. Although in Ecuador the transition to a neoliberal governance model began in 1980, the critique of this model—radical resource nationalism—prevailed from roughly 1990 to 2006. Meanwhile, although the shift away from the neoliberal model commenced with Correa's inauguration in 2007, the shift to an anti-extractivist position among social movements crystallized over the course of the next three years. This is in part because social movements need time to respond to the changing political terrain, which itself is not instantly transformed but gradually remade as new policies are implemented, and in part because critical discourses developed in prior moments may continue to circulate even when the circumstances for and in which they were developed have changed.[94]

Second, in addition to the lag, these critical discourses redeployed (and in the process, resignified) political demands articulated at earlier points in history. Radical resource nationalism encompassed both a statist nationalism that can be traced to the early 1970s (when it was briefly the policy orientation of the nationalist military dictatorship that inaugurated Ecuador as a "petro-state") and the ongoing struggle for the recognition of indigenous territory, which grew out of a longer history of peasant organizing and appeared on the national political stage in the form of a unified indigenous movement in 1990. Although these two ideological strains rested on different understandings of the connection between nation, state, territory, and resources, they could co-exist in the discourse of a given organization or individual activist because they both constituted critiques of neoliberal resource governance. One framed this governance model as an incarnation of capitalism, the other as an incarnation of (neo)colonialism. During the mid-1990s through the early 2000s, indigenous and environmental activists began to call for an end to oil extraction in the Amazon, broadening the demand for the recognition of indigenous territory into a critique of extractive activity. The narrative of neoliberalism and the radical resource nationalism it provoked built up to a critical juncture in the context of which the preexisting elements of *extractivismo* discourse could coalesce into a novel problematic.

For both these reasons—temporal lag and the (re)combination of preexisting elements—the historicity of radical critique is distinct from that of governance in ways that complicate preconceived periods and their imputed unity. Tracing the unique temporality of critique thus offers an alternative narrative logic to historical accounts organized around the ideological orientations of policymaking elites.

In addition to its distinct logic of periodization, the narrative that follows evinces the double temporality identified by Walter Benjamin in his philosophy of history: the present looks backward at the past looking forward toward the present.[95] Written in the present, my genealogy of *extractivismo* is inevitably refracted by the contemporary structure of political conflict. It looks back in time in search of this critique's source discourses, which are resignified elements dating to prior moments of contention, and injects activists' prior statements with the "presence of the now."[96] But, as much as is possible, I will elucidate the perspectives of the past on their own terms, as concrete responses to prevailing conditions that also always exceeded those conditions, pointing to a hoped for emancipatory future.

Reorienting the Study of Extractive Politics

The commodity boom of 2000 to 2014 and the related repoliticization of resource extraction in Latin America sparked a renewal of scholarly interest in the contentious politics of oil and mining.[97] Joining this scholarship, I present a distinct perspective on the relationship between resource governance and anti-extractive protest. I uncover ideological battles within and between state ministries, recount the diffusion of critiques and justifications across the borders of officialdom and resistance, and reveal society to be the historically conditioned assembly of collective subjectivities, with shifting ascriptions of interests and identity. In contrast to predominant approaches, I reject the dualistic image of the state as a monolithic dispenser of public policy, and of resistance as an external force, quasi-organically emanating from society. Instead, I analyze resource politics as an expansive and vibrant field of contention.

The concept of the "resource curse"—the detrimental effect of natural resource wealth on development and democracy—dominates political science literature and public policy discourse on oil (and, to a lesser extent, on mining).[98] In this literature, the state is ambivalent: it is the powerful dispenser of oil policy and distributor of oil rents and at the same time it is the product of oil dependency, unable to resist the easy rents oil abundance provides or the political-economic pathologies it guarantees.[99] Meanwhile, society is portrayed as either bought off by oil money or repressed into submission.

Tying this conceptual framework together is an analytic focus on the allocation and distribution of oil rents. In this framework, fiscal dependency on resource extraction functions as a causal force that shapes regime type or economic development, often operating via the causal mechanism of incentive structures (specifically, the effect of resource rents on the governance and investment strategies of elite actors). This approach necessarily assumes that "natural resources"—or, more precisely, the revenue streams they generate—are homogeneously deterministic and that politics is primarily an elite affair, wherein oil money facilitates rentierism, oligarchic pacts, clientelism, and state repression. The threat to democracy is seen to emanate from rentier states' ability to minimize direct taxation of the population (relying instead on taxes on oil companies and royalties from oil sales), which provides a buffer against citizens' demands for representation.

Other scholarship takes a more nuanced approach, emphasizing that the political effects of resource rents are not unmediated but highly contingent on the relative timing of oil or mineral discovery vis-à-vis the process of state formation or the ownership structure of oil firms.[100] As Benjamin Smith puts it, oil rents constitute a "highly flexible form of revenue" that, depending on features of the political and economic context, can either bolster regime durability or foment political instability.[101] In this vein, and contra the thesis that "oil hinders democracy," Thad Dunning argues that commodity booms can under certain conditions promote democratization. In the Latin American context, wherein the primary threat to democracy has been elites' fear of popular power, oil rents can satisfy popular demands without requiring the redistribution or expropriation of property, thus stabilizing democracy against the threat of elite-organized coups.[102]

What these approaches have in common is a shared focus on the state-centric distributional politics of resource dependency within "rentier states." But, as Timothy Mitchell puts it, all states are "oil states," in the sense that modern industrialized democracies are themselves thoroughly imbricated in the production, distribution, and consumption of oil flows.[103] Further, depending on features of the historical conjuncture, the relationship between the highly compressed forms of energy made available by coal and later oil have both enabled and limited democracy. Technologies of extraction and distribution, the domestic and geopolitical problems confronting political and economic elites, and the organization of labor all shape the political consequences of hydrocarbon resources.[104] In Ecuador, far from undermining democracy, contention around oil extraction and the construction of a large-scale mining sector occasioned novel democratic practices. In the dispute over large-scale mining, both anti-extractive activists and the Correa administration saw the expansion of resource extraction as raising fundamental questions about the practice of democratic sovereignty, and both articulated figures of "the people" and enacted new modes of participation to defend their political positions.

This book joins work in anthropology, political ecology, and geography that takes a broader view of the politics of resource extraction than the elite-centric perspectives of the rentier state and resource curse frameworks.[105] I show that indigenous, labor, campesino, and radical environmental activists did not merely react to the top-down imposition of resource policy. They were central protagonists in the articulation of resource imaginaries and the construction of natural resources as a site of radical politics. They articulated these imaginaries in dynamic relation with state actors: in addition to responding to state policy, they shaped state action, both by provoking new modes of official justification and intervention, and by exacerbating ideological fractures within the state. I demonstrate that leftist presidents in Latin America have contended with resistance from inside and outside their administrations, and that the outcomes of these conflicts shape the possibilities for domestic policymaking and social mobilization. As a corollary, I reject the dichotomy of "good" leftist governments (for example, Chile, Brazil, Uruguay) versus "bad" ones (for example, Argentina, Bolivia, Ecuador, Venezuela), which, in order to array countries in a normative hierarchy, both decontextualizes governments from the broader political field of leftist forces and constructs them as monolithic entities.[106]

My analytic orientation, which regards resource extraction as a historically dynamic field of conflict, is reflected in my methodological approach. Empirically, this book traces the discourses and the political strategies they shape (and are shaped by) across the boundaries of state and society, within the myriad institutional and organizational locations that constitute each. Between

2010 and 2016, I conducted fifteen months of multi-sited ethnographic field-work and archival research. My time was primarily split between Quito, the capital (and Ecuador's second-largest city) and site of central government institutions, social movement headquarters, NGO and corporate offices, and major universities; Cuenca (Ecuador's third-largest city) and surrounding rural communities in the southern highland province of Azuay, home to several planned gold-mining projects; and Zamora Chinchipe, a southern Amazonian province that is the site of a large-scale, open-pit copper mine, and a planned underground gold mine.

In the course of my research, I conducted over 100 interviews with bureaucrats in the Correa administration, opposition politicians, corporate representatives, public intellectuals, professors, NGO personnel, and social movement activists in indigenous, environmental, human rights, student, and labor union organizations. I also observed events as they unfolded, such as: protests (including the two-week long March for Water, Life, and the Dignity of Peoples, which covered 700 kilometers), activist meetings, mining and oil conventions co-organized by private firms and state institutions, NGO-coordinated "dialogues" on resource conflict, a day-long community consultation on a mining project, public fora on mining (usually, but not always, organized by anti-extractive activists), press conferences organized by the national indigenous federation, popular assemblies, community-organized walks (*caminatas*) through mining concessions, court cases litigating the rights of nature, radical reading groups, and community meetings in indigenous territory. Lastly, I conducted archival research at the Library of the National Assembly (specifically the documentation of the 2007–2008 Constituent Assembly meetings, debates, and resolutions, and the Interim Congress debates over the 2009 Mining Law) and using the extensive collection of daily press coverage of indigenous issues curated by the annual publication *Kipu* (published between 1985 and 2014).

Each of these three categories of data—interview, event, archive—provided distinct vantage points on the social processes under analysis. Observing events unfold in real time gave me insights into the granular dynamics of the discursive activity that mediates political practice—and into the interplay between the contingency of strategic decisions and the structured organizational contexts of their articulation.[107] Such seemingly "micro" interactions always draw upon available discursive formations, political ideologies, and institutionalized sources of political and economic power, as well as social status. They are also situated in an asymmetric terrain of political conflict comprising differentially situated allies and opponents. And such interactions can be carried forward in time and outward in space via subsequent interactions, whether face-to-face or textually mediated, in the form of uptake, circulation, reanimation, documentation, dissemination, and storage. Through these socio-technical means of circulation, a given interaction can live a social life beyond its initial context of unfolding and entail consequences of a "macro" political nature. Thus, whether or not an interaction generates enduring effects cannot be determined in advance. Just as events have unpredictable futures, so too do they index pasts both distant and proximate. In this way, real-time observation, the elicitation of individual and collective memory, and the interpretation of archived documentation can be analytically interwoven to approximate the multiplex temporality of social life.

Overview of the Book

This temporally and spatially interwoven nature of my data and of the social processes upon which they offer a vantage point is reflected in the organization of the chapters that follow.

The first two chapters provide a genealogy of the critical discourse of *extractivismo*, and identify the political conditions—and consequences—of its crystallization. Chapter 1 covers a long historical arc, tracing the shift from radical resource nationalism to the critical discourse of *extractivismo*. It threads together three processes: first, the eruption of localized struggles over resources, land, and indigenous territory (from the 1930s to the 1980s); second, the development of state policy regarding the extraction and export of natural resources (1972 to 2017); and third, the articulation of resource radicalisms that critiqued those policies and envisioned alternatives (1990 to 2017).

Chapter 2 demonstrates that the crystallization of the problematic of *extractivismo* triggered a political realignment: activists that once fought for the nationalization of natural resources now opposed all resource extraction, a leftist president found himself in conflict with the social movements who initially supported his political project, and the Left-in-power became synonymous with the expansion of extraction at any cost. In response, President Correa and high-ranking ministers claimed that opposition to oil and mineral extraction was a tactic of imperial powers acting under the guise of environmentalism. The redeployment of anti-imperialist critique highlights the degree to which this was a fight within the Left. Meanwhile, functionaries I call "critical bureaucrats" critiqued resource extraction from inside the state. Articulating a discourse that resonated with that of anti-extractive activists, they sought to both slow down the pace of extraction and to transition to a post-extractive economic model.

The next three chapters follow the dispute over resource extraction as it reverberated through conflicts over the interpretation of the Constitution, the meaning of democracy, and the grounds of epistemic authority. Chapter 3 focuses on the politics surrounding the writing of the 2008 Constitution. This multivalent text empowers both the state and local communities with authority over resource extraction. It calls for a new model of public policy, *buen vivir* (living well), and is the first constitution in the world to recognize nature as a subject of rights. As I show, from the 2007–2008 Constituent Assembly to long after the text was ratified, the Constitution lived through the semiotic activity that cites, circulates, and interprets it. Its normative force and political salience was the product of this multi-sited interpretive process, wherein social movement activists' practices of popular jurisprudence played a particularly important role.

Chapter 4 zooms in on a particularly contentious constitutional right: prior consultation (*consulta previa*), the collective right of communities to be consulted prior to extractive projects. On October 2, 2011, two rural water systems in the southern highland province of Azuay decided to take constitutional enforcement into their own hands. They organized a consultation to enforce their constitutionally mandated right to be consulted prior to the development of a nearby large-scale mine—a right they claimed that public institutions failed to guarantee. The consultation occasioned a dispute over the collective subject of democratic authority. By shifting the struggle over extraction into the terms of democracy, this new form of social mobilization forced state actors to respond. The latter elaborated a vision of *extractive democracy* that justified the expansion of large-scale mining in democratic terms, shored up by new policies of targeted local and national investment that redistributed resource rents.

Chapter 5 reveals how bureaucrats in this leftist administration perceived and attempted to manage anti-extractive resistance. Bureaucrats and industry actors seeking to promote large-scale mining regarded what they call "information" as a panacea for anti-mining conflict. In their discourse, communities oppose mining because they are "misinformed." This discourse resonated with Correa's technocratic vision, which claimed that mining is a "technical" and not a "political" issue. But technocratic discourse failed to depoliticize mining. Instead, officials' claims to technical expertise became politicized, fomenting divisions among state actors. Meanwhile, anti-mining activists challenged the epistemic authority of bureaucrats and mining corporations. They produced counter-knowledge that figures *el territorio* (territory) as an ecological and cultural landscape.

Finally, in the Conclusion I chart the dilemmas and contradictions of resource dependency for both the Left-in-power and the Left-in-resistance, and draw out the implications for resource politics and leftist mobilization in the years and decades to come. I reflect on the tension between *extractivismo* as critique and its generative capacity to construct the conditions of effective collective action in a political context in which socialism—and the form of mass politics it names—and radical environmentalism became decoupled and mutually counterposed as political projects.

1

From *Neoliberalismo* to *Extractivismo*

The Dialectic of Governance and Critique

In July of 2010, Alicia Granda, activist and researcher at the human rights organization Comisión Ecuménica de Derechos Humanos del Ecuador (CEDHU), told me that "extractivism" was responsible for a wide range of problems in Ecuador.[1] She explained to me that oil and mineral extraction dismantles local productive activities in the countryside, like agriculture and fishing, causes migration to the city, and accelerates the urbanization of rural areas. In her view, capital- and land-intensive extractive projects undermine preexisting rural livelihoods and the social fabric they sustain, while also failing to provide equitable economic development. According to Granda, the sale of vast tracts of land for oil and mineral concessions constitutes a "new colonization," evoking the period of state-sponsored migration to the Amazonian provinces in the 1960s and 1970s, during which *colonos* (settlers) as well as oil and lumber companies came into conflict with indigenous groups.[2] Her analysis was not entirely pessimistic, however. She also discussed how the expansion of extractive activity had opened up new possibilities for collective action and the reconstruction of identities. Granda noted, for example, the emergent alliance between *indígenas* and *colonos* in the southern Amazon, two groups historically in conflict, but which now saw a common enemy in the advancing extractive frontier.

The next week, I sat down with Pablo Iturralde in the offices of the National Assembly.[3] At the time, Iturralde was an adviser to assembly members from Correa's party (Alianza País); he was later appointed to the Coordinating Ministry of Economic Policy. He divided the political field into "two grand projects" that "are in this moment in contradiction." On one side was the model of development promoted by the government and President Correa, based on the "super-exploitation of nature and extractivism," which he described as a "sin" that "so many models or regimes, capitalist as much as those called socialist" have committed. As he put it, "the government and Rafael Correa in particular have said very clearly that the post-oil country is a mining country." He contrasted this with an opposing model, which he called Amerindian or "*sumak kawsay* or the so-called *buen vivir*," a model not so much economic as "civilizational," which envisions a total reordering of the relationships between individual, community, and nature according to the principle of reciprocal collaboration.[4]

Both of these interviews evidenced the crystallization of a new political field polarized by commitment and opposition to "extractivism." According to its conceptual architects—environmental and indigenous activists, and public intellectuals—extractivism means "the intensive and extensive exploitation of natural resources; little or no industrialization; export as the principal destination; exploitation that impedes natural renovation . . . the economic form of the 'enclave.'"[5] It is a syndrome comprising the various pathological effects of economic dependency on resource extraction. In the years that followed my interviews with Granda and Iturralde, talk of extractivism coalesced into a widely circulating critical discourse, articulated not only by militant environmental activists and members of national and regional indigenous federations, but even by a subset of bureaucrats within the Correa government, such as Iturralde, who were skeptical about a development model based on oil and mineral extraction. This conjuncture was marked by conflict within the Left over the desirability of resource extraction *tout court* and the possibility of an entirely novel model of development (or even an alternative to "development"). This marked a historic shift: activists who previously struggled for the nationalization of resource extraction now resisted what they called the "extractive model." In response, some state officials called for the transition to a "post-extractive" economy, while others accused anti-extractive activists of being both traitors to the national interest and tools of imperialist powers.

What follows is a genealogy that traces the conditions of the coalescence of *extractivismo* as a novel critical discourse. To understand why the extractive model emerged as an object of political dispute under the Correa administration, it is necessary to trace *extractivismo* discourse back in time, far enough so that it loses the coherence it later assumed and disperses into a set of elements without a unifying grid of intelligibility. As Foucault put it, "the search for descent is not the erecting of foundations: on the contrary, it disturbs what was previously considered immobile; it fragments what was thought unified; it shows the heterogeneity of what was imagined consistent with itself."[6] Such a genealogical reading historicizes *extractivismo* discourse, tracing its constituent elements—the focus on the communities directly affected by oil and mining, the concept of *el territorio* ("territory" defined as a socionatural landscape), the imbrication of environmental and cultural destruction, the *longue durée* time-scale and expansionary imperative—to specific eruptions of social conflict over oil in the 1990s and early 2000s.[7]

This analytic approach reveals substantial shifts over time in radical critiques of extraction and associated processes of resistance, from the radical resource nationalism that predominated in the neoliberal period, to the anti-extractivism that crystallized under the Correa administration. In what follows, I trace the distinct elements of *extractivismo* discourse to the political realignments in which they initially emerged and began to amalgamate. I periodize this process of discursive institutionalization intro three epochs.

First, I present an overview of the longer-term trajectory of peasant-cum-indigenous mobilization against economic exploitation and political exclusion (1930s–1990). These decades of social conflict saw the formation of indigenous organizations and the national indigenous federation, which would emerge as key collective actors in the neoliberal period. It was in this period that two key elements of *extractivismo* discourse began to take form: the "community" figured as a salient site and protagonist of social mobilization; and territorial defense as the strategic orientation of newly formed Amazonian indigenous groups.

I then turn to popular struggles under neoliberal administrations (1990–2006). It was in the neoliberal period that indigenous territory and natural resources became radically politicized. In response to the privatization and deregulation of the oil sector, social movements articulated radical resource nationalism: democratic and national control over extraction. Alongside these demands, Amazonian indigenous groups directly confronting oil companies elaborated an increasingly pointed critique of extraction as a threat to *el territorio*, the land conceived of as both an environmental and a cultural space— and a site of indigenous sovereignty. This critique thus furnished another set of conceptual elements of *extractivismo* discourse, and contributed to the overall radicalization of anti-oil resistance.

Next, I identify the features of the political conjuncture (2007–2010) wherein the problematic of *extractivismo* crystallized and ultimately displaced resource nationalism as the radical response to extraction. In the next chapter, I detail the wide-ranging political consequences of this transformation of social movement discourse and strategy: the radicalization of anti-extractive protest, the proliferation of internal disputes among state actors over resource policy, and the criminalization of resistance.

From the *Ley de Comunas* to the *Levantamiento Indígena* (1930s–1990)

At the height of its political power in the mid-1990s through the early 2000s, the national indigenous confederation CONAIE (Confederación de Nacionalidades Indígenas del Ecuador) was a key protagonist of anti-neoliberal resistance.[8] The movement began as (and in many ways, remains) a fundamentally subnational phenomenon, with the formation of geographically defined federations of indigenous organizations in the highlands and Amazon, and on the coast. In this section, I survey the terrain of popular struggle from the early twentieth century through the ascendance of the national indigenous movement onto the national political stage in 1990, with a focus on the highland peasant unions and ethnically defined Amazonian communities that eventually coalesced to form CONAIE.

Two trajectories account for the political capacity of this internally diverse, translocal federation, as well as for its relative autonomy from state institutions (and, hence, its historic role as an oppositional collective actor). The first was peasant (campesino) mobilization against unequal land tenure and super-exploitative labor relations in the highlands; the second was ethnic organization to defend communal territory against state-led land colonization, and oil exploration and extraction in the Amazon. These processes remained relatively independent of one another until the 1970s, when indigenous leaders from each region began their efforts to create a national federation, culminating in the formation of CONAIE in 1986.

With regard to the first trajectory, beginning in the late nineteenth century and gathering momentum in the 1930s, rural peasant unions forged alliances with urban leftists.[9] These at times tense alliances initially targeted specific abuses in the vast system of haciendas, the repressive agricultural labor regime that dominated the Ecuadorian highlands from the Spanish conquest to the 1960s. Eventually, these protests shifted to a broader resistance against political exclusion and economic exploitation. What Marc Becker calls the first national indigenous federation, the Federación Ecuatoriana de los Indios (FEI), was founded in 1944 as the culmination of these organizing efforts.[10] As a result of these urban-rural alliances that diffused leftist political ideologies, FEI activists wove together a discourse that combined appeals to class, ethnicity, and nationality. Although the FEI primarily framed its members in economic class terms as campesinos and focused on land reform, the very name of the federation—*indios*—suggests an ethnic dimension, which was further reflected in such actions as the establishment of bilingual schools.[11]

The state responses to these waves of rural mobilization generated unintended consequences with lasting implications for indigenous organizing. The 1937 *Ley de organización y regimen de comunas* (Law of Commune Organization) established the legal figure of the *comuna* as a territorial and political unit of rural organization.[12] Importantly, *comunas*, which were settlements of fifty or more people, were granted the right to elect their own local governments (*cabildos*). In 1964, the military government—which had taken power in a coup d'état the previous year amidst renewed FEI militancy—promulgated the *Ley de reforma agraria y colonización* (Agrarian Reform and Colonization Law). The reform ended the *huasipungo* system of semi-feudal service tenancy (itself a replacement of *concertaje*, the practice of debt peonage that was widespread before it was outlawed in 1918), capped the size of haciendas, and expropriated and redistributed land.[13] Finally, the military government of General Guillermo Rodríguez Lara (1972–1976) initiated a more concerted program of land redistribution. This policy was part of a package of reforms that briefly asserted state control over the economy, mainly via the discovery of oil and related increases in state investment.[14]

These three episodes of state reforms were highly ambivalent. Both the *Ley de comunas* and the *Ley de reforma agraria* enabled community organization that were unexpectedly powerful—unexpected both from the perspective of the rural activists who struggled for land redistribution and labor rights, and to the state actors seeking to quell unrest and "modernize" land ownership and labor relations. The stated intent of the 1937 law was to rationalize the *comunas* as the lower level units of rural economic cooperatives. However, the law also provided a language that enabled spatialized practices of "community" that proved remarkably durable means of indigenous identity formation. Due to the limits of state capacity, instead of incorporating these communities into a corporatist state, the law provided the political architecture for a type of rural collectivity that was relatively autonomous from both landed elites and the central bureaucracy. "Community," in short, became a site of what Rudi Colloredo-Mansfeld calls "vernacular statecraft": the local adaptation of a form of state intervention.[15] At the same time, the reform weakened the FEI: state actors had intended the *comunas* to undermine more militant forms of community organization, and as it turned out, the settlements officially recognized as *comunas* were indeed less likely to join peasant unions.[16] The effects of the law thus went far beyond the creation of a new scale of administration or the formal emancipation of peasants from the land (which allowed them to engage in subsistence agriculture or migrate to urban areas). It enabled new forms of rural collective action, while discouraging others.

The subsequent 1964 dismantling of the *huasipungo* regime simultaneously liquidated the existing power structure (the private political-economic authority of the hacienda) and presented another challenge for radical rural activism. The result was a "power vacuum," which was in the subsequent decades "filled with indigenous grassroots organizations," in part with the aid of the post-Vatican II progressive wing of the Catholic Church.[17] Ecuarunari (Ecuador Runacana-pac Riccharimui, or "awakening of the Ecuadorian Indian"), the highland Kichwa federation founded in 1972, was a product of the emergent collaboration between indigenous *comunas* and progressive priests.[18] Ultimately, the 1937 and 1964 agrarian reforms caused a political opening that redirected highland rural life toward a new arena of politics called the "community," and partially protected that community from both private economic power and the penetration of an unevenly developed state bureaucracy. In the process, the reforms contributed to the relative salience of ethnic identity.

Parallel to these conflicts over land and labor in the highlands, state-led land colonization and the rapid expansion of extractive activity in the Amazon provoked the formation of ethnically defined indigenous organizations. Between the 1950s and 1980s, the arrival of oil (state and private), agricultural, and logging companies, all encouraged by state-sponsored colonization, politicized indigenous communities, resulting in the emergence of groups among the Achuar, Cofán, Amazonian Kichwa, Siona, Secoya, Shuar, and Waorani.[19] The efflorescence of indigenous organizing in defense of communal territory (*el territorio*), understood as the socio-natural space of cultural reproduction, constituted the second trajectory in the formation of CONAIE.

The history of indigenous organizing in the Amazon is inextricable from the political economy of resource extraction. In the context of the 1970s-era oil boom, the Rodríguez Lara military government avidly promoted recently discovered oil reserves as a route to national development, and explicitly couched its policies in an anti-imperialist, nationalist discourse.[20] These state-led efforts not only transformed the fiscal basis of the state; they also opened up a new arena of popular mobilization and radical critique. In the 1970s, resistance to oil exploration and extraction remained locally territorialized among indigenous communities in the Amazon. Initially land colonization and logging, and then oil drilling, spurred the formation of trans-community networks that would later provide the organizational infrastructure for regional and national indigenous mobilization. These networks first emerged as a result of conflictual encounters with settlers (*colonos*) who, encouraged by the 1964 colonization law, migrated from the highlands in search of cheap land and economic opportunity. With support from Salesian Catholic missionaries, the Shuar organized the first lowland indigenous organization in 1964. Provincial-level mobilization emerged with the founding of the Organization of Indigenous Peoples of Pastaza (OPIP) in 1978 in response to the dual threats of colonization and oil exploration.[21] Finally, the Confederación de Nacionalidades Indígenas de la Amazonía Ecuatoriana (CONFENIAE) was founded in 1980, which by the early 1990s encompassed the aforementioned seven Amazonian indigenous nations: the Achuar, Cofán, Amazonian Kichwa, Siona, Secoya, Shuar, and Waorani.[22]

The two trajectories—highland and Amazonian—intersected in the late 1970s, when leaders of the two regional federations (Ecuarunari and CONFENIAE) began conversations to form a national confederation.[23] In 1986, they founded the Confederación de Nacionalidades Indígenas del Ecuador (CONAIE). CONAIE's strength lay in its bottom-up assembly, wherein new organizational layers were sequentially grafted onto previously established levels of collective action and identity: base community, regional affiliate, and national federation.[24] Although the distinct origins of highland and Amazonian affiliates manifested in recurrent internal debates over political strategy, CONAIE achieved the status of a national collective actor, united by a shared infrastructure of decision-making and communication.[25] Thanks to this infrastructure, CONAIE gained the capacity to mobilize geographically dispersed communities to contest the policies of every national administration since 1990, and to frame those policies as an affront to indigenous communities— and, beginning in the mid-1990s, as an attack on "the people" writ large. In coalition with other popular sector groups, their combined forces have paralyzed economic activity and forced presidents to resign.[26] Although CONAIE and its member organizations worked in concert with other popular actors, it self-consciously took on the role of the primary articulator of categories of critique (centered on a condemnation of *neoliberalismo*) and positive political-economic visions (*el territorio*, plurinationalism, popular sovereignty, and communitarian economy). These categories and visions proved remarkably enduring. Although they were adapted and modified to respond to particular circumstances and as a result of particular alliances, they helped shape the terrain on which both state and social movement actors articulated post-neoliberal projects.

A key conceptual innovation, with wide-ranging political consequences, was CONAIE's critique of the nation-state and its positive vision of a plurinational polity. Reflecting how class and ethnicity had determined both structures of oppression and indigenous mobilizations, the political programs that CONAIE developed in the course of its first decade disrupted the conceptual frame of the nation-state in two ways. First, against liberal capitalism, they posited a reassertion of democratic, national sovereignty over the economy.[27] And second, against *mestizaje* assimilationism, they demanded that Ecuador be redefined as a plurinational state.[28]

The understanding of indigenous peoples as nationalities (and the corollary that Ecuador is a plurinational state) solidified in the 1990s. According to José Antonio Lucero, this conceptualization of indigenous identity functioned to strike a balance between the representation of the highlands and the Amazon within CONAIE.[29] Lucero traces the concept of indigenous *naciones* to the Comintern's use of the language of nationality in the 1920s to refer to oppressed minorities, which arrived in the region via the influence of Soviet social scientists as well as Soviet-educated Latin Americans.[30] As an organizing framework, it was particularly useful in negotiating between the two primary subnational regions that constituted the federation: the more populous but monolithically Kichwa highlands, and the less populous and more ethnolinguistically diverse Amazon. In the late 1990s, indigenous leaders debated how to achieve equitable internal representation, and resolved to distinguish between *pueblos* and *nacionalidades*.[31] The highland Kichwa nationality would henceforth be subdivided into various peoples (Saraguro, Otavaleño, Cayambi, among others), which would have equal representational weight as each of the more numerous Amazonian nationalities (Shuar, Achuar, Cofán, among others). Lucero argues that the division of indigenous peoples into *naciones* and *pueblos* was a remarkable achievement on the part of CONAIE and served as a vehicle for CONAIE's ability to "set the terms for indigenous representation" more broadly.[32]

The 1990s saw four indigenous uprisings (*levantamientos*), in 1990, 1992, 1994, and 1997–1998. Demands for land reform (titling of indigenous territory and land redistribution) and the recognition of Ecuador as a plurinational state dominated the earlier uprisings, while the 1997–1998 mobilizations more assertively called for the refounding of the state via a new constitution. In addition to land, all of these protests focused on broadly shared economic grievances. By the mid-1990s, leaders of CONAIE and Ecuarunari (its highland sub-federation), in an emergent coalition with a broad range of popular sector groups called the Coordinadora de Movimientos Sociales, had identified neoliberalism as the contemporary incarnation of capitalist imperialism.

But despite the protests' unification around the theme of neoliberalism, they also evinced the distinct organizing strategies and rhetorics of highland and Amazonian regional indigenous federations, with important implications for subsequent anti-extractive protest under the Correa administration. Indigenous organizations based in the Amazon mobilized to gain legal recognition for their ancestral territories, which were threatened by agricultural colonization and oil extraction.[33] Amazonian groups articulated a broad conception of territory (*el territorio*) as a geospatial, ecological, and cultural landscape—a conception that would later become a foundational element in the critique of *extractivismo*. In contrast, highland indigenous organizations had historically articulated their own conception of land (*la tierra*) and demands for redistribution in economic terms, given the legacy of the hacienda economy, unequal land tenure, and debt peonage. Yet as Deborah Yashar shows, the political coordination between these two groupings of indigenous nationalities resulted in the diffusion of the language of *el territorio* from Amazonian groups to their highland counterparts, and its adoption as a shared organizing framework.[34]

Direct actions taken by highland indigenous communities over unresolved land conflicts snowballed into the June 1990 *levantamiento*. This uprising took political elites (not least among them, President Rodrigo Borja) by complete surprise. Borja's election (in 1988) had represented a relative swing to the Left after the hardline neoliberal administration of León Febres Cordero (1984–1988). But the contrast between his rhetoric—he campaigned as a critic of neoliberalism and a supporter of social democracy and multiculturalism— and his piecemeal market reforms, combined with his unwillingness to meet with indigenous movement leaders to discuss land policy, provided a political impetus for mobilization. The ten-day *levantamiento* was concentrated in the highland provinces of Cotopaxi, Tungurahua, Chimborazo, and Bolívar, where strategic roadblocks cut off commercial transport, and CONAIE activists presented sixteen demands to the government.[35] Reflecting the dual conceptions of *tierra* and *territorio*, the second demand was for both granting land and the legal recognition of territories.[36] Other demands included price freezes for basic necessities, the declaration of Ecuador as a plurinational state, the completion of public works in indigenous communities, the legalization of indigenous medicine, a solution to the problem of water access, and environmental protection, among others.[37] Although the 1990 uprising dramatically altered the political terrain—the indigenous movement had now become a key political actor—the specific demands of CONAIE were left unresolved, and it was only the beginning of over two decades of mobilization.

From the 1930s to 1990, social struggles engendered conceptual elements and organizational forms that endured beyond the political realignments in which they initially emerged. These intertwined critiques and processes of resistance contributed to the future crystallization of anti-extractivism. Conflicts over rural land distribution and labor regimes resulted in the institutionalization of the local community (*comuna*) as a level of political mobilization; land colonization in the Amazon provoked indigenous groups to defend *el territorio* as a socio-natural space of cultural (re)production; the transformation of Ecuador into a petro-state transformed oil into a salient arena of policymaking and protest; and the imperatives of forming a national indigenous federation resulted in the definition of indigenous groups as *naciones* and *pueblos*, bolstering claims to sovereignty and self-determination. However, these elements would not immediately cohere into a militant rejection of extraction on the part of indigenous and other popular sector groups. As political and economic elites unified in support of neoliberal policies, popular forces—key among them the indigenous movement and oil workers' unions—responded by rallying around a radical resource nationalism, demanding democratic control over oil wealth.[38] But, alongside this grassroots nationalism and in the midst of heightened conflict over oil in the southern Amazon, indigenous groups began to articulate a more pointed critique of oil extraction. It is to the consolidation of radical resource nationalism and the concurrent radicalization of anti-oil resistance that I now turn.

Resource Nationalism as Anti-Neoliberal Critique (1990–2006)

Across Latin America, beginning in the 1980s and gaining momentum in the 1990s through the early 2000s, social movements of many stripes have identified their target as *neoliberalismo*.[39] Definitions of neoliberalism have varied in scope, ranging from a narrow set of economic policies (privatization, deregulation, liberalization, austerity) to a broad hegemonic project advanced by domestic and international elites, reshaping social relations and even subjectivities.[40] In Ecuador, processes of economic reform from the early 1980s up until Correa's election in 2007 were hotly contested in the legislature and on the streets. In comparison to what was achieved elsewhere on the continent,

Ecuador's adoption of neoliberalism was thus truncated and uneven. Even so, the "language and political logic" of neoliberal ideology constituted the prevailing orientation of state actors.[41] Social movement activists—especially from the indigenous movement—played a central role in articulating the concept and critique of neoliberalism.[42] In a dialectic of governance and critique, natural resources such as land, water, oil, and, eventually, minerals, constituted key sites of neoliberal policymaking—and for forging rebellious visions and practices of plurinationalism, eco-socialism, indigenous self-determination, and leftist populism. The tensions between these radical visions would only come to a head in the context of Correa's administration (2007–2017), which would be marked by conflict between an extraction-based model of development that combined elements of neoliberalism and resource nationalism, and an increasingly militant anti-extractivism.

From the early 1990s to the early 2000s, oil extraction became an increasingly salient target of anti-neoliberal critique. This critique comprised two distinct ideological strands. The predominant one, articulated by the largest and most diverse social movement coalition, was a radical resource nationalism demanding the expulsion of foreign oil companies, the nationalization of oil, and the channeling of oil revenues to meet social needs.[43] In their critique of neoliberalism, indigenous and other popular sector groups, as well as left-wing and nationalist political figures, drew on past national experiences with resource nationalism as a policy paradigm and an official state ideology. Indeed, I add "radical" to resource nationalism in part to distinguish the discourse and political strategies of social movements from those of the military government of Rodríguez Lara. That government articulated a vision of resource nationalism that constituted a substantial departure from the policies of prior governments, but its vision remained contained within a statist developmentalism and stopped short of a critique of capitalism.

A second strand was more critical of extraction *simpliciter*. I refer to this as "proto-anti-extractivism"—an admittedly inelegant, and inherently retrospective label. In the course of conflicts with oil companies, Amazonian communities in particular identified resource extraction as a threat to their territorial integrity, self-determination, and natural environment. This subset of critical discourses demanded, at a minimum, indigenous control over extraction (for example, veto power over particular projects), or, maximally, opposed oil extraction entirely (especially where it affected indigenous territories) and proposed economic alternatives such as ecotourism.

The neoliberal turn in oil policy commenced with the transition to democracy under the Osvaldo Hurtado administration (1981–1984).[44] Like many other new democratic governments across the continent, his administration inherited the interrelated debt, liquidity, and balance of payments problems that had come to a head under the 1976–1979 military regime, as well as sharply declining oil prices and low prices for other exports. In this context, Hurtado—despite being the founder of the initially center-left Popular Democratic Party—implemented short-term austerity policies and signed an agreement with the IMF.[45] In addition to declining prices, Ecuador's oil sector—the primary source of state revenue—faced stagnant production (in no small part due to corporate boycotts) and the depletion of reserves (due to domestic fuel consumption at subsidized prices).[46] In this context, Hurtado worked with Congress to pass the 1982 Hydrocarbons Law, which reflected an emergent policymaking consensus that there was no way out of the economic crisis without attracting foreign investment in the oil sector.[47] The reforms established a risk-sharing contract, which lowered taxes, reimbursed investors once exploitable fields were discovered, and opened up new blocks for bids on exploration contracts.[48] The era of official resource nationalism was over, and a new era of confrontation between neoliberal resource governance and radical resource nationalism would soon begin.

In what follows, I analyze protests against specific oil projects and oil companies from 1990 to 2006, with a particular emphasis on the period between 2002 and 2006. These latter years were characterized by a high level of oil-related conflict, which found expression in both nationalist and proto-anti-extractivist registers, and an increasingly vocal opposition to oil extraction on the part of Amazonian indigenous groups. In the critical discourse that planned, mobilized for, and was interwoven with this contention, elements of radical resource nationalism and proto-anti-extractivism coexisted without explicit recognition of their contradictions: they were at times entangled in the same utterance, at other times mapped onto distinct tendencies within a given political group, and sometimes they erupted into intragroup conflict over programmatic differences. Both radical resource nationalism and proto-anti-extractivism constituted responses to the prevailing regime of deregulated and privatized resource extraction, their common target. Radical resource nationalism posed the problem in terms of ownership, sovereignty, and the popular will, whereas proto-anti-extractivism resisted a model of development on the timescale of modernity. Elements of *extractivismo* discourse were first "drafted" in the course of these struggles over oil exploration in the 1990s and early 2000s. But several years later, in a new political context, these elements were stitched together into an encompassing critique of the extractive model and the damage it wreaks.

The Double Movement: Neoliberal Extraction
and the Radicalization of Protest (1992–2006)

In 1992, the Organization of Indigenous Peoples of Pastaza (OPIP), comprising Kichwa, Achuar, and Shuar indigenous groups from the oil-producing Amazonian province of Pastaza, marched for thirteen days to Quito.[49] They voiced two principal demands: the legal recognition of indigenous territory and the constitutional recognition of Ecuador as a plurinational state. Although these demands resonated with those that had been previously articulated by CONAIE, they were also inflected with concerns specific to Amazonian indigenous identity: the conception of *el territorio* (as opposed to land, *la tierra*) as a space of cultural (re)production (rather than as primarily a means to economic livelihood).

This territorialized understanding of cultural identity was historically grounded in Amazonian peoples' relative autonomy from the state (and often, other indigenous settlements) until the 1960s, as described above. Claiming land as a cultural right grounded in historic use, the 1992 march thrust both the concept of territory and the issue of oil extraction onto the national stage.[50]

Although the marchers employed environmentalist rhetoric, OPIP did not position itself in opposition to oil extraction per se, but rather demanded more substantial participation in environmental and social policymaking, as well as in the economic benefits extraction brings.[51] However, their discourse soon shifted toward a stance more critical of oil extraction. In 1994, in coordination with the radical environmental group Acción Ecológica, OPIP protested the Seventh Round of Oil Tender, which opened up ten new concessions, four of which were in indigenous territory in Pastaza province. The organization's principal demand was a fifteen-year moratorium on oil extraction.[52] Their language linked social and ecological justice under the framework of what Joan Martínez-Alier calls *ecologismo popular*.[53] While not yet elaborated into full-fledged *extractivismo* discourse, OPIP's 1994 statements identified oil extraction as the source of environmental and social ills. OPIP thus contributed to the evolving ecosystem of critiques of resource extraction, which environmentalist and indigenous activists would subsequently draw upon when they retooled their strategies in the context of a left-of-center, pro-extraction administration.

Throughout the 1990s, in a Polanyian double movement, both neoliberal reforms and protests explicitly targeting neoliberalism picked up pace.[54] President Sixto Durán-Ballén (1992–1996) aggressively implemented neoliberal policies. He slashed consumer subsidies, social insurance, and public services, often by decree, and instituted labor reforms that decreased the power of an already fragmented labor movement.[55] However, structural changes (financial sector liberalization, tariff reductions, and privatization of the state telecommunications firm) were more challenging to implement since they required legislative approval, and midterm elections left Durán-Ballén without congressional support.[56] From the outset, his administration was caught between an oppositional congress and a militant CONAIE, which worked in alliance with the relatively weak national labor federation, the Frente Unitario de Trabajadores (FUT), and, increasingly, the new umbrella organization of union and popular sector organizations, the Coordinadora de Movimientos Sociales (CMS), formed between 1994 and 1995.[57] Anti-neoliberal discourse crystallized in early 1994 as Durán-Ballén pursued stabilization policies that included a 70 percent fuel price increase, which CONAIE successfully framed as an attack by "the ruling class" against "the union workers movement, the Indian-peasant movement, that is, all the Ecuadorian people."[58] Protests against the policy drew up to half a million people across major cities, as well as roadblocks in the rural highlands. Though Durán-Ballén refused to rescind the measure, the Constitutional Court declared it unconstitutional in the face of destabilizing social unrest.

With regard to oil policy, Durán-Ballén withdrew Ecuador from OPEC, thus freeing the country from the cartel's production quotas. He also reformed the Hydrocarbons Law to further reduce state involvement and increase private investment in the sector, allowing foreign companies to explore new marginal fields, participate in operating the Trans-Ecuadorian Pipeline, and exploit gas in the Gulf of Guayaquil (previously reserved for the state company Petroecuador).[59] In addition, a new model of production-sharing contracts vastly reduced the state oversight that had been previously required in order for oil firms to seek reimbursement for their investment. In 1994, these legal reforms were put into practice, and met with protest, during the Seventh Round of Oil Tender (discussed above).

Another wave of resistance to the perceived onslaught of neoliberalism came in June 1994, with the *Movilización por la vida* (Mobilization for life), which CONAIE called in response to an agrarian reform bill that would effectively end land redistribution, liberalize the land market by allowing for the division and sale of previously unsaleable communal land, and privatize communally managed irrigation water.[60] The protest lasted twenty days and included marches with up to 30,000 participants in major cities. The demands of CONAIE were couched in their recently published political program, which called for a new constitution to found a "plural and democratic nation."[61] While it recognized the "historic experience of the permanent struggle of Indigenous Peoples" against colonialism, republicanism, and imperialism, it addresses a broader audience of "peasants, workers, women, students, professionals, intellectuals, the religious, soldiers, and democratic and humanist politicians."[62] The document repeatedly invoked plurinationality, envisioned as having not only cultural but also democratic and economic implications, such as the replacement of capitalism with a "planned ecological communitarian economy."

At this juncture, CONAIE's political project was at once *indigenista* and popular-democratic. The federation claimed to speak on behalf of a broad bloc of the oppressed conceived of in both democratic ("the people") and class ("the poor") terms, and defined against a class of political-economic elites ("the oligarchy").[63] This identity articulation was not purely aspirational: it reflected on-the-ground alliances between indigenous and non-indigenous groups. Nationally, the coalition between CONAIE and the CMS was a key example, but such connections were forged at the local and provincial level as well. As Sawyer's ethnographic work shows, during the 1994 *movilización*, the communiqués of the Indigenous-Campesino Alliance of Pastaza Province (which included CONFENIAE and OPIP) addressed *indígenas*, campesinos, and—most expansively—"all people."[64] She continues, describing a scene outside a branch of the National Development Bank (Banco de Fomento) in the capital of Pastaza: "With his thick glasses and short-cropped hair, one CONAIE leader rallied protesters in front of the Banco de Fomento. 'Who are the majority?' 'WE ARE,' yelled the predominantly campesino crowd of a hundred or so. 'Who are WE, the rich or the poor?' 'THE POOR,' the street responded."[65] This figuration of the people and their enemies was in turn conducive to a radical resource nationalism. Resources, long stolen by profit-seeking foreign capital in collusion with the domestic ruling class, were conceived of as the people's collective subterranean patrimony. In this critical discourse, the problem was not extraction or even export, but the ownership and regulatory regime that funneled revenues into private coffers, leaving poverty and underdevelopment in its wake. The political program issued by CONAIE in 1994 did not declare a struggle *against* extraction, but instead reclaimed indigenous-cum-national sovereignty over natural resources, which should be "exclusive property of the Plurinational State."[66]

In an alliance with the CMS called the Patriotic Front, CONAIE demonstrated its political capacity again in the protests of February 5, 1997, against the right-wing populist president, Abdalá Bucaram (1996–1997), eventually driving Congress to remove him.[67] Organized into deliberative "people's assemblies," activists demanded a new constitution. In response, the interim president, Fabián Alarcón, called an election for a Constituent Assembly.[68] The resulting 1998 Constitution fell short of the demands of the indigenous movement, such as recognizing Ecuador as a plurinational state, but it did recognize new collective rights.[69] These rights provided a preliminary legal basis for the expansive understanding of *el territorio* articulated by Amazonian indigenous groups. Subsequently, Pachakutik, the political arm of CONAIE founded in 1996, won enough delegates to make it the third-largest party in the country. Pachakutik participated in a minority left bloc to develop legislative proposals informed by CONAIE's political project.

Importantly, in addition to the promulgation of oppositional discourse both inside and outside the assembly, the rewriting of the constitution provided a forum for political elites to justify representative democracy and neoliberal economic policies. Bowen refers to this elite "discursive strategy" as "multicultural market democracy," and it was most forcefully espoused in working papers published by the Corporación de Estudios para el Desarrollo (CORDES), a Quito-based think tank focused on development issues and founded by the president of the Constituent Assembly, and former national president, Osvaldo Hurtado.[70] More generally, the discursive strategies developed by both elites and activists during the mobilizations of the 1990s—themselves building upon longer term trajectories of statecraft and resistance—constituted a more lasting success than the neoliberal policies they respectively supported and opposed. As Bowen puts it, "although elites may have little interest in specific neoliberal reforms, the language and political logic of neoliberalism have proven useful in blocking CONAIE's more redistributive demands."[71]

Likewise, anti-neoliberal discourse endured and even proliferated beyond the context of mass protest in which it was crafted, reshaping politics for years to come. After their climax of mobilization and electoral success, CONAIE experienced a decline in capacity and legitimacy, but its trenchant critique of neoliberalism would continue to circulate, and resonate with a broader and broader public. The political weakening of CONAIE was in large part due to their collaboration with the military in the 2000 coup, led by Coronel Lucio Gutiérrez, that deposed the then president, Jamil Mahuad. They were further discredited when President Gutiérrez, who was subsequently elected in 2003 on the promise to reverse neoliberal policies and eradicate political corruption, implemented structural adjustment policies and co-opted individual indigenous leaders.[72] Monica Chuji, an Amazonian Kichwa activist and later member—and then opponent—of the Correa administration, refers to this as "one of the most paradoxical and contradictory moments" in the history of the Ecuadorian indigenous movement.[73] In April 2005, confronted with mass mobilizations known as "the rebellion of the *forajidos* (outlaws)" and the abandonment of his allies, Gutiérrez resigned.[74] The street protests and popular assemblies ranged from relatively spontaneous gatherings of individuals with no party or organizational affiliation to more formal events organized by established NGOs, and even the mayor of Quito.[75] Notably, neither CONAIE, which had hitherto been the main articulator of political discontent and coordinator of protest, nor existing leftist political organizations, played a role in this particular rebellion (although, as described below, indigenous resistance persisted in the Amazon). Rafael Correa entered the November 2006 presidential race riding the coattails of these mass mobilizations. He capitalized on his already established anti-system credentials, including his participation in the *forajido* movement and his brief tenure as minister of the economy, the latter under the interim Alfredo Palacio administration (2005–2007), which had earned him a reputation as a strong critic of neoliberal policies. And, crucially, he redeployed the very critique of neoliberalism voiced by CONAIE and their popular sector allies over the past decade and a half.

"A Problem of Sovereignty": Oil Strikes, Oxy, and Indigenous Territory (2002–2006)

Amidst this multifaceted crisis of political representation, oil extraction was a recurrent source of political and social conflict. In what follows, I focus on 2002 through 2006. These five years were characterized by the intense radicalization of resource nationalism in the capital and the northern Amazon, and, alongside it, the development of more vocal opposition to oil extraction on the part of indigenous groups in the southern Amazon. Despite their distinct geographic sites, protagonists, and demands, groups articulating their demands in the rhetorics of both resource nationalism and proto-anti-extractivism claimed to act in the name of "sovereignty": the former invoked popular national sovereignty against foreign capital, while the latter asserted indigenous territorial sovereignty against oil extraction. Crucially, in defending their territory against oil, the Sarayaku, Shuar, and Achuar extended the object of their critique to embrace not only foreign capital, but also the state-owned oil company Petroecuador and the various state agencies that provide the regulatory framework for (and, in violent confrontations, the armed defense of) extraction. This discursive and strategic shift constituted a key advance toward the elaboration of *extractivismo* discourse and the opposition to extraction *tout court*.

Between 2002 and 2006, oil workers were key proponents of radical resource nationalism. In February 2002, environmental justice groups, such as the Amazon Defense Front, and the oil workers' union FETRAPEC (Federation of Ecuadorian Petroleum Workers) led an eleven-day oil strike in Lago Agrio, a northern Amazonian city whose history is intertwined with decades of oil extraction, to protest the construction of a privately owned and operated pipeline operated by Oleoducto de Crudos Pesados.[76] President Gustavo Noboa's administration (2000–2003) responded forcefully, declaring a state of emergency and militarizing the region. Grievances encompassed the state's neglect of socio-environmental harm due to decades of oil exploration, extraction, and transport, as well as the loss of national sovereignty over oil resources (a critique especially emphasized by oil workers).

In June 2003, members of FETRAPEC and CETAPE (Committee of Petroecuador Workers) flooded the streets of Quito to protest the threat of oil privatization under the Gutiérrez administration. In an agreement with the IMF, Gutiérrez had pledged to privatize some of Petroecuador's oilfields, and had instructed the minister of energy, Carlos Arboleda, to accelerate the process for the four most productive fields.[77] In response, oil workers went on strike, and in August 2003 they staged a massive anti-privatization demonstration in Quito, where they were joined by many other popular sector groups. They framed both the privately owned pipeline and oilfield privatization as "selling out national patrimony" facilitating the "plundering of resources," asserting that "petroleum belongs to the people, not the IMF."[78] As Marcelo Román, president of FETRAPEC in the mid-1990s and a leader of the 2003 protests, explained during our interview, "Imagine if the principal vein of your body was operated by a private company, and not you."[79] Here Román wove together several tropes of radical resource nationalism: in figuring pipelines as veins and oil as blood, he framed privatization as a corporate colonization of the anatomical infrastructure of the national body.[80]

The 2003 strikes and protests were met by state repression (including the arrest of the president of FETRAPEC, and legal charges of terrorism and sabotage against many other union leaders, including Román) and systematic "defamation campaigns" in the media, orchestrated by Minister Arboleda.[81] These campaigns—which Tom Perreault and Gabriela Valdivia argue contributed to the political weakening of the oil workers' unions—inverted and redeployed oil workers' nationalist appeals, accusing protesting workers of "being antipatriotic and terrorists."[82] During this turbulence in the capital, in the zones of extraction both indigenous communities and mestizo *colonos* entered into increasingly militant confrontations with oil companies. In January 2005, as the Ministry of Energy and Mines attempted to expand oil extraction to the central and southern Amazon, the debate over oil divided the Amazonian indigenous federation CONFENIAE. Indigenous communities in the south, who were more skeptical of oil extraction, were pitted against those in the northeastern Amazon, whose much longer experience with oil activity had resulted in greater acceptance of extraction.[83] According to newspaper coverage, the Sarayaku people (part of the Kichwa nation, whose territory overlapped with oil concession Block 23), and the Shuar and Achuar nations (whose territory overlapped with Block 24), "[led] resistance to this extractionist [sic] activity."[84] These three groups emerged as especially vocal opponents of oil extraction—and key architects of proto-anti-extractivism.

Marlon Santi, who would later become president of CONAIE and was then president of the Sarayaku Association, stated that CONFENIAE leaders should demand "the declaration of the untouchability of their [the Sarayaku's] reserves and support their [the Sarayaku's] Plan of Life, based on ecotourism."[85] He also called for a constitutional reform mandating that "subsoil wealth would be administrated by indigenous [peoples], within their reserves."[86] A few months later, after talks broke down between Shuar communities, the minister of energy and mines, and the state oil company Petroecuador over the operations of the oil company Burlington, FISCH (the interprovincial Shuar federation) announced a "state of emergency." They declared their opposition to "extractive activities" but also, as stated by the president of FISCH, Enrique Cunambi, signaled an openness to oil extraction "if and only if it is controlled (*ejecutada*) by the Shuar inhabitants themselves."[87] Santi's and Cunambi's statements combined, first, an opposition to resource extraction and, second, the call for indigenous control of resource extraction. At the time, these demands were compatible as a set of critical responses to the neoliberal governance of an oil-dependent economy. Retrospectively, their distinct logics are apparent: the critical discourse of *extractivismo* implies a radical rethinking of the extractive basis of the economy, while the demand for indigenous control potentially leaves that basis unaltered, merely shifting ownership and control.

In a similar "state of emergency" declaration on the part of the interprovincial Achuar organization OINAE and FISCH, the two groups characterized themselves as "the only ones who know the Amazon," which they described as existing in a pre-extractive idyll ("remote . . . intact, uncontaminated") that would be irreversibly altered by "the exploration and exploitation of oil." Over time, the document warns, not only would these indigenous nationalities be extinguished, but a whole range of "negative social, cultural, environmental, and other impacts" would be set in motion. Although Amazonian indigenous opposition to oil extraction remained ethnically and geographically circumscribed ("our" collective rights over "our" territory), the focus on the wide-ranging socio-environmental effects of extraction would later become a key element of *extractivismo* discourse.

Protest against oil companies and oil extraction picked up momentum in August 2005 with a bi-provincial oil strike in the northeastern Amazonian provinces of Orellana and Sucumbíos.[88] In 2000, Occidental Petroleum violated Ecuadorian law and its contract by transferring 40 percent of its economic interest to another oil company without first receiving ministerial approval.[89] Occidental (or "Oxy") became symbolic of the loss of sovereignty to foreign capital. The strike, which took place from August 13 to August 21, was organized by residents and local elected officials.[90] Hundreds marched in Amazonian cities, declaring "we too, are Ecuador."[91] Strikers prevented oil from leaving by occupying airports, roads, and oil wells, and demanded the termination of the contract with Occidental. They further called for the nationalization of oil to fund social and economic needs; more public investment in, and direct transfer of 25 percent of oil revenues to, the two provinces; and the cessation of oil contracts signed without Amazonian communities' and local governments' consent.[92] In response, "police and army forces were sent to control the spaces of disruption, using tear gas bombs, water cannons, and mass arrests," including of local elected officials.[93] On August 25, negotiations with the Palacio administration resulted in more oil revenue for and public investment in the two provinces, but not in the expulsion of multinationals.[94]

Radical resource nationalism guided social movement response to the prevailing resource regime, and, in the case of the oil strike and anti-Oxy protests, yielded concrete political gains. But alongside resource nationalism, indigenous activists were expanding their position from a limited critique of particular oil companies to a more encompassing critique of oil as a model of development. They began to craft the historical narrative that would later become a hallmark of *extractivismo* discourse, a framing that would allow anti-extractive activists to link the moment of colonial conquest to the resource policies of a self-identifying leftist president. On October 12, 2005, CONAIE and a range of social movement groups joined a continent-wide day of coordinated protests against the 513th anniversary of the Spanish conquest, dubbed *El día de resistencia de los pueblos*. Across the region, indigenous groups mobilized to reject a series of free-trade deals (linked to the ultimately failed continent-wide Free Trade Area Americas agreement).[95] In Ecuador, October 12 also occasioned oil-related demands. Participants called for oil companies, particularly Oxy, to leave Ecuador, and for the nationalization of oil.[96] However, despite the familiar resource nationalist demands, viewed retrospectively through the prism of contemporary disputes over extraction, October 12 constituted a point of inflection in the genealogy of *extractivismo* discourse. On that day, indigenous protesters explicitly connected oil extraction to a centuries-long history of colonialism. As CONAIE leader Blanca Chancoso put it, "[transnational companies] continue with the same process of exploitation as 513 years ago. . . . They want to take all of the natural resources of the country and the indigenous people are the most affected."[97] This historical arc recontextualized resource extraction in the *longue durée* of conquest. Although she articulated her critique in the register of sovereignty—natural resources rightfully belong to the people (*el pueblo*), itself ambivalently defined as national ("the country") and indigenous ("the most affected")—by connecting the present of extraction to the past of plunder, Chancoso elaborated the sweeping temporal logic that would come to characterize *extractivismo* discourse. By 2006, Oxy and free trade became more tightly linked as twin symbols of neoliberal hegemony. On January 11, labor and environmental activists, along with former government and military officials (such as Edgar Isch, who had served as Gutiérrez's minister of environment) came together for the "Oil and Sovereignty" meeting. Their manifesto framed the problem of oil in terms of popular sovereignty. Neoliberalism, implemented by national elites and foreign capital, "alienated our hydrocarbon wealth." Participants demanded the nationalization of oil, the nullification of several oil contracts, and an end to extraction in environmentally protected areas.[98] They also expressed solidarity with indigenous groups resisting oil extraction in the Amazon. In the Amazonian region, ongoing mobilization in Shuar and Achuar communities, in coordination with non-indigenous-identifying *colonos*, culminated in an anti-Oxy and anti-free-trade protest in the capital on May 8, 2006. Organizers named the demonstration "In defense of sovereignty, natural resources, and national dignity," and received support from Acción Ecológica, CONAIE, a national umbrella federation of unions (Frente Patriótico), the oil workers' union FETRAPEC, and Pachakutik.[99] Although the Palacio government played down the size of the protest, on May 15 it terminated the contract with Occidental.[100]

May 2006 was the climax of radical resource nationalism. Months later, the conjuncture set in motion by the election of the self-identifying "twenty-first century socialist" Correa and, soon thereafter, the convening of a popularly elected Constituent Assembly to rewrite the Constitution, transformed the political terrain. In this critical juncture, key components of what had become a militant opposition to oil extraction among indigenous communities in the southern Amazon gained salience: extraction as ecologically and culturally destructive; *el territorio* as socio-natural space and the site of indigenous sovereignty; and local communities as empowered under constitutionally recognized plurinationalism to veto extractive projects. Indigenous and environmental activists, and allied intellectuals, would recombine these elements, sedimented by the struggles of preceding decades, under the banner of a critique of "the extractive model," a term popularized by environmentalist critics of the Latin American new Left, and deploy it against the Correa administration and his promotion of new extractive projects.

The Critical Juncture (2007–2009)

Parallel to this series of protests against Oxy and against free trade, Pachakutik, CONAIE, and Ecuarunari were embroiled in internal debate over the upcoming presidential elections. Between late April and mid-June 2006, these indigenous organizations engaged in heated discussions over whether to enter into a political alliance with Correa or to run an indigenous leader such as Luis Macas (president of CONAIE from 1991 to 1996 and from 2004 to 2008) or Auki Tituaña (cofounder of Pachakutik and one of Ecuador's first indigenous mayors) as an independent candidate.[101] The possibility of sharing a ticket with Correa as the vice-presidential candidate to an indigenous presidential candidate was also floated.[102] As these discussions unfolded, multiple lines of fracture divided indigenous activists as they wrestled with a long history of alliances with non-indigenous leftists. These alliances had been present from the origins of the first regional and national indigenous organizations, but had more recently resulted in cooptation and delegitimation (most notably, in the politically disastrous alliance with Gutiérrez). Meanwhile, negotiations with Correa became increasingly tense, and terminated when he refused to participate in a primary process along with Pachakutik candidates.[103] Ultimately, the indigenous political party nominated Luis Macas, one of the founders of CONAIE and of Pachakutik.[104] Just a few years later, viewed from the other side of a critical juncture, an alliance between Correa, Pachakutik, and CONAIE would seem impossible.

Correa, elected on November 26, 2006, in the context of mass discontent with established political and economic elites, came to power in a discursive field shaped by over a decade of anti-neoliberal resistance. Correa claimed that his administration constituted a definitive rupture with neoliberalism, and that he would reassert national control and coordination over the economy, particularly over resource extraction. In response, anti-neoliberal social movements gradually rearticulated their position as opposition to extraction *simpliciter*, and away from a nationalist rhetoric of resources for the people.

Extractivismo discourse became salient at the intersection of two processes: first, the longer-term realignment of social movement strategy in the context of a new leftist president; and, second, that president's aggressive promotion of the large-scale mining sector.[105]

The following sections focus on the 2007–2008 Constituent Assembly's Mining Mandate and the protests that erupted over the 2009 Mining Law. These moments marked two key turning points in the genealogy of *extractivismo* discourse and accompanying political realignments. In the course of the debates surrounding the Mining Mandate, a critique of resource extraction that exceeded the categories of anti-neoliberalism gained momentum. The mandate took aim at the "hemorrhage" of mineral concessions that were a product of the sector's deregulation under the neoliberal regime of resource governance. Although the mandate remained inscribed within the language of national sovereignty, by instituting a moratorium on mining activity it raised the possibility of a political program centering on opposition to resource extraction, even if nationally owned.

If the 2008 Mining Mandate was the product of a tenuous leftist coalition supporting the reassertion of national sovereignty over the economy, then the 2009 Mining Law represented the limit of that political alignment and the exhaustion of anti-neoliberalism as a guide to social movement strategy. In the time that elapsed between the mandate and the law, the administration's commitment to developing the mining sector was made clear. From the perspective of its critics, this commitment came at the cost of the rights of indigenous peoples, affected communities, and nature alike. If this was what post-neoliberalism looked like, then new discourses, tactics, and alliances were necessary.

El Mandato Minero and Subsoil Sovereignty

The 2007–2008 Constituent Assembly provided a venue for the articulation of two political projects: a nascent anti-extractivism, and radical resource nationalism. The final text of the 2008 Constitution retains vestiges of both. It empowers communities affected by extraction, and it grants rights to nature. It also asserts the state's exclusive control over subsoil resources and biodiversity itself.[106] When the assembly was convened, resource extraction did not yet divide the Left. But as the assembly unfolded, a debate grew among leftist delegates from both Alianza País (AP) and Pachakutik over the model of development. Even as delegates interwove anti-extractivism and radical resource nationalism, their emergent stances laid the groundwork for these two resource radicalisms to eventually confront one another as mutually exclusive positions.[107] As the years wore on, resource nationalism would be reduced to a contract model that increased the state's take and the redistribution of revenues—a far cry from the popular sector vision of democratic control.

In the Constituent Assembly, those critical of resource extraction primarily posed the problem as one of ownership and regulation, and the solution as the recuperation or expansion of state authority. Although their speech was peppered with the terms of what would soon consolidate as *extractivismo* discourse—multiple delegates spoke of the "extractivist model" and its wide-ranging consequences—the discussion remained inscribed within the problematic of anti-neoliberalism, understood as the abdication of state authority to coordinate and regulate economic activity.[108] The pushback from right-wing delegates reinforced the problematic of neoliberalism. Rallying to defend the free market against state intervention, they warned that the Mining Mandate's moratorium would undermine the legal certainty (*seguridad jurídica*) required for investment and the legal sanctity of the contract itself, fundamental to both the "model of economic development" and a "State of Law."[109] These right-wing delegates also inadvertently provided arguments that would later be recycled in the Correa administration's pro-mining discourse.

On April 18, 2008, delegates discussed and voted by overwhelming majority in favor of Constituent Mandate Number Six, known as the "Mining Mandate."[110] The mandate revoked without compensation all mineral concessions in which no investment had been realized, that were located in protected natural areas, that had been granted to state functionaries in mining-related ministries, or that had been granted to any individual owner who already had at least three other concessions.[111] It declared a moratorium on new concessions, suspended mining activity until the new constitution "entered into force," and established a state-owned mining company.[112] The mandate represented a political position—critical of but not opposed to mining, in favor of more regulation and slower expansion—that would all but disappear a few years later. This position would soon dissolve into two poles: complete opposition to extraction, and a state-corporate alliance to aggressively promote it.[113]

Acción Ecológica's critical response to the Mining Mandate testified to the continued salience of anti-neoliberal discourse. Their press release stated that although they understood that the act was an attempt at the "recuperation of national sovereignty over natural resources," the "spirit of the mandate adopts a position favorable to the push for mining in this country."[114] The press release went on to state that "instead of burying neoliberalism, its long night is prolonged."[115] To conclude, they proclaimed, "Ecuador will not be a mining country." Despite their active participation in anti-mining resistance, Acción Ecológica articulated their criticism of the Mining Mandate in the terms of anti-neoliberalism rather than *extractivismo* discourse. Similarly, when CONAIE wrote a letter of opposition to the government a month later, they did not use the term extractivism, and wrote instead of their resistance to "the neoliberal model" implemented by the Correa administration.[116]

But the Constituent Assembly also provided an institutional setting for the dissemination of *extractivismo* discourse. The possibility of an anti-mining or, more broadly, an anti-extractive position appeared on the discursive horizon, legible but just out of political reach. During his intervention in support of the Mining Mandate, the president of the Constituent Assembly, Alberto Acosta (AP), stated: "I would propose something, comrades, if I could and if I had the votes, I would propose that in Ecuador, we eradicate open pit metallic mining, large-scale open pit metallic mining. But maybe I don't have the votes and I am a realist, why don't we propose a popular consultation, so that the people define their future without fear, sincerely (*sin tapujos*), everything for the fatherland, nothing for us."[117] For Acosta, demanding the eradication of large-scale mining was not yet realistic.[118] However, in the longer speech in which that statement occurred, he put forth an analysis that contained all of the elements of *extractivismo* discourse. He argued that the economic effects (concentration of wealth, speculation), environmental effects (deforestation, soil erosion, water contamination), and social effects (displacement of indigenous communities) of mining and oil extraction are symptomatic of the "extractivist model of development." He hinted at the possibility of a post-extractive future: "we cannot permanently live from the rent of nature." Martha Roldós, a delegate from the center-left party Red Ética y Democracia (RED), also raised the possibility of a national vote on extractivism: "I hope that, in some moment, we have the opportunity that in a referendum, the country decides which is the model of development in which it wants to live, the country decides whether it wants extractivism or not."[119]

The next week, the Natural Resources and Biodiversity Committee (presided over by the Amazonian Kichwa activist and AP delegate Monica Chuji) presented a "diagnosis" that stated that the "primary export model, fundamentally extractivist, in the past 130 years has generated in Ecuador a territorial order (*un ordenamiento territorial*) articulated around the overexploitation of natural resources demanded in the metropoles."[120] Weaving together concepts from dependency theory with the territorialized socio-ecological devastation more recently emphasized by southern Amazonian indigenous groups, this historical narrative of the pathology of extraction swept across colonialism, the establishment of the republic, the incorporation into the world market, and the internal colonization of the northern Amazon, culminating in oil exploitation. It identified the political logic of the extractive model, which undermined the regulatory capacity of the state, resulting in environmental degradation, and reduced politicians to spokespersons for extractive industries.[121]

From the Mining Mandate to the Mining Law

On November 14, 2008, Correa submitted a draft of a new mining law to the interim Congress. A few days later, pockets of protest against the proposed law erupted in Quito and in areas either potentially affected by large-scale mining or with a history of indigenous mobilization around water. On January 7, the CONAIE and Ecuarunari leadership announced a "grand national mobilization in defense of water, the land, food sovereignty and for life" scheduled for January 20, 2009. The language of anti-neoliberalism suffused the announcement: "We express our support for the communities and peoples (*pueblos*) that struggle against the privatizing and neoliberal project of the Mining Law that threatens the life of the peoples and national sovereignty and favors the transnationals."[122] But as the protests unfolded, activists increasingly articulated an anti-extractive stance.

In his weekly radio address, Correa threatened to veto the law and present it as a national referendum if representatives "succumb[ed]" to modifying the law under "pressures" from opposition groups.[123] On January 12, a majority of delegates voted in favor of the law, and it was sent to Correa the next day.[124] The law was poised to be signed by the president when protests swept the country.[125] Participants presented a long list of grievances, but crucially it was the law's perceived infringement of indigenous rights—specifically the right to prior consultation and the protection of communal territories recognized in the recently ratified Constitution—that connected the issue of mining to the historic struggles of the indigenous movement.[126]

Ecuarunari's press release on the day of the march situated the protest in their long struggle for "the defense of human rights, of collective rights and of *Pacha Mama*."[127] They demanded "a true process of change," which would transform the "Neoliberal State" and "construct a Plurinational State." They wove together anti-neoliberalism with a critique of extraction: "The overcoming of the grave effects produced by the neoliberal model cannot be achieved with policies of a developmentalist and extractivist model that promotes the extraction of economic resources at whatever cost and reproduces, in practice, a social-economic structure of inequality, injustice, discrimination, and the exploitation of human beings and nature." In their third grievance, they argued that the law "promotes a model based on the sacking of natural resources (extractivist) and favors transnationals." These demands evidence the shift to a wholesale rejection of resource extraction as the basis of Ecuador's political economy.

Although the final version of the bill was signed into law on January 26, national (the CONAIE and Acción Ecológica), regional (Ecuarunari), and local (UNAGUA, a water users committee in the southern highlands) organizations considered the march a success.[128] First, the law served as a focal point for an emergent coalition of previously locally fragmented anti-mining groups in the southern sierra. Second, these groups gained an important ally in their anti-mining struggle: CONAIE, which saw the law as a direct violation of constitutionally recognized indigenous rights. (As I discuss in Chapter 3, in March 2009, CONAIE brought a case challenging the law's constitutionality to the Constitutional Court.)[129] Third, the demonstrations against the law tested the recently elected president of CONAIE, Marlon Santi, who represented a significant shift for the federation's leadership.[130] He was the first president in eight years to have been elected from CONFENIAE, the Amazonian affiliate of the national indigenous federation.[131] Santi is a member of the Sarayaku indigenous people, who had been engaged in a five-year-long conflict with Argentinian-owned oil company CGC.[132] The combination of Santi's background in oil-related mobilization and a national administration bent on expanding oil and mineral exploitation pushed the indigenous movement to focus on opposing resource extraction.[133]

The consensus represented by the 2008 Mining Mandate—between radical resource nationalism and a nascent critique of extractivism—was no longer viable. For environmental, water, and indigenous activists, the new law revealed that the state-coordinated expansion of mining would be prioritized over indigenous rights and environmental protection. As prominent environmentalist and indigenous rights lawyer Mario Melo explained to me, the uniqueness of the dispute over resource extraction in Ecuador was in large part a product of the administration's attempt to construct a new extractive sector. As he put it, "large-scale mining would be a continuity of this model; rupture would be an alternative model of development. It appears as two distinct paths since large-scale mining is not yet at the extraction phase."[134] Large-scale mining, a sector barely off the ground in a historically oil-dependent country, had become an urgent site of statecraft and resistance. In this new conjuncture, the threat of large-scale mining enabled the consolidation of a radical critique and organizing strategy centered on militant opposition to resource extraction in all forms.

2   *Extractivismo* as Grand Narrative of Resistance

In the wake of the Constituent Assembly and anti-Mining Law protests, *extractivismo* discourse circulated through the conduits of an activist communicational infrastructure. In meetings, texts, public events, and informal conversations, indigenous, environmentalist, anti-mining, and anti-oil activists crafted strikingly similar narratives. When Amanda Yepes of the radical environmental group Acción Ecológica took the stage in a June 2012 debate over mining in the northern city of Ibarra, she recounted a sweeping history of extractivism, dating it to 1534, the year of the Spanish conquest of Quito and the moment of its "insertion into the world market," then sped ahead through the colonial period and independence, noting the continuity of the export-oriented accumulation model that was only reinforced when the first barrel of oil was extracted in Ecuador in 1972. The nascent large-scale mining sector was just one more link in a never-ending chain.

Extractivismo discourse often results in what Bruno Latour refers to as an "acceleration" of analysis.[1] Mimicking the ever-expanding frontier of oil and mineral exploitation that it seeks to describe, *extractivismo* links phenomena across vast expanses of time and space. These phenomena, whether the export-oriented production of cacao, the short-lived oil-funded developmentalism of the 1970s, or the still-under-construction large-scale mining sector, are only so many manifestations of the same essence of extractivism, which is, as Alberto Acosta put it at a November 2011 event in Cuenca, itself the "essence" of "development," understood as the "500-year history" of Western modernity. Its duration in time is matched by the proliferation of damage across space. Extractivism is seen to produce effects at many scales: the distortion of local land use, disordered urban growth, the loss of national sovereignty, and pollution.[2] And, most dramatically, activists indicted the extractive model for causing the death of cultures and ecosystems (see Figure 2.1).

Even within this sweeping account, for anti-extractive activists and intellectuals, the Correa administration was the most extractivist regime in Ecuador's history.[3] This reveals the extent to which the concept had become the linchpin of critiques made by Latin American leftists. These critiques ranged from reproaching Pink Tide governments for sacrificing stated commitments to indigenous rights and environmentalism on the altar of resource extraction, to making the stronger case that the political-economic logic of "leftist" (this too is called into question) administrations was fundamentally "extractivist." According to those that espoused the latter, Correa's discourse of post-neoliberalism, combined with the increase in social spending, merely ideologically legitimated the consolidation of extractivism.[4]

As polarization between the Correa administration and oppositional social movements exacerbated, anti-extractivism and opposition to the government became increasingly intertwined and interchangeable. The first three resolutions adopted at the CONAIE assembly on June 18, 2013, show the tight link between an anti-Correa stance and an anti-extractive stance: "Maintain our political autonomy and independence from the government of President Rafael Correa," "Maintain the unwavering (*inclaudicable*) struggle against the extractivist model," and "Declare Ecuador 'Free of Large Scale Mining' especially in sources of water and watersheds."

As *extractivismo* discourse and opposition to Correa consolidated, indigenous, environmental, and local anti-mining and anti-oil groups—CONAIE, CONFENIAE, Acción Ecológica, Fundación Pachamama, UNAGUA, Asamblea de los Pueblos del Sur, among others—acted to obstruct every phase of what was now seen as an interconnected "extractive model." *Extractivismo* discourse highlighted how the environmental effects of extraction travel to locales distant from oil or mining projects. This occurs through the physical infrastructure that extraction requires (highways, tunnels, pipelines, tailing basins), which causes widespread deforestation, as well as through the media of air and water, which transport contaminants. But, seen through an anti-extractive lens, this model was just as importantly a set of political-economic relationships between points of hydrocarbon or mineral extraction and points of consumption—whether in the form of burned fossil fuels or the redistribution of resource rents as social investment. In the view of anti-extractive activists, these pathways were carved

Figure 2.1 "Mining companies, out!" Note the use of skull and crossbones, a symbol of death, to represent mining companies. The mining helmet bears the name Kinross, a Canadian multinational company that at the time was pursuing a gold-mining project in Ecuador. The crossbones are a mining shovel and pick.

out by the constant egress of crude oil or semi-refined copper ore and the constant ingress of dollars to affected communities, whether to build schools or pay off local officials, and were reinforced by political support concentrated in urban centers. Through the signifying practices of their protest actions, these activists constructed resource extraction as both *a singular point of origin* of a range of social, economic, and environmental pathologies, and as a process comprising *multiple sites of intervention* on the part of state and corporate actors, and, therefore, multiple opportunities for resistance.

The two-week-long March for Water, Life, and the Dignity of Peoples, which departed from the southeastern Amazon on March 8, 2012, and arrived in Quito on March 22, politically repurposed the circuits of the extractive model. I accompanied the marchers, a few hundred at first, as we traversed 700 kilometers on foot and in unwieldy caravans, the number swelling to 25,000 in Quito (see Figure 2.2). We began in the town of Pangui, within what bureaucrats and corporate actors call the "zone of influence" of the Mirador mine, the first large-scale mine with an exploitation contract—which was suspiciously signed just days before the march commenced.[5] We zigzagged through the southern Andes, home to more planned mining projects in the highland wetlands (*parámos*), which supply water to rural farmers and urban consumers. We were subsequently joined by brigades from the northern Amazon, traveling in same direction as the crude that flowed through notoriously faulty pipelines, and finally we arrived in Quito, where the state coffers, voters, and armed forces formed the complex of incentives, democratic legitimacy, and sanctions that activists claimed kept the model in motion.

In the words and imagery disseminated throughout the mobilization process, marchers proposed an alternative model: a post-extractive vision in which the polity was not a machine that ran on fossil fuels but a plural collectivity comprising cultures and ecosystems alike. They declared: "We are water. We will flood Quito." In the most widely circulating poster, the variously sized drops of water were arranged such that they formed one big drop, and were superimposed on a map of Ecuador crisscrossed by blue lines representing its waterways (see Figure 2.3).

The composition invoked an aquatic Leviathan: like the sovereign whose authority both contained and was constituted by his subjects, the image refigured Ecuador as a republic of water in which elements of nature were not only rights-bearing subjects (as per the 2008 Constitution) but active members of the polity. As the pamphlet on the march published by the collective Minería Muerte stated, "We want to march for Water, Life and the Dignity of

Figure 2.2 "Water is the blood that nourishes the earth." Arriving in Quito during the 2012 March for Water, Life, and the Dignity of Peoples. Photo Credit: Elisa Levy.

Peoples, march toward splendid life, to a new civilization, to the true *Sumak Kawsay*, where we recognize ourselves as the sisters and brothers of the tree, of the bird and the bacteria, brothers and sisters of the drops of rain, indigenous to the planet Earth, daughters and sons of the only Mother, sisters and brothers with equal rights."[6] Anti-extractivism radically decentered human beings: crude and ore were political protagonists; wetlands and mountains were moral agents. It was a truly *post*-neoliberal project: the activists and intellectuals who crafted this discursive-political strategy sought not only to transform the regime they had labeled neoliberalism but also to transcend the repertoire of anti-neoliberal resistance. The problematic of *extractivismo* shifted the focus away from the classic concerns of both Marxism and egalitarian liberalism: the mode of production, the property regime, the pattern of distribution, the regulation of the economy, or the means to socio-economic development. In its purest form, the perspective of *extractivismo* discourse regarded these concepts and their political targets as not only insufficient but as reproducing the developmentalist pathology that was the essence of Western civilization.

Figure 2.3
"Drops of water" poster.

MARCHA POR EL AGUA, LA VIDA Y LA DIGNIDAD DE LOS PUEBLOS

fecha de salida 8 de marzo de 2012
mineriamuerte.wordpress.com

Bureaucrats in a Bind

In the wake of the protests against the mining and water laws, and especially after the March for Water, Life, and the Dignity of Peoples, state officials found themselves operating on a new political terrain. Social movements deployed militant rhetoric in opposition to resource extraction, and, though still geographically fragmented, had demonstrated their ability to obstruct the development of a large-scale mining sector, whether by building coalitions around the issue of water in Azuay, electing an anti-mining prefect in Zamora Chinchipe, physically blockading bureaucrats and corporate representatives from entering a project's zone of influence, or protesting mining at the halls of state and corporate power in Quito (see Figure 2.4).[7]

In the face of this opposition, bureaucrats were tasked with implementing a post-neoliberal resource policy in which the state asserted control over its resources and directed the proceeds of extraction to local and national development. Furthermore, there were new, if still ill-defined, constitutional and legislative standards for policymaking: to construct *buen vivir*, to ensure

Figure 2.4 "Megadiverse country. Perverse mining plan." Graffiti, Quito, August 2011.

equity across the regions of Ecuador, and to expand state authority over the private sector while at the same time encouraging local cooperatives and small businesses (the "popular and solidary economy"). Meanwhile, large-scale mining was still a nascent industry, and to get it off (or out of) the ground, foreign corporations needed to be convinced that Ecuadorian projects were a profitable and secure investment. In addition to these multiple pressures, the task of bureaucrats was made more challenging by the institutional complexity that pervaded mining regulation. Officials positioned in a wide range of agencies, each with distinct missions and organizational cultures, were involved in the multifaceted process of creating and controlling this new economic sector.

The internal diversity of the bureaucratic field was evident in the array of discourses around resource extraction and at times contradictory policy initiatives.[8] The functionaries at agencies tasked with longer-term planning and the management of socio-environmental conflict most consistently used the language of *extractivismo*, raised concerns about the detrimental effects of extractivism, and were the most committed to a post-extractive economy. In sharp contrast, those involved in the negotiation of contracts or the environmental approval of projects, as well as the president and his circle of advisers, deployed a series of arguments about the economic blessing of natural resources and the mitigable socio-environmental impacts of their exploitation. As protest against extraction intensified, this latter group made the more provocative claim that resistance to oil and mineral projects was tantamount to treason.

The range of official positions on resource extraction was a product of the politicization of resource extraction and the challenge this posed for state actors. But this range also cautions against viewing (anti-)neoliberalism and (anti-)extractivism as two discrete periods of statecraft and resistance. The commitment to the recuperation of state sovereignty over national resources strongly inflected official policy and discourse around mineral resources. Anti-neoliberal discourse had become institutionalized, and persisted beyond the immediate objectives for which it was crafted. Correa administration officials—especially those who pushed for the expansion of resource extraction—redeployed the anti-neoliberal discourse first elaborated by activists in the 1990s. In their protest of neoliberal policies, indigenous, labor, urban barrio, and campesino activists had claimed oil as the collective subterranean patrimony of the people. State actors re-signified this radical resource nationalism: they replaced its popular sector coalition with the sovereignty of the state, and they abandoned its deeper critique of capitalism, emphasizing instead the technocratic regulation of the economy in the interest of a homogeneously defined public. Further, and in effect consolidating the link between national sovereignty and natural resources initially forged in anti-neoliberal rebellion, pro-extraction state actors cast those opposed to extraction as enemies of the state. These state actors characterized anti-extractive activists as the tools of imperial forces, and accordingly pursued legal action against protesters, the prosecution of whom was explicitly framed in terms of protecting the state from its enemies.

Caught between increasing "socio-environmental conflict" (the favored corporate-cum-bureaucratic term for protest related to mining or oil), wary investors, and a president committed to new extractive projects, these various bureaucratic discourses were themselves modes of state intervention in the emerging field of practice defined by the problematic of resource extraction. In this sense, following Vivien Schmidt, written and spoken discourse produced by state actors "is what enables agents to change institutions, because the deliberative nature of discourse allows them to conceive of and talk about institutions as objects at a distance, and to dissociate themselves from them even as they continue to use them."[9] At this "second order" level, discursive activity ("to deliberate and persuade") enjoins policymaking and institutional reform. As James Ferguson demonstrates with regard to the "development discourse" that was pervasive in his case study of Lesotho, the patterned talk of bureaucrats is bound up in their practice, insofar as discursive regimes supply the problems and solutions—the sites and modes of intervention, respectively—of statecraft.[10] This resonates with Foucault's insights regarding the emergence of the state as a specific form of reflexive practice, a development that he dates to the end of the sixteenth century, wherein the activity of writing and talking about the state was pivotal in connecting what had previously been disparate institutions into a unified field of practice henceforth understood as *the* state.[11] For these authors, studying the patterns of state discourse—both the discourse of state actors, and discourse about the state—is inseparable from the study of the constraints and possibilities of state action.

This is especially the case in the context of the design of new institutions or policies, where actors must articulate their objectives in dialogue or contention with others in order to realize—or resist—plans for what does not yet exist. In the case of Ecuador, it was the exigencies of the construction of a new extractive sector that forced actors on all sides to retool their strategies for political action. The study of the debate over extractivism therefore not only brings our attention to the discursive dimension of the assembly of political institutions, but also points to the importance of attending to a broader array of phenomena in the study of the political economy of resource dependency, often ignored in the narrow focus on the distribution of resource rents in much of the social science literature.[12]

State actors' orientations toward resource extraction were refracted through their efforts to construct a post-neoliberal political economy—and, therefore, through their specific critique of the "neoliberal era." For bureaucrats, neoliberalism referred to the political era that had ended with Correa's ascent to power. In their view, the neoliberal period was marked by the absence of the state or, more specifically, as the lack of state planning and coordination of the economy.[13] Lorena Jacombe, a functionary at SENPLADES (Secretariat of National Planning and Development) who worked in the area of public investment, captured how this historical narrative inflected the present task of post-neoliberal transition.[14] As she described it, the neoliberal state "was a weak state, it was a minimal state, it was an inefficient state, it was a chaotic state, a product of all of the neoliberal stabilization policies . . . In comparison with that, what we hope for is a strengthening of the state . . . a revitalization of the state. It is a regulatory state, a state that recovers its capacities, its authority to govern, to issue public policy, to be able to regulate and control, a state that sets limits when limits must be set." In affinity with their professional identity as *técnicos* (experts), Jacombe and her colleagues framed neoliberalism in technocratic terms, shorn of any ideological reference points. It is telling that she not only characterizes the neoliberal state as "weak" and "minimal" but also as "chaotic" and "inefficient"; as a corollary, a post-neoliberal state would be an authoritative and efficient regulator of economic life. This technocratic rendering contrasts sharply with more radical conceptualizations of neoliberalism—as a set of policy responses to a global crisis in capital accumulation, a class project to reassert the power of capital over labor, an ideology that valorized entrepreneurial individualism, or a socio-economic technology enabling commodification on an unprecedented scale—as well as with analyses of neoliberalism that challenge the very notion that it was a withdrawal of the state by pointing to the augmentation of the state's repressive apparatus, or to the adoption of new regulations to protect markets from democracy.[15]

The temporal logic of Jacombe's narrative resonated with Correa's repeated statement that his administration spelled the end of the "long night of neoliberalism." Neoliberalism was a thing of the past. As proclaimed in Correa's campaign slogan-cum-official government motto, the "Citizens' Revolution," through an amalgam of popular mandate and bureaucratic fiat, had triumphed. However, in the process of policymaking, the rupture cleanly separating past and present gave way to the more complex temporality of transition, shot through with continuities both inertial and intentional in nature.

For bureaucrats who saw their task as planning the transition away from both neoliberalism *and* extractivism, resource extraction posed a vexing paradox: in the short and medium-term, building a post-neoliberal economy necessitated the intensification of extraction and the fiscal capture of extraordinary profits; in the longer term, however, post-extractivism would require transforming the model of accumulation. The top environmental adviser at the Coordinating Ministry of Patrimony explained to me that this transition comprised two simultaneous processes that were in tension with one another. First, the "extractive model is intensified" to convert "natural resources" into "investment and redistribution."[16] Second, there was a gradual but decided transition from an "extractivist model" based on "primary exports" to a new "axis of accumulation" centered on the "biodiversity" of "a diverse, plurinational country." Over the course of my fieldwork, several bureaucrats articulated this complex political economy: they argued that extractivism was entrenched in such a manner that it could only be overcome by squeezing out every last drop of resource rents. The 520-page official development plan and socio-economic treatise, "El plan nacional para el buen vivir: 2009–2013," repeatedly describes the *longue durée* of Ecuadorian history as characterized by an extractivist primary commodity export mode of accumulation, and elaborates the consequences: inequality, territorial fragmentation, economic dependency, environmental degradation, among others.[17] As the plan states, "To date, Ecuador has had 20 constitutions. Except for the developmentalist period, which did not prosper for multiple reasons, the development strategy . . . has consisted in generating wealth through the export of primary agricultural or non-renewable (oil) goods. It has been an extractivist primary export strategy."[18] The resonance with activists' critique is striking—and it testifies to the broad circulation of *extractivismo* discourse, as well as to the enduring influence of dependency theory on both social movements and state officials.[19] But for bureaucrats, there was a twist: since "leaving this model in an immediate manner is unviable," oil and, in the near future, mining would remain key components of a "sustainable endogenous strategy" to satisfy basic needs.[20] This logic renders large-scale mining necessary for a post-extractive transition. The dissemination of this plan in turn circulated this logic among bureaucrats in the nexus of central ministries in Quito as well as the decentralized agencies in the provinces, home to new mining and oil projects.

Multiple high-level bureaucrats at SENPLADES, a key site of the production of official interpretations of concepts such as *buen vivir*, articulated some variant of the argument that intensified resource extraction was a necessary means for overcoming extractivism. For these officials, extractivism was at the heart of the complex temporality of the Citizens' Revolution. As Eugenio Paladines from the SENPLADES Sub-Secretariat of Decentralized Planning put it, mining must be "planned so that what happened with oil doesn't happen again."[21] Mining has the potential to "develop new activities, industries, it will get linked (*encadenarse*)," meaning that the sector will not remain an enclave economy in the classic dependency theory sense, but will stimulate the growth of non-extractive sectors.[22] For Paladines, the point of inflection toward a post-extractive economy was not a "future transition" but a current problem to be acted on immediately. Mining would both provide revenue for pressing needs and trigger *encadenamiento*, the process of coordinated economic linkage that had become a bureaucratic mantra. Large-scale mining, a sector still in the early stages of construction, was to be the beginning of the end: "a post-oil vision," as María Belen, in the same division as Paladines, told me—or, as an official at the Ministry of Political Coordination phrased it, "the last moment of extraction."[23] But how long is a moment? Belen added yet more layers of temporal complexity to the transition. On the one hand, as she explained, the structure of ownership of the territory and its resources remained inscribed in a neoliberal logic: after "forty years of [mineral] concessions, of private rights . . . we haven't recuperated control over our territory. We don't have clarity over the wealth of our subsoil. We haven't achieved sovereignty."[24] On the other hand, despite the actuality of concessions that testify to a prior era of deregulated and privatized governance, she asserted that mining policy should be oriented toward the future: "The perspective must be twenty-five years after mining. Neither the government nor the movements have this holistic point of view."

Bureaucrats engaged in long-term planning often expressed a sense that they felt constrained by larger forces. They characterized themselves as well-intentioned *técnicos* hemmed in by competing demands that emanated from inside and outside the state. As Paladines said, "There are groups that want to exploit everything, there are others that want nothing. In these two interests the state must intervene. The government is between two extremes." While Belen characterized the conflict as between state and non-state actors, Paladines left the "groups" undefined, raising the possibility that the state may in fact need to intervene against itself. Their colleague German Guerra concretized this latter possibility: "You have a confrontation between a more extractivist vision and a more conservationist vision . . . within the government itself."[25]

This multifaceted confrontation—between past and future, between extraction and post-extraction—is particularly intense for the bureaucrats stationed in the provinces directly affected by mining projects. This became apparent when I spoke with Mariuxsi Flores, the provincial director of ECORAE (Institute for the Eco-development of the Amazon) in Zamora Chinchipe, home to the only large-scale mining project in the country. The contract for the open-pit copper mine was signed with ECSA (owned by a consortium of Chinese state-owned companies) days before the March for Water, Life, and the Dignity of Peoples commenced in Pangui, one of the towns in the officially designated zone of influence of the project. Zamora Chinchipe was also home to the most prominent anti-mining elected official, Provincial Prefect Salvador Quishpe. Flores found herself navigating this tricky political terrain. She framed her policy positions as a product of a specifically "Amazonian" vision, in contrast to bureaucrats in the central ministry offices located in Quito. Speaking quickly and with intensity, she listed the components of an "agenda of transformation" for the region: "bio-knowledge, bio-commerce, coffee, cacao, sustainable ranching," which, combined, would transition from an "extractivist model" (*matriz*) to an "ecosystemic model."[26] Then, without a pause, she proceeded to explain her support for mining. Animating a collective territorial voice that papered over the contention in her province, she said, "We as the Amazon view mining as an opportunity to adopt a development model with a clear mining policy . . . so that the state does not lose and the environment is preserved." She thus combined a commitment to a post-extractive transformation, framed in explicitly ecological terms, with an unwavering support for extractive projects.

In contrast to these bureaucrats, who reappropriated elements of *extractivismo* discourse and deployed them as a justification for intensified extraction (as the path to a post-extractive future), President Correa frequently insisted that mineral resources were a blessing, not a curse.

Sometimes, however, he allowed that if properly managed, mineral resources in fact could provide the solution to the very negative consequences that environmentalist and indigenous activists attributed to their extraction. As he put it in a July 2012 televised interview on the state-owned TV station, "with the resources from mining we can conserve the environment, because they give us the resources to construct urgent [public] works"—referring to the sewage systems he had just mentioned. He continued, "It doesn't destroy the environment. Intelligent mining will conserve the environment, and will help us get out of underdevelopment. So you have to be intelligent, not think with the gut [points to his stomach], but instead, with reason, and heart [points to head and chest]."[27] Despite the pro-extraction stance, in the same interview Correa also asserted that his policies were aiming for a post-extractive transition. Addressing "those who always talk of leaving the extractivist economy," he said, "we are going to convert ourselves for the first time in the world to an exporter of services, in this case energy services—what's more, clean energy." Sidestepping for a moment whether the export of hydropower counts as "post-extractive"— precisely the types of distinctions at stake in the debate over the extractive model—what is noteworthy here is that Correa insisted on such a transition at all. This was a rare exception to his otherwise vehement support for expanding oil and mining, and as such is a testament to the political power of *extractivismo* discourse.

More frequently, Correa and functionaries from the Ministry of Nonrenewable Resources and Ministry of Environment justified the intensification of resource extraction without any such appeal to a post-extractive future. Instead, their discourse centered on the here and now, highlighting the immediate benefits of extraction and downplaying its socio-environmental costs. As I was told by every Ministry of Environment official I interviewed and as I heard in every state-industry mining convention I attended, "every human activity impacts the environment," and any negative impact could be mitigated such that it did not become a "liability" (*pasivo*). Or, if a future was relevant, it was never a post-extractive future. The policy framework outlined in the Ministry of Nonrenewable Resources' "Plan nacional de desarrollo del sector minero 2011–2015," a publication frequently invoked in mining-related public events, does not use the term "extractivism" at all, and while it speaks of a "future" to be constructed, that future consists of "a new mining culture" rather than a future free of resource dependency.[28] The contrast in language and policy orientation with SENPLADES's "Plan nacional para el buen vivir" is striking.

Similarly, when Wilson Pastor, then minister of nonrenewable resources, was asked in a newspaper interview about the government's "extractivist economic model," he denied the relevance of the problematic by responding that, since a manufacturing sector "that has never existed cannot be invented," therefore "we have to continue with natural resources as the main source"— presumably of state revenue and/or economic development. When he insisted that "the model is changing, and radically," the term "model" referred not to the source of state revenue but to the structure of investment, as well as the regulatory and technological apparatus.[29] By "radical change" he meant the use of technology that results in less environmental harm, as well as the reinvestment of oil income in hydroelectric plants "to [make] clean energy."

For Correa, the debate over extractivism was not merely a disagreement over economic policy. More fundamentally, it revealed a rupture within leftism over the means and ends of radical transformation. In an interview with the journal *New Left Review* in fall 2012, Correa reflected on this internecine conflict:

> It is madness to say no to natural resources, which is what part of the left is proposing—no to oil, no to mining, no to gas, no to hydroelectric power, no to roads. This is an absurd novelty, but it's as if it has become a fundamental part of left discourse. It is all the more dangerous for coming from people who supposedly speak the same language. With so many restrictions, the left will not be able to offer any viable political projects . . . We cannot lose sight of the fact that the main objective of a country such as Ecuador is to eliminate poverty. And for that we need our natural resources. There are people here who seem ready to create more poverty but leave those resources in the ground, or who even see poverty as something folkloric.[30]

Correa stressed the "novelty" of anti-extractive discourse at the same time that he dismissed it as "madness" and "dangerous" precisely because it was articulated as leftism. While Correa's language further polarized the conflict between his administration and his former allies among social movement organizations, it also pointed to an important obstacle to popular mobilization along anti-extractive lines. Under the Correa administration, both the economic growth caused by the commodity boom and the influx of oil revenues enabled increased social spending, resulting in dramatically reduced poverty and inequality. In our informal conversations, environmentalist and indigenous activists noted that these socio-economic gains posed a symbolic and practical challenge to broad-based mobilization against resource extraction—especially to including the urban *mestizo* populations in cities like Quito and Guayaquil, who do not face the immediate environmental and social impacts of extractive projects.[31] Correa reanalyzed this political challenge as anti-extractive activists' failure to confront poverty, and, even worse, to see poverty as "folkloric," part of a romantic image of indigenous communities. Against this image, Correa presented his modernizing project as one of eliminating poverty through state spending.

The apotheosis of this rejection of anti-extractivism was the argument that opposition to oil and mineral extraction is a tactic of imperial powers acting under the guise of environmentalism. This redeployment of the anti-imperialist strand of Latin American critical thought highlights the degree to which this was a fight within the Left. As conflict over extractive projects intensified, Correa elaborated on his characterization of anti-extractive protesters as at odds with leftism. During the summer of 2013, in the midst of resistance to the planned expansion of oil exploration and exploitation into the southern Amazon, he increasingly accused activists of being tools of imperialism. In December 2013, during one of his weekly Saturday addresses (*sabatina*), he cited the work of Bolivia's vice president, Álvaro García Linera, who he called "one of the great thinkers" of the continent.[32] He was most likely referring to García Linera's long essay about power and capitalist accumulation in the Amazon, published a year before, which systematically attacks anti-extractivism.[33] While there are important differences between the positions of García Linera and Correa, they both characterize *extractivismo* discourse and political strategy as an invention of foreign NGOs, who—as representatives of wealthy nations—have a vested interest in undermining the economic development of poor, resource-dependent nations.[34] According to this argument, foreign NGOs (as Correa puts it, "the little *gringos* with their full stomachs") enlist indigenous organizations to resist resource extraction and to declare themselves in opposition to the government.[35] The issue of territorial control is a key component of this argument. For Correa and García Linera, since the state has never fully consolidated control over its Amazonian territory, foreign NGOs represent a continuity of the rule of private economic interests over the region, further impeding the reassertion of state sovereignty that is central to Correa's political project.[36]

This discourse circulated through presidential addresses and ministerial offices, in both speeches and in documents, such as an April 2010 report of the Secretariat of Peoples, Social Movements and Citizen Participation, which frequently invokes the specter of NGOs as the source of "anti-mining discourse."[37] Despite its anti-imperialist thrust (by invoking foreign capital as a cause of weak territorial control on the part of state institutions), the delegitimation of *extractivismo* discourse via its attribution to foreign environmentalist NGOs was also articulated by corporate representatives, as well as by NGOs aligned with the government. It was frequently voiced at mining industry conventions and mining company headquarters, as well as at events or workshops organized by these NGOs. Each moment of discursive relay and reproduction invited the possibility of innovation and re-signification. For example, some of the private-sector actors modified the analysis: they claimed that foreign NGOs were financed by rival mining companies with an interest in undermining their competition.[38]

The redeployment of anti-imperialist discourse against anti-extractive activists took the form of a multilayered political irony. Some of the same social movements and intellectuals that Correa attacked as the tools or accomplices of imperialist organizations had, prior to his rise to power, advanced similar critiques of the political-economic interests of NGOs and their complicity in state retrenchment from social welfare provision in the neoliberal period.[39] Just as some state officials marshaled the concepts of *extractivismo* and *post-extractivismo* to justify resource extraction, mining company representatives decontextualized the argument against environmentalist NGOs from any critique of capitalism. Furthermore, although this discourse usually invokes foreign NGOs—and indeed their external provenance is key to the argument's avowed anti-imperialism—in practice it was most forcefully applied against domestic organizations that have transnational linkages, allies, donors, or employees, which is to say most environmentalist or indigenous groups. To the extent that the critique of NGOs and their ostensible role in propagating *extractivismo* discourse is reflected in policy decisions, the targets are Ecuadorian organizations. Acción Ecológica was dissolved in an executive order in March 2009 on the accusation of unspecified "violent acts," alleged deviation from its mission, interference in public policy, and threatening national security; following a reversal of that order, it was shut down again in December 2016.[40] And in December 2013, Fundación Pachamama was dramatically forced to shut its offices after the Ministry of Environment alleged its participation in physical confrontations and verbal abuse during a protest against the Eleventh Round of Oil Tender.[41] In the state-owned press, the NGO was characterized as controlled by foreigners.[42] More generally, the characterization of protesters as treasonous has been accompanied by what activists refer to as the criminalization of protest: following its inauguration in 2007, the Correa administration pursued legal action against approximately 200 individuals for their participation in protests against resource extraction.[43] About a third of these were arrested during the demonstrations against the 2009 Mining Law and 2010 Water Law. The charges for what were almost exclusively acts of nonviolent protest are telling: sabotage or terrorism. On December 14, 2016, after a police officer was killed during a violent conflict with members of the Shuar community in Nankints over the San Carlos copper project (a planned open-pit mine in the Amazonian province of Morona Santiago), Correa issued an executive order declaring a province-wide state of emergency. He sent in soldiers and police to forcibly clear a mining camp that had been occupied by Nankints residents in response to their territorial displacement by the copper project, as well as to raid the homes of neighboring Shuar communities.[44] The state of emergency ended on February 14, but the military checkpoints that had been set up were not removed.

Conclusion

From 1972 to 2017, Ecuador saw dramatic transformations in resource governance and resource radicalisms. These existed in a relationship of dynamic, albeit asymmetric, co-constitution. In addition to establishing the state-owned oil company and the institutional framework of sectoral policy, the Rodríguez Lara military government embraced an ideology of resource nationalism, articulated in anti-imperial and developmentalist terms. Although short-lived, this inaugural orientation bequeathed an organizational and ideological legacy. After a few years, under attack from foreign oil companies and domestic elites, and in the midst of declining prices, the official resource nationalist governance regime was dismantled, and neoliberal oil policies were implemented. In this context, popular organizations such as oil workers' unions and the national indigenous federation articulated their own variant of resource nationalism: radicalized and from below, they wielded it as a forceful critique of *neoliberalismo*, and transformed resource extraction into a site of radical politics. They claimed oil as the people's patrimony, and demanded the termination of contracts with foreign oil companies and democratic control over the economy.

At the same time, in the central and southern Amazonian provinces, the Sarayaku people, along with the Achuar and Shuar nations, were in a battle with foreign and state-owned oil companies. In the course of the struggle to defend communal territory from yet another form of encroachment and displacement (the earlier iterations being state-led land colonization, and logging), these indigenous communities identified oil extraction as a threat to their cultural survival. Alongside the radical clamor for nationalization and redistribution, in these conflicts a different critique of resource extraction began to emerge, focusing less on ownership or regulation, and more on localized socio-environmental devastation and the threat to indigenous territorial integrity. In 2006, these struggles in the streets of the capital and in the rainforests of the Amazon, combined with mass discontent with neoliberalism and existing political parties, brought the Left to national electoral power. But, despite his embrace of resource nationalism (rhetorically, and to an extent in policy reforms), the victory of leftist Rafael Correa did not spell the end of resource-related protest. On the contrary. His election was a key element in a political-economic conjuncture that occasioned the radical re-politicization of resource extraction. Drawing on the recent history of indigenous resistance to oil extraction in Amazon, a range of groups elaborated a wholesale rejection of the extractive model of development and developed a new repertoire of resistance strategies to target each of its nodes.

The state response to this strategic shift was bipolar, and each pole was inflected by resource radicalisms present and past: one set of bureaucrats adopted the language of *extractivismo*; another doubled down on resource nationalism. For the first faction, the post-extractive transition constituted a concrete problem for state practice; for the second, anti-extractive resistance posed a threat to national development and was aligned with the interests of imperial powers. If Correa's election was the condition of possibility of a shift in the prevailing radical critique of extraction, two more elements of the conjuncture would consolidate both the radicalization of anti-extractive resistance and the internal dissensus within the state over the question of extraction. These were the 2007–2008 Constituent Assembly, and the Correa administration's avid promotion of large-scale mining—the subjects of the chapters to follow.

Before continuing to trace the contours of this emergent political terrain, it is worth pausing to reflect on the possibilities and limitations of each of the two predominant resource radicalisms. Radical resource nationalism posited an expansive political subject ("we the people") against the widely despised figure of the foreign capitalist. It concretized resistance to neoliberalism and solidified a popular-sector coalition, tying together groups with distinct histories of struggle: indigenous federations, labor unions, urban movements. Even if CONAIE, one of the key protagonists of radical resource nationalism, struggled for plurinationalism, their political project explicitly encompassed the grievances and the demands of a broader bloc of the oppressed that included the non-indigenous. It called for concrete changes in the structure of ownership and regulation and framed these as necessary to address the unsatisfied basic needs of the population. Its narrative structure was progressive and teleological: a bright future of reclaimed sovereignty lies ahead.

Extractivismo discourse presented a different set of demands, identities, and temporal structure, and even redrew the cartography of popular struggle. Many indigenous and environmental activists declare their opposition to extraction in all forms, but rarely define the limits of this category: Does agriculture count? What about small-scale mining? Post-extraction is also hard to pin down, and the vision can slide into a montage of imagined precolonial pasts and hazy extraction-free futures (organic agriculture and ecotourism are frequently alluded to). Meanwhile, the very territoriality of extraction, while enabling the obstruction of projects at the sites of exploration, construction, and extraction, is less conducive to mass mobilization in densely populated cities.

However, despite and because of its radical reframing of the leftist problematic, *extractivismo* has served to guide social movements to concrete victories, and has upended accepted notions of the prerequisites for collective action. Several specific campaigns have forged urban-rural coalitions, and in the process rescaled who counts as "directly affected" by extractive projects. Inhabitants of Cuenca, the third-largest city in Ecuador, joined campesino activists (often organized in community water councils) in the rural highlands right outside municipal lines to resist mining projects that would affect their shared water supply, which both irrigates dairy and vegetable farms and slakes urban demand. Bureaucrats confessed that their multifaceted anti-mining mobilization contributed to stalling development of the planned Quimsacocha gold mine, one of the government's five "strategic" projects. In 2013, a decentralized network of activists across the country mounted an impressive campaign to prevent oil extraction in the Yasuní National Park, a UNESCO Biosphere Reserve and home to numerous indigenous communities (some living in voluntary isolation). The administration had previously adopted a civil society proposal to *not* extract oil in the park, in exchange for $3.6 billion in donations from the international community to fund sustainable development (framed as the "ecological debt" owed by the Global North to the Global South). When the government failed to attract enough donations by the deadline, Correa decided to proceed with oil extraction, sparking the formation of the activist network YASunídos.[45] The campaign drew huge protests in major cities far from the sites of extraction.[46] Despite not achieving their goals, the resistance to oil extraction in Yasuní reached a scale in numerical size and territorial expanse comparable to the large protests against Occidental Petroleum and free trade in 2005 and 2006.

Importantly, the YASunídos campaign also directly contested Correa's claims that exploiting the Yasuní is necessary to fight poverty, and proposed alternatives such as increasing taxes on the wealthy. By broadening the territorial base of anti-extractive protest and incorporating the historic economic concerns of the popular sectors, contention over the Yasuní expanded the repertoire of anti-extractive resistance, and opened up the possibility of a class-based critique of Correa's oil and mineral-funded political project—a point to which I return in the Conclusion.

3   *Consulta Previa*

The Political Life of a
Constitutional Right

The 2007–2008 Constituent Assembly pro-
vided a venue for the articulation of two political projects: a nascent anti-
extractivism and radical resource nationalism. The resulting 2008 Constitution
is a fundamentally contradictory text. It empowers both local communities
and the central state to make decisions regarding resource extraction. It
grants rights to nature, and it asserts the state's exclusive control over subsoil
resources and biodiversity itself. The document bears the traces of its origins
in decades of social struggle, as well as emergent disagreements among leftists
over the substantive content of leftist rule: was it post-neoliberal, or socialist, or post-extractive—or all three? The Constituent Assembly did not settle
these internecine debates, but instead staged a dispute over the relationship
between the state, the national territory, its natural resources, and the collective identity of the democratic "people" that continued to reverberate long
after its ratification.[1] Its preamble and 444 articles, along with subsequent
laws, executive decrees, and Constitutional Court decisions, infused the
conflict over resource extraction with a new "language of contention" with
which state and social movement actors justified and critiqued, governed and
resisted.[2]

Based on an analysis of archival documents, this chapter traces the Constituent Assembly debates, focusing on the contentious drafting of the right
to prior consultation: the collective right of affected communities to be consulted prior to resource extraction. This right was a flashpoint in conflict
over the "extractive model." I then draw on ethnographic research and

interviews conducted between 2011 and 2014 to examine the subsequent political life of the 2008 Constitution, and of this constitutional right in particular, after its ratification. Throughout, I argue that the political life of the constitution—its salience and normative force—is an emergent outcome of its invocation in political practice. I demonstrate that *constituent politics*—the multiplex activity of refoundation and legitimation—is not limited to "rare periods of political innovation and original constitutional making."[3] Rather, it is an ongoing process that predates and outlives constitutional drafting, and comprises the context-specific relations between assertions of constituent power, the written constitutional text, and constituted governments.

The Constituent Assembly occasioned highly contentious debates over prior consultation, plurinationalism, resource extraction, the rights of nature, and the recognition of Kichwa as an official language, among other issues.[4] These debates drove a wedge between Correa and historically mobilized popular organizations, and contributed to the internal fracture of his political party, Alianza País. The final document only partially implemented the political platform of CONAIE and allied movement organizations. In the lead-up to the popular referendum to approve the Constitution, CONAIE member organizations criticized the text's shortfalls and debated whether to support ratification. Ultimately, the so-called "critical yes" strategy prevailed: CONAIE members were encouraged to vote in favor of ratification at the same time that the CONAIE leadership voiced criticisms of its limitations. As detailed below, however, in the wake of the landslide vote to ratify the text, and during the protests against the 2009 Mining Law, these same activists shifted their position, fully embracing the Constitution and linking it to historic social mobilizations. In the ensuing battle over resource extraction, indigenous, environmental, anti-mining, and anti-oil activists, and allied intellectuals, constantly referenced constitutional articles, and explicitly described themselves as the document's vigilant defenders.[5] But these activists were not textual literalists. They read selectively, highlighting new collective rights while ignoring the state's "inalienable" control over nonrenewable resources. More significantly, their language often resuscitated proposals that had been rejected in committee or on the plenary floor, such as binding prior consent and territorial self-determination. Popular movements enlisted this reading of the constitutional text in their fight against extractivism. In the process, they claimed constituent power—the collective capacity of self-authorization that at once undergirds, exceeds, and limits the power of constituted governments—through the creative deployment and interpretation of the constitutional text.[6]

The degree of intentionality of this "misreading" of the Constitution is empirically unrecoverable and, I would suggest, besides the point. My field experiences convinced me that indigenous, environmental, anti-mining, and anti-oil activists, and allied intellectuals, truly believed that what they called "the Constitution" was on their side. But, for them, "the Constitution" referred not to the 217 pages of inert constitutional text, but to an evolving set of constitutional interpretations that invoked specific textual fragments and enlisted them in a political struggle over the model of development. These constitutional interpretations were "strategies without a strategist": concrete semiotic practices embedded in a historically specific social field that pragmatically intervened in an ongoing, relationally defined terrain of political struggle.[7] These activists and intellectuals did not operate in a vacuum. Historically, their constitutional interpretations indexed past struggles; politically, they deployed these interpretations in their encounters with state and corporate actors. State and corporate actors, meanwhile, tended to circumvent the aspirational and transformative language of the Constitution, substituting it with laws, decrees, and regulations that provided a legal basis for a technocratic vision of the relations between state, society, natural resources, and economic development.

More generally, these competing interpretive strategies evidence the degree to which legal codification—whether in a constitution, ordinary laws, ministerial regulations, or executive decrees—does not mark the conclusion of constituent politics. Instead, the enactment of legal norms in practice requires interpretive strategies that link abstract language to concrete instances of enforcement or resistance. In Ecuador, these acts of constitutional interpretation took place in a wide variety of venues, consisting not only, or even primarily, of courtrooms, but also of ministry offices in the capital and in the provinces, state and corporate information centers in affected communities, social movement organization headquarters, anti-mining and anti-oil demonstrations, popular assemblies in repurposed auditoriums and soccer fields, and texts of various genres.[8] These sites, events, and texts constituted the material and relational infrastructure of the circulation of constitutional discourse—and the lifeblood of its political effectivity. When state officials, corporate actors, politicians, and anti-mining activists invoked and interpreted a constitutional right, they did not merely ascribe meaning to an inert document. Rather, I show that it was only through such semiotic activity that constitutional mandates had a political life at all.

Constituent Politics

My analytic perspective conjoins recent debates on constituent politics in Latin America, with ethnographic and law-and-society approaches that situate the production of legality in broader social milieux, and investigate the non-legal sources of law's power and transgression.[9] In Venezuela, Bolivia, and Ecuador, leftist presidents convened popularly elected constituent assemblies empowered to rewrite constitutions.[10] Presidents Hugo Chávez, Evo Morales, and Rafael Correa framed these constituent processes as necessary to refound the state and to decisively sever their administrations from the legacies of colonialism, exclusion, and neoliberalism that had historically structured the political order.[11] In each case, constituent assembly processes involved novel forms of social movement and citizen participation, and resulted in texts that dramatically expanded social, economic, and indigenous rights, established new participatory institutions, and strengthened executive authority over strategic sectors of the economy, such as resource extraction.[12]

While scholars have attended to these moments of refounding as well as the social struggles that preceded them, less attention has been paid to the everyday forms of political activity that imbued constitutional texts with continued political salience and normative force long after their ratification. This chapter traces the 2008 Constitution as a document that lives through temporally and spatially dispersed political activity, and that is continually redefined by its concrete deployment in political struggle. This is what Kim Scheppele refers to as a "constitutional ethnography": a method that analyzes "the *strategies* through which governance is attempted, experienced, resisted and revised, taken in historical depth and cultural context."[13] As Upendra Baxsi puts it, ethnographic approaches to the "making, working, and unmaking of constitutions" can account for both the jurisprudence of officially sanctioned "lawpersons" and popular interpretive practices.[14] In this vein, Kregg Hetherington's ethnographic analysis of the legal practices that Paraguayan campesinos deployed in their struggles for land redistribution highlights how the law was enacted and enforced in the course of contention in the countryside, and in turn linked to sites of official legal production in Asunción via the circulation of people, discourses, and documents.[15] Reflecting on the interactions between police and protesting campesinos, he writes: "The irony is that for all their references to upholding the constitution, the law was not some pre-given code that campesinos were simply respecting in the camp. Instead, *the law was being made* in these encounters with the police, and not symmetrically. The rules of protest were improvised, and they were legal only because police consent made them so. In other words, the campesino protest not only reinforced the law as the only legitimate terrain of struggle, but also revealed the law as subject to the dictate of violence."[16] In Ecuador too, in their clashes with state and corporate actors, popular movements both appealed to and contributed to the production of constitutional legality. And, as in Paraguay, the terrain of struggle was asymmetric, not only because official interpretations of the law are backed by force—which has been deployed in confrontations with anti-mining and anti-oil protesters—but also due to unequal access to financial, institutional, and communicational resources. Depending on the facet of the debate in question, however, it is by no means assured that the state—itself internally heterogeneous—or corporations will prevail over the efforts of anti-extractive groups. The account below testifies to the ability of activists to craft and circulate compelling counter-narratives as well as physically obstruct extractive policies, just as it attests to the consolidation of a technocratic vision among state actors that aimed at, but never fully achieved, the exclusion of popular democratic practices from the arena of resource extraction. In any particular contentious episode, the terrain of debate was both tilted and in motion, and analysis must proceed slowly to trace the connections between actors, strategies, and political objectives.

Drafting *Consulta Previa*

In Ecuador, social movements in declared opposition to the Correa administration frequently enlisted the 2008 Constitution in their struggles. They constantly claimed to defend the Constitution against state policies, at once invoking and producing the text's legal authority. These constitutional citations constructed a shared referential ground, consisting of the document as a whole as well as particular articles and terms: the collective right of *consulta previa*, the rights of nature, plurinationality, *buen vivir*, among others. Activists' sense of allegiance to the Constitution is not surprising; the document bears the traces of its origins in social mobilization. But a close look at the period of contentious politics that led up to the Constituent Assembly, the debates that took place within it, and the final text itself reveal that the process and product of constitution-making were at once outcomes of popular struggle, and key elements in the reassertion of state control over the national territory and its resources.

The 2007–2008 Constituent Assembly was convened in response to longstanding social movement demands and a series of more proximate political crises: the April 2005 "rebellion of the *forajidos*," and CONAIE's protests against a proposed free-trade agreement with the US and to demand the nullification of the contract with Occidental Petroleum in spring 2006.[17] During this period of heightened social mobilization, both indigenous activists and *forajidos* demanded a new constitution.[18] In the eyes of CONAIE members as well as other sectors of the Left, the 1998 Constitution, despite also being a product of social movement pressure (in which CONAIE and its political party, Pachakutik, played a major role) and a crisis of representative politics, had not fundamentally altered Ecuador's political-economic structure.[19] Correa entered the 2006 presidential race riding the coattails of these mass mobilizations and capitalized on his already established anti-system credentials.[20] He promised to transform the country via a new constitution and made good on this pledge with a popular referendum on April 15, 2007, in which 86.79 percent of voters voted in favor of rewriting the Constitution. Elections for the Constituent Assembly delegates were held on September 30, 2007; Correa's party, Alianza País (AP), won 80 of the total 130 seats. The delegates met for eight months and 69 percent of voters approved the document.[21]

The preceding years of protest, combined with indigenous, environmentalist, campesino, and labor activists' efforts to submit proposals to the assembly and serve as advisers to the delegates, substantially shaped the content of the 2008 Constitution.[22] The Constitution redefined Ecuador as a plurinational state oriented toward *buen vivir* ("a new form of citizen conviviality . . . in harmony with nature") and recognized a series of new rights of humans and nature alike. Plurinationality had been a central demand of the indigenous movement for over a decade, as reflected in CONAIE's 1990 and 1994 political programs, both of which accompanied massive national uprisings that represented the emergence of the indigenous federation as a nationally organized political actor.[23] The inclusion of *buen vivir*, a translation of the Kichwa concept of *sumak kawsay*, was also the result of a CONAIE proposal that Pachakutik delegates had promoted in the assembly.[24]

However, as Correa has consistently made clear in his discourse, rewriting the Constitution was also a key part of his administration's transformative political project. In crafting their policy platform and constitutional proposals, President Correa, AP elected officials, and high-level bureaucrats reinterpreted and repurposed activists' critique of neoliberalism as a call for a stronger and more developmentally inclined state, eschewing its more radical potential as a rejection of both capitalism and *mestizo* nationalism.[25] From the perspective of these state and government actors, a new constitution would lay the groundwork to establish the state as the central economic regulator, in contrast to its historic subordination to national and international capital during the "long night of neoliberalism."[26] This state-led coordination of the economy took the form of oil and mining contracts that increased state revenues and, along with increased taxation of the wealthy, funded a range of welfare programs, social services, and infrastructural projects.[27] The 2008 Constitution provides a legal basis for this policy paradigm. The same document that recognizes nature as a rights-bearing subject also repeatedly stipulates that nonrenewable natural resources and even biodiversity itself are the exclusive, inalienable "patrimony of the State."[28] This state-centric interpretation of post-neoliberalism was elaborated in explicit debate with social movement actors, who increasingly defined themselves as in opposition to state-led resource extraction.[29]

The Constitution's ambivalent and contested status was abundantly clear in the process of its drafting. The Constituent Assembly debated the relationship between the state, the national territory, its natural resources, and the collective identity of the democratic "people." This debate reflected nascent internal divisions among delegates from the president's party, AP, as well as pre-existing tensions between AP and Pachakutik delegates. These intersecting disputes erupted during the protracted drafting of the collective right to prior consultation of communities affected by extractive projects. The right to prior consultation had already been recognized via Ecuador's ratification (in 1998) of ILO Convention 169, which establishes that indigenous peoples must be consulted whenever a legislative or administrative measure could directly affect them or their environment.[30] The 1998 Constitution subsequently established two forms of prior consultation: first, the collective right of indigenous and Afro-Ecuadorian communities to "be consulted about plans and programs of prospection and exploitation of nonrenewable resources found in their lands"; and second, the right of all communities, regardless of ethnic or racial identity, to be consulted regarding "state decisions that can affect the environment."[31]

In the 2007–2008 Constituent Assembly, the Natural Resources and Biodiversity Committee was tasked with drafting the right to environmental consultation of affected communities in regard to activities with environmental impacts. It soon became apparent that neither committee members, nor their colleagues in the assembly at large, agreed on the content of this right. Between January and late April 2008, the majority proposal (prior consultation) and a minority proposal (prior consent) were debated in committee and on the plenary floor. A right to prior consent would go further than the already existing right to prior consultation by requiring that the outcome of such consultations be binding (that is, that the consent of the community would be a prerequisite for the development of extractive projects). Both the president of that committee, longtime Amazonian Kichwa activist Monica Chuji (AP), and the president of the Constituent Assembly, Alberto Acosta (AP), supported significantly strengthening the right to environmental consultation, which despite its inclusion in the 1998 Constitution had been unevenly implemented in practice.[32] They advocated for the recognition of the right to prior consent, which would have granted local communities binding veto power over projects that affect their environment. But despite the support of these high-ranking AP delegates and of organized social movements, powerful actors, including President Correa himself as well as many other AP delegates, opposed the stronger right to prior consent. And for both sides, the implications extended far beyond the content of this right, raising fundamental questions about democratic authority in the context of an extractive economy—and about the relationship between the state, the nation, and the plurality of nationalities, peoples, and communities that the national territory encompasses.

Supporters of the majority proposal argued that a binding right to consent would allow a sort of tyranny of the minority, in which the "particular interests" of a specific community—or, worse, of the forces that might "manipulate" them—would prevail over "the national interest." In this formulation, the state, as the owner of nonrenewable natural resources, should channel the revenues generated by extraction toward national socioeconomic development. The requirement to obtain consent would jeopardize extraction-funded public works that "tend to benefit the majority," as Jorge Calvos (AP), a proponent of the majority proposal, warned. His intervention captured what was at stake in the wording of this right: "We cannot tie the hands of the present or future government . . . What would happen if . . . to carry out a project . . . we had to consult that community and if that group opposed itself to the national interest? The national interest must be kept present, the public interest is higher than private interests, higher than particular interests . . . We would be allowing for a mechanism of extortion and blackmail, so that the projects that have to be for the benefit of the majority would be abandoned because of minority interests."[33] Delegate Gorki Aguirre (AP), also in favor of the majority proposal, characterized the "consent thesis" as a "political and social risk" that would subordinate "the interests of the State, of the people in general" to the "partial" interests of those with "fundamentalist arguments, who preemptively reject all forms of natural resource exploitation."[34] The use of the term "fundamentalist" to describe those who criticize oil or mineral extraction subsequently became a common characterization on the part of pro-mining officials as well as corporate actors in the oil and mining sectors.[35]

The fear that collective rights come at the expense of the national interest was also voiced during the 1997–1998 Constituent Assembly debates. A high level of protest activity—including the installation of people's assemblies—led up to and accompanied that constituent process, and occasioned a broad debate over the basis of political legitimacy and the substance of democracy.[36] In response to calls for an expanded bill of collective rights and new forms of participatory democracy, promoted within the assembly by Pachakutik delegates, delegates from the dominant right-wing bloc consistently defended elections as the only legitimate mode of representation and raised the possibility of minoritarian co-optation of the democratic process.[37] In the 2007–2008 assembly, AP delegates deployed similar arguments, but this time the exploitation of natural resources figured more prominently, due to both the Correa administration's goal of reasserting the state's role in resource extraction and the nascent critique of extractivism among environmental and indigenous activists. Alongside and in tension with this critique, Correa operated in a discursive field in which national sovereignty had been successfully linked to control of subsoil resources in the popular imaginary.[38] His administration redeployed this formulation against the social movements who forged it, just as those same movements have rearticulated their position as opposition to extraction.

Returning to the 2007–2008 Constituent Assembly, proponents of the right to prior consent challenged Aguirre's one-to-one mapping of the interests of the nation—the undifferentiated, unified "people" that were simultaneously being problematized by the proposal to redefine the state as plurinational—onto those of the state. Committee President Chuji, the most consistent and ardent defender of the right to prior consent, presented the minority proposal on the floor of the plenary. Chuji and her allies put the collective right to consent in the context of an almost two-decade-long cycle of contention around natural resource extraction and the defense of indigenous territory, and pointed to the persistent failure to enforce consultation despite its inclusion in the 1998 Constitution as evidence of the necessity of a more substantive right. They also emphasized that consent was a demand in several social movement organization proposals and interpreted it as part of an ongoing process of democratization of the state. In contrast, they claimed that the majority proposal was the product of pressure from above, from the central government or President Correa himself.[39] Fernando Vega (AP) recast the majority proposal supporters' understanding of democracy as a form of top-down, unilateral decision-making. With a rhetorical question—"Why do we fear the people?"—he in effect linked the majority proposal to a long political history of antidemocratic justifications of the status quo. He proceeded to argue that extraction was not in the interest of some homogeneously defined public, but always involved specific communities making sacrifices so that others might benefit.

In contrast to majority proposal supporters' appeal to a univocal nation, via the repeated invocation of *the* national interest, supporters of the minority proposal articulated diverse figurations of the relevant collectivity. Despite the ostensible application of environmental consultation to *all* communities, references to indigenous peoples as the bearers of collective rights and as the historic protagonists of mobilization suffused the arguments in favor of prior consent. Supporters of prior consent referenced international legal instruments that apply to indigenous peoples, cited examples of indigenous mobilization against oil exploitation (such as the Sarayaku case), and pointed out the vulnerability of indigenous territory in the face of an expanding extractive frontier.[40] At other points, consent was cast as a more universal right—although even then, indigenous communities were still highlighted. As the minority report stated, consent would be "a real exercise of sovereignty and democracy by Ecuadorians, and in particular ancestral nationalities and peoples."[41] Elsewhere, it would rectify the marginalization shared by indigenous and peasant communities alike, but the former in particular confront an "indifferent and racist State."[42] Some proponents of the minority proposal explicitly clarified the inclusive nature of the right they were drafting. As Gilberto Guamangate (AP) put it: "Careful, they are going to be thinking that this is an issue only for indigenous people. No, sir. If we want to make a real citizens' revolution, let's start doing it." Carlos Pilamunga (Partido Sociedad Patriotica) reiterated: "Do they keep thinking that when one speaks of prior consent it is only for indigenous peoples? I don't think it's like that. We are proposing, from the indigenous movement . . . that it should be . . . [for] all Ecuadorian citizens."[43]

With the explicit support of the president, the majority proposal for prior consultation prevailed over the minority proposal for prior consent. The new Constitution, approved by 69 percent of voters in a referendum held September 28, 2008, guaranteed a slightly modified version of the same two consultation rights that appear in the 1998 Constitution: prior consultation for indigenous communities and environmental consultation for all communities. Both rights explicitly state that community opposition to extractive projects or to policies that can affect the environment does not constitute grounds for not implementing the project or policy. The 2008 Constitution recognizes the collective rights of indigenous and Afro-Ecuadorian peoples to "prior, free and informed consultation, within a reasonable period, about plans and programs of prospection, exploitation and commercialization of nonrenewable resources that are found in their lands and that can affect them environmentally or culturally. . . . If the consent of the consulted community is not obtained, the Constitution and the law will be upheld."[44] Given the latter clause, the article "recognizes and at the same time negates the substantive content of prior consent."[45] Environmental consultation is included in the "Regime of living well" (*el buen vivir*): communities must be consulted about any "state decision or authorization that can affect the environment" and will be "thoroughly and opportunely informed."[46] This also stipulates that, in the event of "a majority opposition of the respective community, the decision whether to execute the project or not will be adopted by duly justified resolution" on the part of the relevant state authority.[47] Adding to the legal ambiguity, the Constitution also guarantees the full implementation of all international instruments that expand human rights.[48] This would include the 2007 UN Declaration on the Rights of Indigenous Peoples (UNDRIP), to which Ecuador is a signatory, and which establishes that "States shall consult and cooperate in good faith with the indigenous peoples concerned through their own representative institutions in order to obtain their free, prior and informed *consent* before adopting and implementing legislative or administrative measures that may affect them."[49]

Guamangate's and Pilamunga's warnings regarding the ambiguity of the collective subject of prior consultation were prescient: the constitutional text did little to provide clear instructions to those tasked with its implementation or newly empowered by the rights it stipulated. After ratification, the unsettled parameters of the "community" and their decision-making authority were at the heart of the contention over prior consultation. The subjects of this collective right were "names that set out a question or a dispute (*litige*) about who is included in their count," a dispute that moves back and forth between legal inscription and pragmatic verification.[50] This dispute continued due to the efforts of indigenous, campesino, and environmental activists—including those residing in communities potentially affected by planned mining and oil projects. Through their contentious actions, these activists kept constituent politics alive: they enlisted the Constitution in their struggle over resource extraction and claimed to defend it against the very state that it had refounded. They crafted a creative reading of their constitutional rights that intermingled the constitutional text with provisions that the assembly had not adopted, and with their own historic demands for expansive collective rights. Armed with this interpretation, they asserted their right to a form of consultation stronger than appears anywhere in the text itself.[51]

A Mobile Constitution

The March for Water, Life, and the Dignity of Peoples of March 8–22, 2012, which I accompanied in its entirety, was initially planned as an anti-mining demonstration. But it quickly became a forum for indigenous, environmentalist, and labor activists, and opposition politicians, to articulate a wide range of grievances against the Correa administration (see Figures 3.1–3.5). To express these grievances, marchers frequently relied on the Constitution's aspirational language. For the entirety of the two-week march, from its commencement at dawn in the main plaza of the southern Amazonian town of Pangui to the final day in Quito's Parque el Arbolito, the Constitution lived among us. Cited in countless speeches, analyzed in side conversations, and prominently featured in the first of the marchers' nineteen demands, it was made present through allegations of its violation and calls to its defense. The Constitution was invoked as a whole, *la constitución*, and by reference to its salient parts: plurinationality, the right to water, the rights of nature, Article 405, Article 163. It was at times misquoted. Nowhere in the 2008 document does the phrase "the sovereignty of indigenous communities" appear, a "constitutional" right that march organizer and anti-mining prefect Salvador Quishpe claimed the government violated in response to his rhetorical question, "Why the march?"—posed in the small community center of San Lucas, a village populated by the Saraguro people, of which his short black pants, poncho, and wide-brimmed hat marked him as a member.

The constantly moving marchers provide a particularly apt instance of, and metaphor for, the circulation of constitutional discourse, as well as the ongoing interpretive work entailed in linking the text to diverse political projects. This interpretive work is politically productive in two senses. First, by invoking the Constitution as already normative—as a set of prescriptions that ought to regulate political action—they generate the very legal authority to which they appeal. Second, when they link their anti-extractive position to the Constitution, activists legitimate their political project by grounding it in the legal act that refounded Ecuador and was itself popularly ratified. The contrast between this interpretive strategy and the fraught internal debates around ratification reveals the extent to which such interpretations are crafted in the midst of evolving political circumstances. Four years before the march, in the lead-up to ratification, CONAIE held an "extraordinary assembly" in which they harshly criticized the Correa administration and, among other declarations, demanded the constitutional recognition of a binding right to prior consent.[52] They resolved to "defend this right at all costs" since, as the

Figure 3.1 Water ceremony in Pangui to mark the start of the March for Water, Life, and the Dignity of Peoples. Photo credit: Elisa Levy.

resolutions read, it is an essential part of "the struggle to decolonize democracy and the State."[53] During those internal debates, Humberto Cholango, then president of the highland indigenous organization Ecuarunari, was one of the architects of the so-called "critical yes" vote strategy.[54] He advocated for unilateral support of the Constitution combined with explicit critique of several official policies, including the promotion of large-scale mining. After ratification, however, this moment of internal dispute and the "critical yes" vote strategy it produced were supplanted by a wholesale embrace of the Constitution and the deployment of the text as a tool of resistance—especially against the government's perceived failure to implement prior consultation for extractive projects.

This deployment of the Constitution decoupled it from the proximate conditions of its production and ratification. It also flattened the contradictions between its articles, ignoring constitutional provisions that were less congruent with their political project, rather than outright rejecting or reconciling them.

Figure 3.2 Marching through Latacunga. Ecuarunari president Delfín Tenesaca appears in the center; Salvador Quishpe, prefect of Zamora Chinchipe, at the far left, alongside Lourdes Tibán, Pachakutik assemblywoman. Photo credit: Elisa Levy.

The combined effect of these citational practices was to position "*the* Constitution" as the coherent, unified, and final arbiter of political life. In locales far from the courtrooms populated by officially sanctioned "lawpersons," these activists engaged in the intertwined acts of refounding and legitimation, and contributed to the production of constitutional authority.[55]

On the sixth day of the march, during a meeting in the southern highland city of Cañar convened to finalize the list of marchers' demands for an upcoming press conference, the political committee was engaged in heated discussion. Some worried about the sprawling nature of the demands, which addressed resource extraction, land policy, university education, and reproductive rights, among other outstanding grievances. There was also a brief back and forth over the addressee of the document. Abel Arpi, anti-mining activist and leader of the Assembly of the Peoples of the South, pointed out that addressing the demands to President Correa would inadvertently contribute to the

Figure 3.3 Arriving in Quito. Photo credit: Elisa Levy.

very centralization of power that activists so frequently criticized. To attend to these two concerns, the political committee added an additional demand, now the first of nineteen, which articulated a unifying theme and appealed to an authority seen as more foundational than that of the president: "the full enforcement (*vigencia*) of the Constitution and the abrogation of all unconstitutional laws, norms and regulations."

The ascendance of an interpretive strategy that centered on the defense of "the Constitution" did not, however, preclude subsequent deliberation over how to apply its abstract principles to concrete political demands. As with any circulating discourse, each moment of relay is also an opportunity for re-signification and, under certain circumstances, critical reflection. On the penultimate evening of the march in the semi-flooded high school auditorium in southern Quito where we had camped out for the night, Luis Contento (vice president of Ecuarunari), Abel Arpi, and I debated the text's ambiguity. What did it mean, Contento and Arpi wondered, that in Article 408 it stated that the products of the subsoil, including minerals, belong to "the State"? Arpi offered an interpretation that reconciled state ownership of non-renewable resources

Figure 3.4 "The rainforest is life and life should be defended." Marching through Quito. Photo credit: Elisa Levy.

and his anti-extractive political stance. "We are all the state," he said, broadening the collective subject from the central government to a plurinational public. If "we all" own natural resources, he concluded, we can decide whether or not to extract. Although Arpi's attempt to reconcile contradictory elements of the Constitution was in my experience unusual, his interpretation exemplified the complexity of social movements' deployment of "the Constitution" to both ground their political authority ("we are all the state") and legitimate their political project (resistance to the extractive model).

Reflecting on the march a month after its final day in Quito, Humberto Cholango, then president of CONAIE, described the birth of a "social force" that "assumes as its strategic objective . . . the fulfillment of the Political Constitution of the State, which includes a large part of the program of struggle [of] social movements."[56] The Constitution had refounded state and society alike: "now we have a new Constitution and one has to depart from it to think about the State . . . Society must be thought of in the framework of a plurinational State." His statement captured the centrality of the text to the formulation of grievances and the construction of a political program, and suggested

Figure 3.5 "Kimsakocha: free of mining." Marching through Quito. Photo credit: Elisa Levy.

the ongoing work required to generate the Constitution's authority: indigenous activists "must" rethink about politics according to the framework laid out by the document, and its "fulfillment" should be a conscious goal of their political activity.

The following year, I met with the president of Ecuarunari, Delfín Tenesaca, in the small offices of the highland indigenous federation's headquarters, housed in a faded concrete building ironically named El Conquistador at the northern edge of Quito's colonial center.[57] Along with Correa's recent reelection, which had sent waves of depression and critical reflection throughout the networks of social movement activists and allied intellectuals, the topic of *consulta previa* was at the forefront of the Kichwa leader's mind.[58] A few months before, the Ministry of Nonrenewable Resources and the Ministry of Environment had consulted indigenous communities affected by the new round of oil tenders in the southern Amazon, a process that provoked conflict between indigenous leaders and state officials. Meanwhile, the National Assembly was in the midst of conducting pre-legislative consultation regarding the proposed Water Law, marking the first ever application of the constitutional guarantee that indigenous communities and Afro-Ecuadorians be consulted prior to any law that could affect any of the collective rights enumerated in Article 57.[59] But Tenesaca did not see these state-led processes as truly honoring the Constitution. Referring to the pre-legislative consultation to make a broader point, he told me, "In Ecuador, they have not done a single consultation. After all of this struggle, recently they have begun to consult, after the first [legislative] debate. It is not a prior consultation, nor is it binding, it is simply a game of internal and external politics." He continued, using the language contained in the Constitution and in international conventions: "They don't do a consultation that is prior, or informed, or free"; instead, "they do blackmail consultations . . . it is just a justificatory action." For Tenesaca, "justificatory" meant that the consultations were not substantively "prior," but merely a means to constitutionally justify an already decided upon policy.

He contrasted these official consultation processes with his own interpretation of the constitutional text, an interpretation deeply embedded in the indigenous movement's historic and contemporary campaigns. "Collective rights are sacred in the Constitution. We are going to exercise these collective rights, all twenty-one numerals," he insisted, referring to the list of rights of indigenous, Afro-Ecuadorian, and Montubian peoples. He recounted a history of indigenous mobilization demanding consultation, specifically citing the demand to ratify ILO Convention 169 on indigenous and tribal peoples. He retrospectively reanalyzed the 1990 indigenous uprising—viewed by scholars and activists alike as the movement's entrée onto the national political scene—as a call for consultation in the areas of "land, [resource] exploitation, and education," even though the word "consultation" does not appear among the sixteen points that CONAIE presented to the government at that moment.

Tenesaca voiced a claim advanced frequently by anti-extractive activists as well as allied politicians and intellectuals: the Ecuadorian government did not carry out constitutionally mandated consultations. Monica Chuji, the former Constituent Assembly member and an ardent defender of prior consent, asserted that "in these five years" of the Correa administration, "we do not have one example" of the application of the right to prior consultation, leading her to conclude that it is merely "a right written on paper that is not enforced."[60] She told me that this violates explicitly guaranteed rights as well as Article 417 of the Constitution, which stipulates the "direct application of international instruments related to human rights and ratified by Ecuador" (such as ILO Convention 169 and UNDRIP). In his office in Zamora, a few hours away from the "zone of influence" of the first and only large-scale mining project with an exploitation contract, anti-mining prefect Salvador Quishpe flipped through his small, worn copy of the Constitution, as he said, emphatically, "They haven't done consultations. They didn't do them."[61]

In these interviews, informal conversations, and public events, conversation slid from accusations of the violation of the right to prior consultation to assertions of the Correa administration's wholesale "trampling" of the Constitution, in effect linking the document to a history of social struggle and its transgression to a political-economic model with proximate (neoliberal) and distant (colonial) origins. A month before the march, at the Binational Forum on Community Consultations in Resistance to Mining, held in Cuenca in February 2012, and featuring Peruvian and Ecuadorian activists, Dr. Carlos Castro Riera, dean of the University of Cuenca Law School, told the audience that "the Constitution is the result of [indigenous] peoples' long struggle from colonialism to the present . . . It is a constitution full of rights, a *garantista* constitution. Consultation is a fundamental right of communities. The Constitution is a key component of the democratic structuring of the state. They don't even correctly read what the Constitution says. The laws are against the Constitution. We have gone from a discourse of rights to an authoritarian discourse." In this context, he stated, social movements' "strategy" must be to "defend the Constitution . . . in the face of a government that has distanced itself from it." Alicia Granda, of the human rights and social justice organization CEDHU (Comisión Ecuménica de Derechos Humanos del Ecuador), accused the Correa administration of continuing the "dream of past governments" to make Ecuador a mining country, a "developmentalist, extractivist vision."[62] She contrasted Correa's extractivism with the Constitution's ample recognition of the rights of individuals, groups, and nature. These rights are at once a "hope" for the future and a reminder of a moment when the ruling party was less "monolithic," a reference to the Constituent Assembly, when Acosta and Chuji were still members of Alianza País.

After the march, the question of the relationship between the Constitution and the popular sovereignty it explicitly recognized as the sole source of its authority continued to permeate political discussion.[63] In June 2012, the book release of a volume on environmental law in the new Constitution at FLACSO University in Quito, posited the question of the complex relationships between constituent power, constitutional text, and political strategy. Alberto Acosta, one of the event's panelists, asserted that "the Constitution is a toolbox for citizens to construct a new society," thus locating interpretive authority in the citizenry, explicitly defined in contrast to an overreaching president and extractivism (which "goes against many articles of the Constitution"). But the event also revealed the document so confidently marshaled to be a work in progress, imperfectly suited to the needs of social movements and thus always requiring a selective interpretation. For example, Acosta uncharacteristically problematized the isolation of the constitutional text from the contentious process of its drafting. In reference to ILO Convention 169, which recognizes the right of indigenous people to prior consultation, he related that the "guarantees of international agreements were a source of much debate in the assembly, as Monica Chuji"—seated in the audience—"knows." Constitutional lawyer Julio César Trujillo, another panelist, flagged prior consultation as in particular need of careful exegesis. He noted that the right of indigenous communities to prior consultation requires a prior specification of the collectivity to which it applies: "The great challenge is to make [Ecuador] a plurinational state, from right to reality. To which groups do we apply the name 'nation'?"

Trujillo's rhetorical question echoed the concerns that delegates Guamangate and Pilamunga had voiced during the Constituent Assembly debate between prior consultation and prior consent. Both delegates warned of the pitfalls of narrowly defining the subjects of consultation as indigenous communities, especially given that the very right they were drafting applied to all communities whose environment would be affected by extractive projects. Meanwhile, as I discuss in the next section, bureaucrats tend to bypass constitutional language altogether, instead relying on Executive Decree 1040 to delineate who counts as an "affected community." The tendency of state officials to avoid constitutional language only highlights the ongoing work of anti-extractive activists to render constitutional dictates relevant to politics. It also highlights the fact that constitutional interpretations are always articulated in a relational field populated by competing political projects. This is especially true of the 2008 Ecuadorian Constitution, a fundamentally ambivalent text produced at the intersection of an ongoing dispute between two closely related, but mutually opposed, leftist political projects.

Decree 1040 and the Logic of Substitution

Parallel to indigenous and environmental activists, bureaucrats too were engaged in the multi-sited process of constitution-making. Functionaries at the Ministry of Environment and the Ministry of Nonrenewable Resources routinely enlisted the technocratic language of Executive Decree 1040 to define and implement *consulta previa*. On April 22, 2008, while the Constituent Assembly was debating between prior consultation and prior consent, President Correa signed Executive Decree 1040 to regulate "mechanisms of social participation" in regard to state decisions that can affect the environment.

This decree was a revealing example of the mode of executive governance that Angélica Bernal refers to as the "constituent president": a leader who simultaneously convenes popular constituent process in response to pressure from below and plays a top-down "protagonist role" in that same process (in this case, to limit the substantive content of prior consultation).[64]

The decree is also emblematic of what I call the logic of substitution: an interpretive strategy that responds to the expansive legal demands of social movements by circumventing the constitutional text and supplanting it with technocratic regulations.[65] Though the bureaucrats I interviewed told me Decree 1040 defines prior consultation, the word "consult" does not appear in the decree.[66] Instead, the decree envisions a "tripartite effort" between state institutions, citizens, and the promoter of the project (that is, the company holding the concession) in accordance with undefined "principles of 'legitimacy and representativeness.'"[67] This vision, however, directly violates the 2008 Constitution (in the process of being ratified at the time), which stipulates that only state institutions can carry out consultations and does not recognize a role for a corporate "promoter" in these processes.[68]

I now turn to an analysis of the content of Decree 1040 and its implementation during the process of "social participation" for the Mirador project, an open-pit copper mine in the southern Amazonian province of Zamora Chinchipe. I also discuss the legal battle over the 2009 Mining Law, a dispute that centered on rights to prior consultation and pre-legislative consultation. I then demonstrate the pervasiveness of the decree in bureaucratic discourse and follow with an analysis of a contentious episode in which anti-mining activists physically blockaded a state-led consultation in Azuay. Each of these elements—decree, court decision, bureaucratic discourse, state practices, and the resistance they occasion—constitutes a site of interpretive activity, a conduit through which the Constitution is made and unmade through its invocation in concrete political struggles.[69]

The Decree

The first article of Decree 1040 consists of a list of definitions. The array of technical terms sets up a particular space of justification that allows bureaucrats to distinguish between the collectivities that count as "affected communities" and those that do not. Affected communities are the "human groups that inhabit the area of direct influence."[70] The decree tautologically defines the "area of direct influence" of a project as the "area or territory potentially affected by an activity or project . . . which will be defined by the competent authority" (that is, the Ministry of Environment and/or the Ministry of Non-renewable Resources). *Afectación* (literally, the action of having an effect, often translated as "impact") is defined as the "negative impact" of an activity on the community or the environment. Meanwhile, environmental impact is defined as "the positive or negative alteration of the environment" caused by the project in a "determined area." Given this distinction between impact and *afectación*, it follows that a community could be "impacted" but not "affected." Such impacted but unaffected communities would *not* be guaranteed the right to consultation that both the 1998 and 2008 Constitutions guarantee to "affected communities," a term neither constitution defines. As became clear in the Mirador process discussed below, these definitions have concrete implications, and are eminently political and potentially contentious.

The decree establishes a technocratic vision of community participation. As opposed to a participatory process that is "prior" to, and determines the viability of, the project in question, the decree emphasizes informing community members about an already decided upon project.[71] It defines "social participation" as "the mechanisms to present" environmentally risky projects and "the impact studies, the possible mitigation measures and the environmental management plans, to an affected/interested community."[72] The decree invokes a two-way flow of information, in the course of which state decisions are made transparent to residents and the state learns the opinions of the community, opinions which are ultimately the "basis of the governance and development of environmental management."[73]

Citizens are expected to conform to a technocratic model of participation. Decree 1040 stipulates that citizens' "opinions and observations" will only be incorporated in the final version of the environmental management plan when they are "technically and economically viable," such that projects are developed in "an appropriate way," "minimizing and/or compensating impacts" with "the aim of improving the environmental conditions for carrying out the activity or project."[74] Voicing concerns or questions in a technical register is thus a requirement for consequential participation in decision-making around extractive projects. As a corollary, participants' opposition to a project—implicitly marked as not "technically or economically viable"—does not entail its suspension or cancellation. The decree addresses two types of community opposition: first to the process itself, and second to the planned project. Regarding the first type, it states: "In the event that the subjects of participation do not exercise their right to participate having been duly convened or oppose its realization, this fact will not constitute grounds for the nullity of the social participation process and will not suspend its continuation, obliging the promoter to present the report of systemization of opinions."[75]

"Participation" can proceed despite the absence of participants. Meanwhile, in the event that community members attend the information sessions and voice their opposition, the project can still be developed if the "competent authority"—one of the two aforementioned ministries—"insists."[76]

The Ironies of Information

The question of what constitutes implementation of this collective right, and the paradoxical possibility that communities could be "consulted" without their knowledge, was at the heart of the constitutional battle over the 2009 Mining Law. The law entered into force on January 29, 2009, following two weeks of anti-mining protest in the northern and southern highlands that had aimed to block its passage.[77] The law addresses the right to prior consultation in a chapter entitled "Of Social Management and Community Participation." Like Decree 1040, the law conceives participation in informational terms. It states that the objective of participation is "to promote the sustainable development of mining activity, ensuring (*precautelando*) the rational exploitation of mining resources, respect for the environment, social participation in environmental matters and the development of the localities located in the areas of influence of a mining project."[78] On March 17, 2009, ten months after declaring their opposition to a wide range of the Correa administration's policies, CONAIE challenged the law's constitutionality.[79]

Along with the water users' association and anti-mining group UNAGUA, and with the support of the radical environmental group Acción Ecológica, the national indigenous federation brought their case to the Constitutional Court. In claiming their rights via the institutional channel of the court, CONAIE and its allies signaled their allegiance to a constitution that they perceived as legally validating their anti-extractive project. This marked an important shift in a trajectory that began with internal debates over whether or not to support the document's ratification, to the victory of a "critical yes" voting strategy, to full-fledged embrace of "the" Constitution, mediated through a complex interpretive strategy that linked it to their historic struggles and asserted their constituent power as indigenous *pueblos* to deploy it in political battle with the state.

In the 2010 court case, CONAIE alleged that the state was constitutionally obligated to consult them prior to the passage of the law, since it was a legislative measure that affects the collective rights of indigenous peoples.[80]

Furthermore, they claimed that the law's framework for the consultation of indigenous peoples prior to mining projects was unconstitutional. This is because, like Decree 1040, the law does not use the constitutional language of the collective right to prior consultation, and instead emphasizes the provision of information with the explicit goal of promoting mining. Finally, they claimed that the law violates international instruments to which Ecuador is a signatory because it does not stipulate that participatory processes should aim for consent.[81]

The arguments put forward by CONAIE raised the question of who governs resource extraction, and the court case staged a conflict between the authority of affected communities and the authority of the recently refounded state.[82] In advancing this claim, CONAIE's legal strategy focused on the territorial and temporal dimensions of the right to consultation. Given the historic centrality of territorial claims in indigenous discourse and practice in Ecuador, the federation was concerned about how both mining projects and the state's participatory processes would contribute to the extractive penetration and fragmentation of indigenous territories.[83] According to CONAIE, the law's terminology of "areas of influence" (instead of their preferred language, "the community or communities, nation or nations that live within the territorial area that will be intervened") leaves the location of the consultation "to the discretion of the consulting entity" and constitutes an "imminent risk" due to the alleged state practice of "consulting everyone, except the community directly involved."[84] Moreover, since the Mining Law grants the freedom of mineral prospecting (that is, the earliest stage of exploration) to all natural or legal persons, public or private, foreign or national, CONAIE claimed that it would be impossible to identify potentially affected communities in advance since prospection could happen at any moment.[85]

In response to these allegations, the administration simultaneously claimed that "we do not need to consult" and "we have already consulted." These contradictory claims rested on two distinct senses of consultation. On the one hand, the argument that indigenous communities need not have been consulted prior to the passage of the Mining Law relied on an understanding of consultation as a form of binding authority (that is, veto power) that, if implemented, would privilege minority interests over the public good.[86] On the other hand, the argument that consultation had already been carried out relied on a narrow and information-centric understanding of consultation.

Regarding the first argument ("we do not need to consult"), Fernando Cordero, president of the National Assembly's Legislative Committee, stated: "It would be absurd for laws such as the Civil Code, the Penal Code, procedural codes (*los Códigos Adjetivos*) or economic laws to have to be previously consulted because they can affect any of their collective rights; this would threaten (*atentar*) the unity of the Republic. The claim of the plaintiffs would violate the principle of the generality of the Law."[87] Instead, he argued, the state must "put the general interest before the particular." In this view, pre-legislative consultation would amount to tyranny by the minority, obstructing the public good (implicitly equated with the promotion of mining, which was the explicit aim of the Mining Law at issue).

However, in seeming contradiction to these strong arguments that the consultation of indigenous communities prior to the passage of the Mining Law was unnecessary (and indeed would threaten the very unity of the nation-state), the administration also argued that such consultation had already occurred. To substantiate this argument, Cordero presented documents that "[include] the opinions and observations of the communities, indigenous peoples of the Amazon, mining cooperatives and associations, mining chambers, among others; with which it is evidenced that the project of the Mining Law was general knowledge."[88] Attorney General Dr. Néstor Arboleda also insisted, "the National Assembly, through the Economic Development and Production Committee, carried out consultation workshops in various cities . . . in which the CONAIE participated." Dr. Alexis Mera, President Correa's legal consul, reiterated the point: since the Legislative Committee "received many arguments on the part of citizens, among them the CONAIE itself," it is "inadmissible that the claimants indicate that a consultation directed in a particular manner to the sectors they represent should have been carried out."[89] These state officials pointed out that on December 2, 2008, CONAIE, along with several other social movement organizations, called for the suspension of the law due to its unconstitutionality and proposed a national dialogue to evaluate the advisability of large-scale mining in Ecuador. They thus invoked indigenous leaders' allegations of unconstitutionality as evidence of their substantive participation in a pre-legislative consultation. Paradoxically, CONAIE's initial allegations of the law's unconstitutionality would provide the legal basis for its constitutionality.[90]

On March 18, 2010, the Constitutional Court issued its ruling. It stated the necessity of a new law (as opposed to the existing decree) to regulate pre-legislative consultation and, in the interim, established minimum procedures for its application as well as for that of prior consultation.[91] This ruling suggests that the court did not want the process of pre-legislative consultation of the Mining Law (that is, the general informational process described by the administration's representatives), nor its content regarding prior consultation for mining projects, to serve as a legal precedent. But, despite these concerns, the court ultimately accepted the official argument that indigenous communities had been sufficiently consulted and upheld the "conditional constitutionality" of the Mining Law. The court thus ratified an information-centric understanding of participation. As I describe below, the social participation process for the Mirador mining project, along with the continued circulation of this technocratic vision in bureaucratic practice, further crystallized the official definition of *consulta previa* as the provision of information.

The Mirador Project

According to the Ministry of Environment's final report, Decree 1040 provided the legal framework for the process of social participation for the Mirador open-pit copper mining project in the southern Amazonian province of Zamora Chinchipe. The process took place between October 29 and November 12, 2010, in three information centers in the canton of Pangui.[92] Although the report cites other bodies of law in the "Legal Framework" section, including both the 2008 Constitution and ILO Convention 169, there are several additional citations of Decree 1040 in other sections of the document, and the language and mechanisms employed closely match those set out in the decree. The central role of the Chinese-owned mining consortium ECSA throughout the process indicates that bureaucrats continued to follow the decree's vision of a "tripartite dialogue" between state, community, and project proponent (also referred to as the "promoter").

Following Decree 1040, each step of the Mirador process was planned in advance by the Ministry of Environment via a "facilitator" (an external consultant chosen by the project proponent from a registry of certified individuals). During the community hearing on November 5, representatives from both the Ministry of Environment and ECSA were available to address concerns, and the logos of both entities emblazoned every page of the ministry's final report.[93] The role of ECSA in the process violated the 2008 Constitution, which stipulates that only the state can consult affected communities. It was also in tension with the government's state-making project, which aimed to reassert public authority over multinational companies in strategic economic sectors, including large-scale mining. The ministry's final report evinced anxiety over the role of a private company in the process. It urged bureaucrats to "clarify that the socialization process of these studies is the responsibility of the Ministry of Environment as the National Environmental Authority, and in this way, avoid subsequent confrontations . . . deceptions . . . [and] bad interpretations."

This anxiety resurfaced periodically throughout the regulatory and contract negotiation process. On March 7, 2012—two days after the contract for the mine's exploitation phase was signed, and one day before the aforementioned two-week long march—the Ministry of Nonrenewable Resources tweeted that "the personnel that carried out the process of social participation were not paid by #ECSA, but by the Ministry of Environment," most likely in response to criticism that alleged the opposite.[94]

The documentation of the social participation process reveals that neither community members nor project promoters fully mastered the undefined "technical" register that the decree demands of participants. Over the course of the two weeks, in the comment registry available in the three information centers as well as during the public hearing, community members raised concerns around pollution, wildlife, jobs, energy, transportation, corporate-community relations, economic benefits, communication and information, and education.[95] Responses on the part of Ministry of Environment and ECSA representatives were short, repetitive, and vague, systematically refusing to admit any negative impact of the project. For example, in response to the question, "What benefits will these projects have for the community?" the response reads: "All projects have advantages and disadvantages. The benefits would be: jobs, growth in people which implies economic growth; roads and bridges for entry." No employment statistics or economic growth rates are specified.

Despite the fact that the Ministry of Environment report states that the social participation process for the Mirador mine was "well attended" and notes the lack of "opposition," a concern about the project's "sustainability"— political, not environmental—pervades the document. This concern echoes the Mining Law's stipulation that the aim of social participation processes is the "sustainable development of the mining activity." In the section "Possible Socio-Environmental Conflicts," the report describes a local group in "radical opposition" to the project. A week after the public hearing, in a letter addressed to the provincial offices of the Ministry of Environment, the Consortium of Social Organizations of El Pangui requested the nullity of "ECSA's hearing" for several reasons, among them, the violation of Constitutional Article 398 (due to the participation of the promoter, ECSA), the lack of outreach to affected populations (such as Saraguro and Shuar indigenous communities), and, perhaps most importantly, the failure to provide the full environmental impact assessment for community review, as required by law (instead, a summary was presented).[96] The official response to this episode demonstrated the pervasiveness of the decree's technocratic and informational vision of participation among bureaucrats tasked with its implementation. The report suggests that a "possible solution" would be "to offer them a technical and environmental justification" and, more generally, that "informative talks" will avoid both "false expectations" and "future conflicts."

1040 Talk

Every time I asked a bureaucrat involved in implementing public policy around large-scale mining about *consulta previa*, they referred to Executive Decree 1040. In our conversations, the transformative vision of a plurinational polity, oriented toward *buen vivir*, with new rights for human collectivities and nature alike was only present in its notable absence. The mobile Constitution that lived through its invocation and interpretation in the various sites of anti-extractive political struggle seemed to evaporate in the offices of the ministries tasked with implementing the constitutional right of prior consultation.

Whether it was voiced in a justificatory or more critical register, with praise or with regret, state functionaries all agreed that this decree was the only appropriate answer to my question, *¿Como se hace una consulta previa?* (How is prior consultation done?). Sometimes, the decree was named explicitly, whether by its full title or by its number alone (*diez cuarenta*). Diego Arcos, the mining adviser to the subsecretary of environmental quality in the Ministry of Environment, in response to my apparent obstinacy, repeated the document by name several times ("I told you, it is all regulated in Decree 1040").[97] Wilton Guaranda Mendoza, functionary in the Office of the Ombudsman in the area of Human Rights and Rights of Nature, related that Decree 1040 was unfortunately still the guideline for carrying out consultations, despite its many inadequacies.[98] In contrast, at a debate over "mega-mining in Ecuador" in the northern city of Ibarra, which unusually featured both government officials and anti-mining activists, the director of the Imbabura office of the Ministry of Environment, Oscar Mejia, lauded the regulation's democratic potential. "Decree 1040," he said, stipulates "that community participation be real, present, that projects generate development. Otherwise, they are extractive activities."[99] For Mejia, the implementation of Decree 1040 amounted to substantive local participation in oil and mining projects—and, for him, social participation was precisely what distinguished lofty "development" from mere extraction.

In addition to the explicit citation of Decree 1040, the document's technocratic language had crystallized as the predominant official framework for the definition and implementation of prior consultation. The decree constituted a key component of an interpretive strategy that calibrated the state-led promotion of large-scale mining and this constitutionally mandated collective right.

This strategy functioned according to a logic of substitution. Bureaucrats used terms such as "information," "socialization," and "technically viable opinions" instead of the language of the 2008 Constitution or that of international legal conventions.[100] As official actors contributing to the circulation of the decree's content, they positioned themselves in a field of contention over the meaning of *consulta previa*—and over the transformative potential of the Constitution itself.

When I asked the vice-minister of mining, Federico Auquilla, about the right to consultation, he responded emphatically, echoing the administration's position in the 2010 Constitutional Court case: "The concept of consultation must be understood well. The concept of consultation is that the population is fully informed about the process that the government is carrying out, of the development of activities, whether mining or extractive. Therefore, we have carried out all of the processes of socialization, the processes of information . . . For us the consultation is to inform. It is to socialize, I insist."[101] In interviews and public events, pro-mining officials inevitably redefined "consultation" as either information or "socialization." Though the word "socialization" only appears once in Decree 1040, it has a social life of its own. The term, associated with the corporate sector but also common in bureaucratic, NGO, and, less frequently, social movement discourse, denotes the dissemination of information for marketing or promotion, whether of a consumer product or a political campaign. Auquilla's interpretation of consultation involved a series of substitutions, wherein consultation, socialization, and information were rendered interchangeable. But in the process, prior consultation, and the long political struggle for its legal recognition, fell out of view—these other terms added only to replace.[102] And his words and tone implied that much was at stake in the concept being "understood well." His ministry's plan to develop large-scale mining, a strategic economic sector, hung in the balance.

Though his tone was calmer, and his job was ostensibly to regulate and not promote mining, Diego Arcos, the mining adviser at the Ministry of Environment, concurred with Auquilla. According to Arcos, participation consists of the dissemination of information. As he told me, "the law literally says that the objective of the process is to make public or inform the community of the environmental impact study. And how to receive their suggestions, their observations or comments." Esteban Torracchi, the provincial director of the Ministry of Environment for Azuay, a province slated for several mining projects, stated matter of factly, "socialization is the same as prior consultation in the Constitution."[103] The similarity in these officials' responses was not only a product of being versed in the same decree; it was also evidence of their access to a communicational infrastructure that allowed for the efficient dissemination of pro-mining discourse. I observed both Arcos and Auquilla speaking on the same panels at several public pro-mining conventions, events where, if one's eyes were closed, the presentations of state and industry actors were often indistinguishable.

As illustrated by the Ministry of Environment's report on the social participation process for the Mirador mining project, the vision of *consulta previa* as an information session for a predetermined extractive project is evident in the minute details of planning and execution. This vision was also present in the manner that bureaucrats explained the logistical details of implementation. According to Arcos:

> The [project] proponent, once the draft is ready, requests from the Ministry of Environment the designation of a facilitator . . . to coordinate where, when, how these processes are realized. So, this facilitator, to be able to do that, goes to the field beforehand, visits the area, learns about (*se empapa de*) the project, defines where it is most suitable to do these processes, where he, on the basis of his experience, considers it most opportune to make this information public to the community . . . He establishes the date. He establishes the place. He establishes how to do it. Everything based on, I repeat to you, in this agreement, in this executive decree and its instructions of application. So, a whole process of facilitation is coordinated in which, I repeat to you, the Ministry of Environment does not do it directly but it is done by these facilitators . . . obviously in a coordination that will be through the Ministry of Environment. But they [the facilitators] do it with the proponent [of the project].

The planning and execution of social participation is not so much an open-ended exercise in local democracy as a tightly managed procedure, in which the company-selected facilitator enjoys significant control over all aspects of the agenda. As I discuss in the next chapter, bureaucrats were not alone in their attempts to manage the political risks of democratic decision-making. Just as bureaucrats took measures to prevent "socializations" from serving as a venue for anti-mining opposition, anti-mining activists endeavored to ensure that the community consultations they organized displayed opposition against mining projects.

There was, however, a substantial difference between community and official *consultas* regarding the mechanism of participation. While the former relied on a direct vote to register the popular will on a given extractive project and are suffused by calls to contentious political action, the latter limit "participation" to an exchange of technical information and commentary. As Arcos explained:

During this whole process, they [community members] make comments, through forms, or even in the hearing itself . . . according to the law, it explains to you clearly, every opinion, comment, or observation is accepted, but . . . only those comments that are technically and economically viable are included. Because any nonsense can occur to anyone . . . So, if someone from the community, to give you an example, says this, "I disagree that the tailings basin goes there." And why? "Because I don't like it, because no, over there it is going to pollute." Well, the observation is, it is neither technically nor economically justified. The proponent explains to this person from the community, and says, "Look, we have put the tailings basin there because we have done these analyses, there is technical viability, economic viability, legal viability, and we have chosen the best site for it, this study and the other, okay?" So, the counterpoint also has to argue that so that in this case the environmental authority receives this observation and includes it, and says to the proponent, "The tailings basin will not go here, you have to change it."

Bureaucrats often invoked an idealized citizen capable of deliberating the pros and cons of a project in a technical register. But, as Arcos's statement demonstrates, this is a polemical characterization, explicitly deployed in contrast to a pejorative stereotype of community members with nontechnical opinions (in his words, "nonsense"). In his office in the colonial center of Cuenca, the capital of Azuay province, Torracchi contrasted two modalities of citizen engagement: "The people listen, say this is missing, that isn't taken into account, they state their fears. A facilitator does this, sends a report to us. But if they don't give a technical reason, one that is viable . . . But if they say, 'You are going to contaminate a place with species X,' that is something else, that enters into the evaluation of the study of impacts."

The standard of "technical viability" made it clear that democracy has its limits. These limits map onto the distinction between the "technical" and its more or less explicitly defined others: the political, the uninformed, the oppositional, the irrational. But the Ministry of Environment's own documentation of the Mirador process, coupled with the anti-mining group's allegations that they never saw a full version of the environmental impact study, suggests that neither state officials nor community members conformed to the requirements of a two-way flow of technical information and commentary. This failure in practice reveals a contradiction in the figure of the ideal citizen: although the stated aim of the social participation process is to "introduce" citizens to a project that may affect their environment and "inform" them of its impacts, in order for their comments to be taken into account, these citizens must already be informed and have mastered a technical register. The informed citizen is at once a requirement and a product of the process. In spring 2012, the contradictions contained within the vision of participation, and between the vision and its implementation in practice, erupted in an episode of organized resistance to a socialization process.

Stones and Sticks in Shaggly

On May 3, 2012, Ministry of Environment officials and representatives of Cornerstone, a Canadian mining company, arrived in Shaggly, a rural parish in Azuay two hours from the city of Cuenca.[104] They had come to conduct the social participation process for the Vetas Grandes project. Cornerstone had rights to some 44,000 hectares of mineral concessions in the surrounding mountains and was legally required to conduct a "socialization" before proceeding to the advanced exploration stage. But when they arrived, Shaggly residents and anti-mining activists from neighboring rural communities prevented the officials and corporate representatives from entering. In addition to their physical strength and cohesive organization, they enlisted the Constitution to confront bureaucrats and corporate actors. They framed their resistance in constitutional language, often linking it to a history of struggle over the defense of territory and water. Two days before the planned resistance, Abel Arpi—anti-mining activist, resident of a nearby rural parish, and leader of the Assembly of the Peoples of the South—wrote an e-mail communiqué to a list of fellow activists. Under the subject heading "Alert before the 'socialization' of the mining company Cornerstone," he wrote:

> We denounce that the State Institutions and the Mining Company are convoking . . . the supposed socialization of the environmental impact studies, in order to . . . begin the perforation of our territories and water sources, all of this is being attempted behind the backs of the people and the Organizations, forgetting that in agreement with the Constituent [Assembly] Mandate Number 6, Article 3, it clearly says that the expiration without any economic compensation of mining concessions . . . in protected natural areas . . . and those that affect water sources . . . also enshrined in the Constitution, we demand our rights to live in a healthy environment . . . to resistance, and to the self-determination of peoples.

The communiqué concludes by inviting all recipients, as well as the press, to "one more day of resistance" on May 3. On May 2, Arpi was videotaped outside a University of Cuenca event on political ecology saying: "But we are going to decide, there with the people, with the communities, what we are going to do. Because it can't happen that a government does not respect the Constitution, that it doesn't respect the mandates of an assembly with full powers, doesn't respect anything. So, I believe that it is violating the Constitution. We as peoples, as communities, have the right to self-determination, we have the right to water."[105] In both the e-mail and video, Arpi contrasted the state- and company-organized socialization with constitutionally mandated rights and the communities that protect and exercise them. He drew on an understanding of *consulta previa* that circulated widely among anti-extractive activists: communities exercise full "self-determination" over their territory, and therefore have the right "to decide" whether extraction occurs or not. Although the formulation of this particular right exceeds the letter of the constitutional text (and in fact redeploys the arguments in defense of the failed proposal for prior consent), it claims the form of constituent power ("we as peoples, as communities") envisioned in its very first article: "sovereignty resides (*radica*) in the people, whose will is the foundation of authority." Their resistance was thus a complex act of constituent politics: it simultaneously indexed the antinomies of an ambivalent Constitution and invoked that Constitution to assert popular constituent power against the very state that the Constitution ostensibly refounded.

The state response was twofold. On the one hand, there was legal action. The Ministry of Environment brought charges against seventeen suspected protesters for the crime of "obstruction of public administration." Criminal charges provoked further protest. On December 10, hundreds marched on the local attorney general's office in support of the accused. According to CONAIE lawyer Wilson Ordóñez, who led the anti-mining activists' defense team, "the accused had exercised 'the right to resistance before the failure of the Ecuadorian State to comply with the right to prior, free, and informed consultation for natural resource extraction projects.'"[106]

On the other hand, state actors also responded in a more technocratic vein. They took the opportunity to redouble their insistence that consultation consisted of conveying information. As discussed at length in Chapter 5, official and corporate actors ambivalently constructed Shaggly protesters as both in need of more "information" and fundamentally irrational, beyond the reach of informational governance. Anti-mining activists were alternately construed as the victims and sources of misinformation, depending on whether pro-mining actors saw them as members of the "community" or as politically or economically motivated outsiders. In an interview published in the state-owned newspaper, the vice-minister of mining, Federico Auquilla, described the ongoing state efforts in Shaggly as "information processes," with the aim that "all citizens find out, we are embracing (*estamos acogiendo*) the right so that all citizens are informed." In this account, the peaceful process of information diffusion was met with the violent "stones, sticks" of the protesters.[107]

Upon closer inspection, the state response reveals fissures and uncertainties that point to unsettled questions of constitutional rule. Despite his insistence that I avoid raising "politically sensitive issues" during our interview, Torracchi—who was among the Ministry of Environment officials blocked from entering Shaggly the month before—brought up the protest of his own accord. When asked whether he intended to return to the parish to proceed with the legally required participation process, he replied: "We have carried it out in the community due to our dedication, to get to know the people. We could do it via television or radio. We went, they didn't let us in, so, I'm sorry for them. But if the Ministry of Environment authorizes me, I'll say, 'We can't enter, we tried.' I think that they are going to try again, I wouldn't do it, but on the part of [the Ministry in] Quito, they are going to try." Torracchi contrasted what he perceived as two distinct official interpretations of constitutionally mandated participation. Speaking on behalf of the Azuay province ministry offices, he advocated for a relatively minimal definition: "if they do it through other means, the website, a letter, they participate."[108] He juxtaposed this with what he expected to be the stance of the ministry headquarters in Quito, which, as he explained, is more concerned with the central government's image and, relatedly, national political support for mining.

Torracchi's statements draw attention to the fact that the state too is a field of dispute. Competing bureaucratic interpretations of "consultation" and "participation" map onto intra-state disagreements over constitutional enforcement, revealing the state to comprise a multiplicity of bureaucratic practices rather than a unitary monolith. Ministry of Nonrenewable Resources and Ministry of Environment functionaries tend to articulate a more limited and technocratic vision of participation. Given the centrality of these two agencies in the development of extractive projects, this vision constitutes the predominant official interpretation of prior consultation. In contrast, bureaucrats in the Secretaría de Pueblos, Movimientos Sociales y Participación Ciudadana (SPMSPC, Secretariat of Peoples, Social Movements, and Citizen Participation) and the Office of the Ombudsman evinced a more critical stance. While Torracchi straightforwardly explained to me that, "seven days before the socialization on such and such day, workgroups (*mesas de trabajo*) [are convened], and seven days after [the socialization], they state all their doubts," at the Office of the Ombudsmen, Wilton Guaranda Mendoza told me that "fifteen days is insufficient," and that the lack of time and high-quality information results in a "total confusion" among community members about the impacts of mining projects.[109] Alicia Hidalgo, an SPMSPC functionary, agreed, telling me: "Personally, it does not seem sufficient. I have fought with them. They talk of an office, fifteen days before. I have a lot of doubts. It should be a permanent office that allows for permanent socialization."[110] Her co-worker, Romulo Heredia, also spoke of "confusion"—within the state itself rather than among affected citizens:

> Prior consultation, it depends how it is considered. In the Constitution, free and informed consultation, non-binding. They do not make decisions as to whether the project happens or not . . . There is a confusion. Some want to call it consultation, others call it socialization. We [the SPMSPC] accompany the process. Meet, gather together the institutions that have to do with the project, and protect (*vigilar*) the rights of the population. It is very ugly work, between two forces. The state wants to move forward; society wants to protect its rights. Some want to go as far as a binding consultation. Within the government, these people [in support of binding consultation] are very dispersed, not in one institution, and without much power . . . The majority [of officials], as the Constitution says, non-binding, more to inform.[111]

In his account, divisions within the state reflect divisions between the state and society, and hinge on unsettled questions of constitutional interpretation. Hidalgo also spoke of discord among officials: "There is a decree [1040], but there is no longer a consensus within the state itself." She then pointed to the frictions generated by the simultaneous refounding of the state and development of a new extractive sector. Referring to the fact that concessions for slated mining projects predate the 2008 Constitution (although all were temporarily suspended and many eliminated by the Constituent Assembly's Mining Mandate), she said, "the concessions are old, you can't carry out prior consultations, therefore they should socialize the environmental impact assessment," echoing activists' concerns that consultations are after the fact rather than substantively "prior."[112]

In addition to the relatively protected conversational space of an interview, the rare occasions of face-to-face debate between anti-mining activists and state officials provided an opportunity for bureaucrats to engage in critical self-reflection. During the aforementioned debate over mega-mining in Ibarra, the provincial director of the Ministry of Environment, Oscar Mejia, responded to harsh criticism from Acción Ecológica organizer Amanda Yepes, who had questioned his claims regarding community participation. In the process, his stance slid from oppositional to sympathetic, reinforced by a change in tone and affect: "Participation is real. Before, they [the communities] didn't participate, they [the companies] offered something, and continued the activities. Decree 1040 is so that they participate, that they [the communities] sacrifice something but that there is real development. The projects, many times are halfway socialized. The *técnicos* don't have decision-making power, it comes from above." Mejia thus raised another source of intra-state dispute: not across ministries but between lower-level functionaries (*técnicos*) and higher-level authorities ("from above"), most likely referring to ministers and the president himself.

Such moments reveal that otherwise self-assured bureaucrats at times faltered under the pressure of calibrating mining policy and constitutional principles. Having just defined consultation as socialization, and socialization as information, Vice-Minister Auquilla appealed to the language of Decree 1040 to add yet another limit to participation.[113] He told me, "consultation is conceived, is organized, when a project of the national government will affect the interests of the population in a negative manner." When I asked him to clarify that Mirador, in contrast, only required an informational process because the project would not negatively impact (that is, "affect") the population, he repeated, "it will only bring benefits, which is a totally different thing." He relied on the decree's distinction between impacted and affected communities to claim that such a social participation process would not be necessary in the case of Mirador. The following month, Correa publicly insisted that the state had already consulted the communities within Mirador's area of influence. The day after the two-week long March for Water, Life, and the Dignity of Peoples, state-owned media outlets reported on an interview Correa had given with Gama TV, with the headline, "In Ecuador there was prior consultation around mining exploitation" (referring to the Mirador project) in response to march leaders' claims to the contrary."[114]

The unsettled meaning of "consultation" raises the question whether consultations happen at all. While Auquilla claimed consultation was not necessary since the project would not detrimentally impact communities, and Hidalgo questioned whether consultations could be "prior" in a meaningful sense, Correa insisted consultation had already been carried out, and that activists' claims were based on a misinterpretation of the Constitution ("they confuse prior consultation with prior consent").[115] Weeks later, in an interview with the newspaper *El Comercio* that opened with a question about the extent of constitutional rule given the continuity of the "extractive model," the minister of nonrenewable resources, Wilson Pastor, repeated Correa's argument: "What the Constitution asks for is prior consultation, like the diffusion [of] and information about the projects. The Constitution does not ask that the inhabitants of Zamora are given a ballot, so that they mark if they are or are not in agreement with mining."[116] Consultation was a slippery term. In the conflict over resource extraction, definitions of this constitutional right invariably invoked competing interpretations, not only of the Constitution, but of the nature of democratic authority in the context of an extractive economy—and the relationship between the state, the nation, and the plurality of communities within its borders. The attempt to limit the referent of *consulta previa* to "information" did not settle debate—either between the government and social movements, nor within the state.

Conclusion

This chapter drew on the archival documentation of the 2007–2008 Constituent Assembly debates, ethnographic observation, and interviews to analyze how the emerging intra-left dispute over resource extraction intensified in the process of the contentious drafting and enforcement of the 2008 Constitution and, particularly, of the collective right to prior consultation. It demonstrated that constituent politics does not end with constitutional ratification, nor is it limited to moments of refounding. Instead, I traced the Constitution as a mobile document that lives through its invocation and interpretation in the heat of political praxis. This analytic vantage point decenters the politics of constitutional interpretation. Rather than privileging the activity of official jurisprudence, this chapter revealed popular movements as key protagonists in a multi-sited and agonistic process of constitution-making. These movements deployed a politically ambivalent legal document to assert their constituent power over and against state institutions. Despite internal debates among indigenous activists over whether to support ratification, in the wake of the Constitution's popular approval these same activists and their allies characterized themselves as its most ardent defenders. My analysis also attended to the specificity of their interpretive strategy, and that of their political opponents. Social movement activists mobilized a selective reading of the Constitution, and prior consultation in particular, that endowed their fight against resource extraction with constitutional legitimacy. Meanwhile, bureaucrats tasked with the implementation of the constitutional right to prior consultation deployed a technocratic rhetoric that, citing the language of Executive Decree 1040, redefined the right to prior consultation as the right to technical information in an ultimately unsuccessful attempt to depoliticize the question of "social participation."

Social participation in extractive projects might have been intended as, in the words of Alicia Hidalgo, "a strategy to manage conflict." But in the context of the dispute over the extractive model, it instead sparked disagreement over a fundamental political question: Who rules? This disagreement, however, presupposed a shared concern and a degree of mutual recognition: both anti-mining activists and pro-mining officials agreed that a collective democratic subject rules.[117] However, for the former this subject coincided with a local community and governed directly, while for the latter it coincided with the nation that delegated its mandate to representatives and bureaucrats. For one side, prior consultation was democracy; for the other, mass democracy was the limit of prior consultation. The next chapter analyzes how these competing interpretations of the Constitution became linked to these distinct visions of democratic sovereignty.

4

The *Demos* in Dispute

On October 2, 2011, two community water systems in the southern highland province of Azuay decided to enforce their constitutionally mandated right to be consulted prior to the development of a nearby large-scale mine—a right they claimed that public institutions had failed to guarantee. The consultation presented participants with a question that no state official had ever asked the residents of this farming community: Are you in favor of the Quimsacocha gold mine, or not? Over 90 percent of them voted against the mine. President Correa responded swiftly. He dismissed the event as unconstitutional and marshaled his impressive electoral record to assert the democratic legitimacy of resource extraction. This consultation in turn occasioned a dispute over the collective subject of democratic authority, a dispute that resonated with and amplified the struggle over constitutional authority.

This chapter draws on ethnographic observation of the consultation (organized by an umbrella organization of community water associations turned anti-mining group, UNAGUA) and traces the dispute over democracy in its wake. This consultation, like many similar cases across Latin America, involved the popular enforcement of the right to prior consultation.[1] This right is recognized in ILO Convention 169, which Ecuador ratified in 1998 in response to the demands of indigenous groups and to oil-related conflict.[2] Prior consultation was incorporated into the 1998 Constitution, strengthened in the 2008 Constitution, and has been regulated by presidential decrees.[3] In Ecuador, this right is not limited to indigenous communities; a separate constitutional provision extends it to any community whose environment is potentially impacted by policy decisions. But in Ecuador and across the region, many scholars, and environmental and indigenous activists, assert that prior consultation has not been substantively enforced. In response, affected communities have organized community consultations. These consultations often provoke state and corporate actors to delegitimize them as unconstitutional, nonbinding, and the result of "manipulation" by indigenous or environmental groups.

This debate unfolds across the Americas, where the proliferation of new collective rights and institutions of community participation in resource extraction has fueled competing claims to democratic authority. In Guatemala, informal mining consultations like the one I observed have emerged as a successful collective action strategy among indigenous communities emerging from the trauma of civil war.[4] In Peru and Colombia, affected communities (both indigenous and non-indigenous) have pressured municipal governments to hold popular consultations on mining projects, as well as organized informal consultations, and entered into direct conflict with their national governments.[5] In addition, in Colombia the Supreme Court ruled against the government for the failure to properly consult indigenous peoples over mining—and some indigenous groups have in turn criticized the court for what they see as an overly procedural interpretation of consultation.[6] In Bolivia, indigenous communities and state actors clashed over the implementation of prior consultation in regard to the TIPNIS highway project.[7] In Argentina, citizens have voted against mining in popular referenda organized by municipal governments, resulting in conflicts between organized movements at the municipal level and provincial governments that depend on mining rents.[8] In Venezuela, indigenous communities protested the government for failing to consult them prior to an executive decree that expanded mining development in the Orinoco Delta.[9] Lastly, and, most dramatically, in 2017 a social movement coalition, in alliance with the left-wing political party FMLN, successfully pressured El Salvador's Congress to adopt the world's first national ban on metallic mining—an achievement that I discuss at more length in the Conclusion.

At stake in these conflicts is not only the implementation of an international legal norm, but the fundamental question of who rules. In an extractive economy with territorially uneven costs and benefits, who should decide the fate of oil and mining projects? Directly affected minorities or national citizenries geographically concentrated in population centers far away from those projects? From one perspective, there is democratic justice in those most immediately affected deciding the fate of extractive projects. But from another, such local rights fragment democratic sovereignty and threaten the collective good of resource-funded development.

When they implement community consultations (*consultas*), affected communities do more than demand the enforcement of their legal right to prior consultation. They invoke the specter of democracy beyond the nation-state.

By claiming the legitimacy of their non-state democratic practices, they reject the notion that the state's formal institutions are the sole locus of democratic decision-making. Further, they challenge the unity of the nation-state: in an enactment of the "plurinational" state set forth in the Constitution (itself a product of indigenous mobilization and theorization), consultations multiply the sites of democratic decision-making and disrupt the monolithic nation presupposed by state actors who claim to represent the public good (often in explicit contrast to the particular demands of territorialized communities or social movements).

If democracy in its radical form is enacted, and expanded, through the eruption of conflict over the terms of collective life, then the communities affected by resource extraction that claim the authority to decide the fate of extractive projects resonate with a long history of democratic contention.[10] As Sheldon Wolin puts it, "Democracy was born in transgressive acts, for the demos could not participate in power without shattering the class, status, and value systems by which it was excluded."[11] For this reason, Enrique Dussel asserts, "Democracy is a perpetually unfinished system."[12]

In a regional and national context suffused by new forms of popular participation, and newly salient claims to popular sovereignty (often defined against the rule of domestic or foreign economic elites, and/or corrupt political parties), social movements were not alone in their claims to represent the interests of the people. By shifting the struggle over extraction onto the terrain of democracy, these new forms of social mobilization forced state actors to respond, and they did so by elaborating a vision of extractive democracy that justified the expansion of large-scale mining in democratic terms. Elected and appointed officials deployed figures of the demos, shored up by new policies of targeted local and national investment, to forge an intimate link between democratic sovereignty and the exploitation of the nation's subsoil resources.

But who are "the people"? Throughout the *consulta* and the debate it ignited, figures of "the people" proliferated. Although, as specified by UNAGUA's instructions and abided by during the event itself, only UNAGUA members could vote, as the consultation unfolded its collective subject expanded, and organizers and participants invoked larger collectivities. In their response to the event, state actors too slid between justifying resource extraction in terms of its benefits for a nationally construed demos (in explicit opposition to the obstruction of locally affected communities) and claiming local political support for extraction (thereby constructing local protesters as a political minority unrepresentative of affected communities). For both state actors and anti-mining activists, the distinct *territorialities* of mineral extraction on the one hand, and democratic participation and representation on the other, surfaced in alternating claims regarding the spatial bounds of the demos and their constituent power.

Enacting Constituent Power

The October 2011 consultation was organized by UNAGUA, an organization that is at once a means of self-government and a social movement, putting it in a unique position to claim popular authority to make binding decisions in defiance of state policies. The Coordinating Committee for Community Water Systems of Azuay, UNAGUA is an umbrella organization comprising thirty-one community water boards in the canton of Cuenca, including those of the Victoria del Portete and Tarqui parishes that organized and participated in the consultation.[13] The organization was founded as the result of efforts beginning in the mid-1970s to construct and maintain water infrastructure (drinking and irrigation) in response to being underserved by the public water utility company (ETAPA). It is embedded in a multi-scalar federation of campesino and indigenous organizations: it is part of the province-wide Federation of Peasant and Indigenous Organizations of Azuay (FOA), which belongs to the regional highland indigenous federation (Ecuarunari) and, ultimately, the national indigenous federation (CONAIE). Beginning in the mid-1990s, UNAGUA and other community water systems entered into conflict with ETAPA over the control of rural community water systems, defying a 1998 municipal ordinance that handed over control of these systems to ETAPA. Functionaries from ETAPA viewed rural residents as lacking the technical skills to manage irrigation and drinking water, and also worried (with good reason) that such community-level organizations were bastions of political resistance. In the early 2000s, UNAGUA was involved in resisting the privatization of water, and, due to their mobilization, won the recognition of their right to operate rural community water systems.

During the same period, UNAGUA also became active in anti-mining resistance, triggered by the Canadian mining company Iamgold receiving an 8,030-hectare concession to explore Quimsacocha, a planned large-scale gold mine in the high-altitude wetlands (*páramos*) above the two parishes, in 2001. The project, along with four others, was considered "strategic" by the Correa administration, but has to date not advanced past exploration, and in June 2012 was acquired by the Canadian exploration junior INV Metals. The relative cohesion of resistance to the Quimsacocha mine hinges on UNAGUA's efforts and on the involvement of urban environmentalists. The communities that comprise the project's area of influence are within the canton of Cuenca. The municipal center of Cuenca is Ecuador's third-largest city. Rural and urban anti-mining activists have forged alliances by mobilizing to protect the Yanuncay watershed, which supplies farmers and city residents alike. It is also worth noting that, although UNAGUA is linked to the regional and national indigenous movement, its members do not all, and at the time of my fieldwork did not primarily describe their identity in ethnic terms (as indigenous) but, rather, in class terms (as campesinos). In terms of livelihood, many were small-scale farmers, mostly in the dairy sector.[14] However, during the consultation and other protest events, UN-AGUA members deployed symbols and discourses that indexed indigeneity. This turn to indigeneity deepened in recent years and is reflected in the biographical trajectory of Carlos Pérez, president of UNAGUA at the time of the consultation. Pérez has long been active in the indigenous movement: in 1996, he helped found FOA and was elected to Cuenca's City Council as a candidate for Pachakutik, the political party linked to CONAIE. As time unfolded, Carlos's self-presentation became more explicitly indigenous and, in 2017, in the midst of serving his four-year term as president of Ecuarunari, he changed his name to Yaku Sacha Pérez (*Yaku Sacha* means "water of the mountain" in Kichwa). In what follows, I refer to him as Carlos, as that was his name at the time of the consultation and our interviews, and that is how state actors referred to him in the verbal attacks I recount. But more broadly, his story testifies not only to the malleability of identity, but also to the evolving cultural and political salience of indigeneity.

It was just after 2:00 p.m. on a chilly October afternoon in the *páramo*. Six of us crowded into the second-floor office of the parish council (*junta parroquial*) of Victoria del Portete. The *junta* had lent their building to UNAGUA for the mining consultation that day. "National and international observers" seemed a grandiose title for our small group, though it was accurate enough: among us, we held passports from Ecuador, Spain, Holland, and the United States, and we had spent the day observing pieces of paper being neatly folded and inserted through a slit in a cardboard box, only to be just as neatly unfolded hours later, creases smoothed, placed in one pile or another, counted, recorded, and set aside in a manila envelope, destined to be slowly eroded by dust and humidity in some unknown file box, impotent, political energy expended. Our observation period had come to a close with the final tally, and we now turned to one another, to reflect, debate, and craft a provisional consensus, and then draft, print, and sign an "Act of Observation," the textual artifact that at once validated our own activity and that of the 1,037 voters, and that would soon be read aloud on the wooden stage in the plaza below, in turn signaling the moment for music, dancing, and perhaps a surreptitious bottle of aguardiente.

According to the Act of Observation, the consultation was a democratic election: "ballot boxes" in "alphabetical order" required voters to register "with their personal information and identity documents" and "deposit" a "secret ballot." The act characterized the process as "peaceful and orderly, showing the civic attitude of the population of Victoria del Portete" as well as an "exercise of free speech and the right to be consulted in decisions that affect their life." In its documentary form, fit for public presentation and circulation, the debates surrounding the production of the Act of Observation were no longer visible. Indeed, the wording of the text—the use of the verbal noun "voting" by unidentified and homogeneous "participants"—circumvented disagreements among observers and organizers alike over the appropriate vocabulary to refer to the complex of actors, practices, and legal forms at play in the consultation. Are the voters individual or collective? Are they best described as families or water users or titleholders? Did the legitimacy of the consultation emanate from the observers or from the community, or both? Was the process "binding" or "symbolic"? Where does consultation end and verification begin?

The consultation had commenced, as did many acts of protest in Ecuador, with a *ceremonia ancestral*. The musky sweetness of burning *palo santo* infused the air around the concentric circles of fruit, vegetables, grains, and flowers arranged on an electric pink and blue cloth, the same kind that might tie a baby to a mother, transport foraged valerian, or display souvenirs in Quito's *centro histórico*. This tableau, a dense semiotic economy at once Kichwa and mestizo, rural and urban, highland, Amazonian, and coastal, served as a stage for the speeches that commenced the day. Both the makeshift stage and the interventions testified to the recently consolidated relationships between the water users' association, the regional (Ecuarunari) and national (CONAIE) indigenous federations, and an environmental group (Acción Ecológica), as well as fraught alliances with *políticos* (specifically, Lourdes Tibán, the Pachakutik assembly member representing Chimborazo, who was in open conflict with Correa).[15]

When the ceremony ended, voting began (see Figure 4.1). As per the instructions elaborated at a prior UNAGUA assembly, from 8:00 a.m. to 2:00 p.m., UNAGUA members voted "yes" or "no" to the following: Are you in agreement with mining activity in the wetlands (*páramos*) and watershed of Kimsacocha?[16] Members of UNAGUA asserted their political authority over a project that they feared would contaminate the local ecosystem and waterways. This assertion drew on available legal norms—the ballot cited the 2008 Constitution, ILO Convention 169, and UNAGUA's legal status as a water committee—linked to

Figure 4.1 Voting. Photo credit: Sander Otten.

a variety of scales of governance (from the canton to the globe) and scales of democratic subjectivity (from the individual voter to "Mother Earth").

The instructions conformed to the genre of an Ecuadorian constitutional article, law, or decree, and thus enacted a form of "vernacular statecraft."[17] The instructions not only cited legal norms, but also explicitly mimicked their formality. They stipulated the election of a Community Electoral Tribunal, which along with the vote counters and the observers comprised the consultation's electoral institutions. The tribunal presided and the observers watched as water users waited in line, were located on the voting roll, presented identification, and marked their ballots, which were subsequently tallied, recorded, and filed (see Figure 4.2). Due to their resemblance to officially sanctioned suffrage practices, these routine electoral procedures calibrated the consultation to the recently refounded political-legal order precisely. The document stated that "part of the democratic exercise of communities, communes, peoples, and nationalities is the democratic participation at the ballot box to construct and decide transcendental issues," and cited constitutional articles and international conventions. The scalar shifts (from "communities" to "nationalities") recapitulated the federated structure of indigenous ethno-territorial organization in Ecuador.[18] But they also aligned with the political logic of the *consulta*. Through the routine techniques of democratic procedure, a local organization drew on the political legitimacy of a series of broader collectivities and invoked concentrically encompassing units of "democratic participation" to ground the democratic credentials of the two voting parishes.

Throughout the consultation, UNAGUA members imagined the process as enacting the plurinational statehood established in the first article of the 2008 Constitution. They de facto defined *plurinacionalidad* as the multiplication of sites—and scales—of democratic decision-making. The *consulta*, then, was a multiplex act of resistance and rule, of subversion and compliance, at once routine (the organizers called it a "civil" process) and extraordinary ("a marvel").[19] The water users of Victoria del Portete and Tarqui claimed an authority grounded in the "ancestral rights" of a community that "predates the state."[20] But their tactics did not refuse state authority; instead, they repurposed nationally and internationally recognized forms of democratic participation in protest against the government's resource policies. They deployed a constitutionally guaranteed participatory institution to both display and consolidate local resistance to a nationally strategic extractive project.

In addition to legal norms, the consultation procedure was shaped by the water committee's organizational practices. Some 1,037 of the 1,500 water users

Figure 4.2 Counting the votes. Photo credit: Sander Otten.

voted according to the principle of one vote per water right, which usually was one per family but could be up to four. Members of UNAGUA had ratified this vote distribution during two planning assemblies.[21] Decision-making power and responsibilities in other realms of parish life, such as the communal labor practice called the *minga*, are allocated according to the household's water consumption. According to a radio interview on the day of the consultation with the president of UNAGUA, Carlos Pérez[22]:

> The majority has one right. I have one right to water; I have one right to vote. But, as an exception, some large families, have one, two, up to four rights; they have to show up with four people to a *minga* . . . For the contributions to the construction of a potable water plant, if you have four rights, you have to pay for four . . . This is contained in the by-laws, in the internal regulation approved by SENAGUA. It is . . . the product of voting . . . and an assembly . . . This is what the ILO Convention 169 and the declaration of the United Nations about indigenous peoples say, that we have to observe the community's own procedures, which are not necessarily going to be the same as the procedures in general terms.[23]

As Pérez explained, rights are allocated according to household size, including those currently residing in other provinces or countries. (Another member of the household can represent up to four minors, migrants, and/or elders.) For Pérez, delegation ensures full recognition of the right to water, "which is a human right." This vote distribution rule, however, would later be labeled "undemocratic" by official discourse. This vote allocation challenged the most fundamental scale of liberal democracy: the individual citizen, wherein one "unit" of democratic authority (the vote) is mapped onto one discretely embodied subject (the voter).[24]

The results imparted an immediate sense of victory: 93 percent of the 1,037 participants voted against the Quimsacocha mine (see Figure 4.3). The closing speeches characterized the event as an act of democratic sovereignty, and linked it to broader political identities and projects: the participants had registered their "will," writing themselves into "the history of peoples and nations that have chosen this path," a history to be read and reread ("this message must spread, comrades").[25] Ecuarunari president Delfín Tenesaca invoked an increasingly expansive democratic subject: every one of us; our children; *Pachamama* (Mother Earth). However its collective author was construed, the event exceeded neutral proceduralism. It might have been a civil or civic process— the adjective used by organizers, *cívico*, can mean either—but it was also a call to arms. Tenesaca exhorted, "let's unite more, work more, and from here

Figure 4.3 Declaring democratic victory. Photo credit: Sander Otten.

comrades, we have to organize a march to Quito." Humberto Cholango, the president of CONAIE, raising his fist in the air, proclaimed, "No one and nothing will stop our fight in defense of water and in defense of our territories . . . to construct a better Ecuador, without mining in our territories." Cholango cast the UNAGUA members as protagonists in the reconfiguration of the relationship between the people, its territory, and its resources. His statement scaled up the *consulta* from the local and present to the national and historic: it was a means to a "better" Ecuador and an imagined post-extractive future.

The yes/no question on the ballot was more than a neutral technology to relay voters' preferences. It was precisely the deployment of recognizable democratic procedures that allowed for claims to such seemingly disproportionate scales of representation: through the act of voting, 1,037 water users became a nation, a people, Mother Earth. But the moment such claims were made, this series of synecdochic moves exceeded its democratic algorithm and became ammunition in the battle over resource extraction. Oriented to the future, to its reception and replication in other locales, the consultation served as a model for the translocal anti-mining movement activists both advocated and hoped for. The event's *political* status—in Ecuador, "political" was most often construed as pejorative—was quickly seized on by the Correa administration to question the consultation's democratic credentials. State officials would portray the consultation as compromised by procedural irregularities and political manipulation, and the results as failing to represent a democratic will. These portrayals were in turn mobilized to challenge the legitimacy of local participatory democracy, as opposed to national electoral democracy. But in the subsequent contestation around the *consulta*, activists were preoccupied with a distinct set of concerns. For the anti-mining movement, poised somewhere between fragmented local conflicts around particular mining projects and national mobilization, consultations provoked both hope and uncertainty.

The Backlash: Reasserting Constituted Power

When I spoke to Carlos Pérez a month and a half later in his law office in downtown Cuenca, he was optimistic.[26] The consultation had "achieved legitimacy"; its "impact . . . is even at the international level." Three weeks after the *consulta*, President Correa visited Quimsacocha, accompanied by reporters, to explain that the mining project would not pollute the watershed, and to deride anti-mining activists for spreading "lies" and "mental fundamentalisms."[27] For Peréz, the president's visit testified to the national scale of the event. At the local level, consultation seemed contagious: Pérez told me about several more slated *consultas* regarding mining and hydroelectric plants.[28] "The communities have awoken. The leaders have said, you convinced us." For Pérez, a new era of anti-mining resistance had commenced: "Before, it was a taboo to talk about mining, and even worse if one spoke against mining. Therefore, the consultation was key in the resistance process. What before was performed with radical actions like shutting down the streets, shutting down the roads (*vías*), was now organized with a peaceful election. Without shutting down the streets, a route (*vía*) to consultation was opened. And this is where Correa gets the angriest. Correa, because he has been the promoter of consultations. And in this consultation, he lost. It is the first consultation that Correa lost." Peréz played on the multivalence of *vía* as both road and route, imagining *consultas* as a material infrastructure to sustain translocal anti-mining resistance. In a political context suffused by new participatory institutions (including the four national referenda Correa convened), consultations projected democratic legitimacy.

The official response criticized the Quimsacocha consultation on democratic and constitutional grounds. When I arrived in Victoria del Portete along with the other observers, we saw a sheet of paper tacked to a pole near the plaza: its heading read ALERTA. It stated that "The Federation of Indigenous and Peasant Organizations of Azuay" (FOA), the base level organization of Ecuarunari of which Pérez was also president, "has convened, without consultation and in an illegal and illegitimate manner . . . the misnamed 'Consultation' which is in reality a PROSELYTIC ACT of Dr. Carlos Pérez Guartambel." It accused the "deceitful consultation" of presenting a "leading and false question without legal grounds because the Mining Law in Article 87 says that the State is responsible for executing the processes of consultation . . . being an authority non-delegable to any private institution," and that all consultation processes must be approved by the National Electoral Commission.[29] It concluded that the consultation "IS UNCONSTITUTIONAL," a "crude political manipulation on the part of the permanent opposition to the Government."

This anonymous warning contained several tropes of the official response to the consultation. It dismissed UNAGUA's performance of institutional formality, claiming for the state the sole authority to execute consultations and interpret the Constitution. It denigrated the process as political, as opposed to constitutional or legal, and as the work of a politician ("Dr. Carlos Pérez Guartambel"), rather than the community. The warning rejected the scalar logic of the *consulta*, which claimed the democratic authority of the local community via an appeal to more encompassing legal orders, whether national constitutional rights or international conventions. The warning scaled the event down, reframing the *consulta* as the political machination of a single individual. In the weeks that followed, these arguments circulated in the state-owned newspaper.

The Saturday after the consultation, Correa devoted a significant portion of his weekly address to the event.

> Failed *politiqueros* that never win half an election but want to attract attention in any form. But something shameless. I refer to the supposed popular consultation in Quimsacocha against mining . . . Totally illegal. They convoke, they organize, they control, they count the votes, and we are going to see how they marked the votes, how the people voted six times, what type of question it was, no? Do you agree with mining in water sources? Do you agree with loving your mother? Well everybody says "yes" in this case. Are you in favor of mining in water sources? If they asked me, well, no, if in addition in the Constitution that is prohibited.[30]

In addition to outright manipulation, Correa argued that consultation is a political practice that inherently encourages the search for supporters to legitimate a pre-existing objective: "If you imagine what they are proposing, that tomorrow, so that the mayor of Santa Elena [location of speech] puts a streetlight in this corner, he is going to need to consult the neighborhood . . . If the opponents, if they know that in the neighborhood, they will lose, they are going to ask you on the street. If on the street, they lose, they are going to ask the two families in the corner, until they find a group where they win."[31] Correa deflated the consultation's scalar logic: in his framing, rather than enabling a set of individuals to represent a community, and that community to represent an entire nation or Mother Earth, the consultation scaled down (from "the neighborhood" to "the two families") in a never-ending search for the outcome preferred by its organizers. It represented the latter's political agenda instead of a democratic will.

In advance of the Inter-American Court of Human Rights' 2012 decision on a case regarding prior consultation, Correa again emphasized that consultations encourage the search for support among an increasingly narrower base.[32] "That for every step in our country, for our development, for the future of our children, we are going to have to ask for the consent of each community. And, if we lose at the level of the community, half the community, if we lose half the community, then of these three families . . . It wouldn't be democracy of the majority, but of unanimity. And it is impossible to govern like this . . . Democracy is over in this country."[33]

Correa both deflated the democratic aspirations of anti-mining activists and took them seriously in their quest to replicate the Quimsacocha consultation model in every potentially affected community. If such "popular consultations" were carried out in "each community," he asserted that both "democracy" and "development"—themselves linked through the electoral legitimation of extraction—would come to an end. He opposed the national good to local particularism. Effacing the collective labor of UNAGUA members, Correa referred to political leaders who "obstruct any national development project," suggesting that the consultation's local scale favors the rule of the few over the rule of the many.

Concern about local obstruction accounted for the administration's hesitation to substantively enforce prior consultation. Official participation processes ("socializations"), co-organized by state and corporate actors, have been implemented for many oil and mining projects, including the open-pit Mirador mine now in operation in the Amazon.[34] Socializations are informational presentations. Citizens may ask questions and comment, but only "technically viable" statements are included in project evaluation, thus mitigating the risk of creating a forum to oppose projects. While the president and bureaucrats insisted that socializations are nonbinding, they equally insisted that the people rule—and already have ruled in favor of extraction—through national elections that directly communicate their will. Technocratic socializations at the local level are the flip side of unmediated popular sovereignty at the national level.

While the administration sought to limit the potential for local opposition, anti-mining activists aimed to amplify it. In the process, they grappled with the tension that inheres in deploying a democratic institution as a resistance tactic. Precisely because community-organized consultations in Latin America are a democratic exercise, a yes/no question posed by a community to itself, they are a risky resistance strategy. As Carlos Pérez put it during a forum in Cuenca on community consultations in resistance to mining, a "lost consultation"—a community voting "yes" to a mining project—would be detrimental not only to that local movement but to the possibility of consultations as a replicable model. For activists, for consultations to be a successful resistance strategy, they have to communicate unified local opposition. Pérez worried that a defeat would encourage mining companies to carry out *consultas* and "an important tool of resistance would be lost." "Urban consultations" were too risky: the perception among activists was that the inhabitants of Quito and Guayaquil were geographically and politically distant from mining projects.[35] The minutes of a planning meeting in Cuenca for the March for Water, Life, and the Dignity of Peoples reflect this concern: "In relation to mining, we considered various possibilities for the demand: a national consultation, local consultations, the recognition of the Mining Mandate [issued by the Constituent Assembly, which temporarily suspended mining contracts], a moratorium on mining negotiations . . . The proposal of a national consultation was basically eliminated from the options, because it literally puts our life on the line (*jugarse la vida*), since the government controls everything."[36] The phrase "the government controls everything" could refer to the administration's influence over the nominally independent National Electoral Commission that administers referenda, or to the efficacy of the official communicational infrastructure in shaping public opinion. Either way, activists recognized the risk of battling a plebiscitary president on his own terrain.[37] But they also highlighted the pitfalls specific to a national consultation. In community consultations, the notion of "directly affected" delineates the relevant democratic subject, and national and international legal norms ground the community's democratic authority. A national consultation would refigure the democratic subject as the national citizenry, whose "outer edges" are drawn by the boundaries of the national territory.[38] At this scale, the effects of extraction are less "direct," or at least less visible; likewise, "the nation" is not the subject of national or international rights to participation in decision-making over extractive projects.

Activists likely had these contrasts in mind when they dismissed the possibility of national consultations as an anti-mining strategy. However, the links between identities, interests, and democratic scale are not written in stone; the scales of democracy are only ever provisionally settled and can be reconfigured through politically effective action. Two years later, environmental activists launched a campaign to hold a national referendum on oil extraction in Yasuní National Park. While the outcome confirmed activists' fears that "the government controls everything"—hundreds of thousands of signatures were rejected in a controversial counting process, blocking the referendum—the movement against oil extraction in the Yasuní transcended directly affected communities, and was especially active in the urban areas that anti-extractive activists have found challenging to mobilize.[39]

Returning to Correa's speech, he alleged that the "political" orchestration of the *consulta* resulted in a series of procedural irregularities and undermined its democratic credentials. For state actors, the most salient procedural irregularity—and that most relevant to the scale of democratic decision-making—was a woman who ostensibly voted six times. She appeared in this speech and in several articles in the state-owned newspaper: "The result of the community consultation was clearly manipulated, even false. The same person voted more than one time. Here in this image [an older woman with more than one ballot] one can clearly see the fraud. A person voted how many times? It seems like six ballots, for her alone."[40] And in a video screened during the speech:

> NARRATOR: A consultation that did not even have an official electoral roll. A roll that was certainly manipulated by the same leaders that established the count, and proclaimed the results, usurping the function of the National Electoral Commission . . .

> OSCAR SIMÓN, PRESIDENT OF THE NATIONAL ELECTORAL COMMISSION (CNE): Who they were has not been clearly determined, who were the participants in this poll, finally, and what conditions, if the right of all citizens to participate was guaranteed, a guarantee . . . the Electoral Commission has to give when it deals with a popular consultation. We do not know what the procedure was.

As discussed, voting rights were allocated according to number of water titles. The efforts of UNAGUA members and observers to calibrate organizational practices with procedural norms were interpreted as the manipulation of democratic formality to serve "political" ends, projecting an opposition between officially sanctioned democracy and *politiqueria*.[41] These criticisms are not merely procedural. The consultation called into question some of the most fundamental principles of liberal, representative democracy. By allowing multiple votes per person, the consultation suggested that citizenship need not be conceived of as mapping onto a discretely embodied individual. And by "usurping" functions such as voter registration and vote counting, they challenged the notion that the state is the unique locus of democratic rule.

The Elusive Demos

In their political struggle over the future of the Quimsacocha mining projects, consultation organizers and the Correa administration invoked the legitimating force of both the national "people" and the local "community," and claimed that these collectivities had communicated their will through mechanisms of representation: consultations, elections, and referenda. Responding to demands to "democratize democracy" via substantive consultations, Correa pointed to his electoral record.[42] As he stated in a speech a few months after the consultation, "Why do so many people just talk blah blah blah about participatory democracy? . . . How much more participation than this? What other president of the republic in history has been held accountable every week to the Ecuadorian people? . . . Until I understood . . . participatory democracy is that we win the elections, but they govern. And this is not going to happen. If they want to govern the country, they must win elections. This is called dem-o-cracy."[43] For Correa, participatory democracy is, in the usage of activists, a deceptive term that proclaims democracy but means its opposite: a regime in which the unelected govern and, as he went on to say, "impose their fundamentalism and infantilism of 'no to oil' and 'no to mining.'" During his speech immediately after the consultation, he was more specific, focusing on parish-level referenda and election results to demonstrate the democratic credentials of mining projects. He contrasted the unofficial consultation with results from a recent national referendum (also referred to as a "consultation," following constitutional language) and the 2009 presidential elections.[44] Like the CNE president Oscar Simón, Correa compared the number of participants in the *consulta* with the electoral roll that establishes the number of participants in the latter two (voting is mandatory in Ecuador).

I think that one thousand people voted. But here I have the electoral roll. Of the two parishes. There are around seven thousand people . . . And I think that 1000 people voted, 900 in favor, 47 against, that we suppose are with the government. Well it turns out that in the last consultation we won by a landslide in Azuay. We won by a landslide in the canton of Cuenca. We won by a landslide, three to one, in Tarqui . . . [applause]. And in Portete we practically tied, 1200 to 1200. But here we won half a vote [laughter]. Very suspiciously [laughter]. They should look in the ballot box. In the elections in April [2009] . . . we won in a landslide, we beat him, and this man [Pérez] did not win even with the vote of his relatives, and he didn't even have his relatives' votes.[45]

This characterization of the consultation, along with Simón's statements during the video regarding the absence of an official electoral roll, demonstrates confusion about the participants in the community consultation of October 2, but also reflects the shifting claims made by consultation organizers. As stated in the consultation instructions, "Suffrage is a right and an obligation of all of the users of the community water system who make community participation effective, whose surnames and names appear in the electoral roll or user registry."[46] The community here is the community of water users of Victoria del Portete and Tarqui, *not* the entire community of residents of the two parishes. Correa conflated two kinds of consultations: a state-organized national referendum in May 2011 encompassing all registered voters, and the *consulta comunitaria*, convoked by and for UNAGUA members. The conflation—which held the October *consulta* to the impossible standards governing a national election—was further enabled by the ambivalence built into the term "popular consultation." When officials use this term, other contextual clues indicate that they mean an official, binding, and often national, "referendum"—like those convened to ratify the Constitution in 2008 or to reform judicial and communications policy in 2011, both of which Correa (the "yes" vote) won. During his visit to Quimsacocha later that month, according to the state-owned newspaper, Correa "dismissed the possibility of convoking a popular consultation to resolve mining exploitation, especially in the areas where some inhabitants oppose this activity that generates resources for public works."[47]

When activists use the term "popular consultation," they either mean an official, national referendum or they mean the opposite: unofficial, local processes such as the one in Victoria del Portete. When we spoke in his office, Carlos Pérez contrasted "popular consultations" to "community consultations," using the former in reference to a canton in Azuay whose inhabitants were attempting to organize a consultation through the official channel of the CNE.[48] But in the same interview he referred to a planned unofficial consultation in Tungaragua, whose organizers wanted to enlist the help of UNAGUA, as a "popular consultation." Likewise, the invitation to observers uses the term "popular consultation" to refer to processes such as the October consultation.

In the debate over prior consultation, "popular" has an ambiguous status. Depending on the context it can index national (in contrast to local), democratic (by the people), or official (state-sanctioned). In anti-mining discourse, activists frequently jumped from defending localist forms of democracy, wherein affected communities are defined in contrast to a homogeneous national subject, to making assertions about *the* people as an undifferentiated mass. Pro-mining rhetoric, meanwhile, presents these three features as commensurable and mutually constitutive: the people *are* the nation; the official *is* the democratic. But upon closer inspection, this rhetoric too jumped from the local to the national. When Correa referred to the "landslide" victory for Alianza País in both parishes and Azuay province, he marshaled voting patterns on a 2011 referendum on issues unrelated to mining to demonstrate local support for the Quimsacocha project. He then referred to presidential elections in April 2009 to make the same point. In the process, referenda and elections lost their specific content and became interchangeable shows of local support for any decisions the government made.

Correa concluded his critique of the consultation with a pared-down version of his own position. Putting aside the criticisms of procedural irregularities, he asserted that the consultation had zero democratic value in the face of the overwhelming democratic legitimacy of his natural resource policy. Whatever the outcome of the "so-called consultation," by electing him, the people already expressed their democratic will that the nation's mineral resources be exploited. "The [presidential] election of April 2009 is very important. We always said that we are going to develop the mining potential of this country . . . We won in just one round, we won in Cuenca, we won in Azuay, we won in Tarqui, it seems to me in Portete too . . . And, well, that is democracy: vote for a government where we say we are going to develop mining policy and the mining potential of this country . . . I have the constitutional power to establish mining policy."[49] Whatever the outcome of the "so-called consultation," if elections ensure prospective representation, the people had already willed that the nation's mineral resources be exploited—especially, as Correa points out, since he won in the first round, which is an impressive feat in a country with a history of political fragmentation.[50] As a corollary, opposition to mining is opposition to democracy (despite the election of anti-mining candidates at the subnational level, such as the prefect of Zamora Chinchipe, Salvador Quishpe).

The Correa administration's model of resource governance involved a complex set of relations between affected communities and the geographically dispersed national population. His invocation of parish-level election and referenda results suggests that the government prizes local political support. The viability of extractive projects requires local quiescence, or at least tacit acceptance: resistance can scare off investors and disrupt mining activity. Indeed, activists uniformly interpreted the 2012 sale of Quimsacocha from Iamgold to INV Metals as a sign of political success. Although there are other explanatory factors (for example, corporate actors saw the 2009 Mining Law as unfriendly to investment), bureaucrats also worried that local protest—especially the 2011 consultation—had stalled the project.[51] State actors see public investment as key to mitigating resistance. Executive Decree 870 established a state-owned enterprise (Ecuador Estratégico) tasked with "the redistribution of national wealth and to bring development to citizens . . . in whose territory nonrenewable natural resources are located" to "make these communities the first beneficiaries of oil, mining and natural wealth in general."[52]

As Correa stated above, however, extractive projects are a conduit of specifically national development. And since Correa was elected on a pro-mining platform that benefits the national majority, mining is democratic. This vision opposes myriad particularisms ("half the community," or "these three families") to the national interest in resource extraction. When CONAIE challenged the constitutionality of the 2009 Mining Law, Attorney General Dr. Néstor Arboleda claimed, "The State, in search of the *buen vivir* [living well] of its population, and being the property owner of non-renewable resources, has the obligation to seek the general interest over particular interests."[53] For these officials, prior consultation as interpreted by CONAIE would spell the end of democracy. It would, as Correa stated above, be "impossible to govern" because it would fragment the nationally conceived demos and unified territoriality required for state rule. But there is no homogeneous "whole country." The nation is a representation of an unevenly territorialized population whose inner and outer edges shift over time.[54] For indigenous and environmental activists, to prioritize the interests of a homogeneously conceived demos over those of affected communities is to efface the asymmetric territoriality of extraction and the plural composition of the nation. As Monica Chuji—the Amazonian Kichwa activist who served under the Correa administration before resigning due to disagreements over resource extraction and indigenous rights—stated:

"the common good is a pretext to violate the rights of communities that are also citizens. It is contradictory. We are also part of the state."[55]

The official democratic imaginary became a discursive resource for bureaucrats tasked with mining policy. As Mariuxsi Flores, the provincial director of ECORAE, the Public Development Institute for the Amazonian Region, told me: "If the project has a national benefit, prior consultation is not going to reflect the cost-benefit; therefore, all of the state should be consulted. The law is clear that it does not apply to strategic projects. We are talking about the country, benefits for the country. It can't be that a parish decides for the nation. All of the beneficiaries and those harmed, it will have to be all of the nation."[56] Despite being constitutionally required, Flores ruled out consultations for mining projects in the "national interest." She repurposed the logic of "directly affected" to justify the democratic credentials of extraction. Though she referred to "those harmed," she repeated the positive impacts ("benefit," "benefits," "beneficiaries") for "all of the nation." But later in our conversation, she extolled the importance of cash transfers and healthcare in "convincing" indigenous Shuar communities to support mining. Flores's appeal to benefits at the national and local levels reveals how the identity, interests, and scale of democratic peoplehood is partly constructed through the public investment funded by resource revenues. In the context of a dispute over the meaning of prior consultation, such situated interpretations have pragmatic effects. Just as activists' pronouncements potentially consolidate collective action, state actors' understandings of prior consultation shape the law's implementation, enabling particular forms of collective identity.

Conclusion

Whether they aim for a "mining country" (*país minero*) or a post-extractive Ecuador, both sides in the dispute over resource extraction in Ecuador appealed to the legitimizing force of local participation in the service of translocal political projects. Just as state discourse alternated between equating and sharply contrasting local preferences with "the national interest," anti-mining activists alternated between differently scaled collectivities, appealing to multiple territorialities of democratic decision-making and democratic peoplehood. During the consultation, they shifted from defending the democratic authority of affected communities to making assertions about "the people" as an undifferentiated mass. The event instructions specified at the outset that the participants were the users of the "Community Water System of the parishes of Tarqui and Victoria del Portete." The document, however, interpolates this particular collectivity as one example of the "communities, communes, peoples and nationalities" that exercise democratic rights. Meanwhile, the invitation sent to observers refers to the "indigenous and mestizo peoples of Victoria del Portete and Tarqui" and "affected communities." The Act of Observation we drafted is less precise: "participants" and "the population." Speeches addressed an even broader collectivity: "the people," "Ecuador," "comrades," "Pachamama," "our children."

This proliferation of democratic subjects was not arbitrary. A situated political calculus drew and improvised on an available repertoire of collective identities, guiding decisions about referential practice. The invocation of a given identity depended on the audience (participants, observers, domestic or international supporters), the context of reception (the plaza, activist listservs, the press), the actor's objective (mobilizing local activism, building translocal alliances, projecting legitimacy), and other factors. National laws and international conventions encouraged an emphasis on the communities "directly affected" by extraction; the imperatives of movement-building encouraged the invocation of other potentially affected communities; the national scale of resource policy, and the president's plebiscitary bent, encouraged two parishes, the smallest unit of representation in Ecuador, to claim national peoplehood. Political contexts, enduring and ephemeral, shape the substantive content of claims to democratic sovereignty. And, if felicitous, such claims can shore up the collective identities and forms of participation they invoke. This is the performative capacity of political discourse. The variety of figures of the people thus revealed the construction of collective subjectivity to be a situated political practice linked to particular political projects, whether the consolidation of state rule or the task of popular movements to articulate "analogical" relations between differently oppressed groups.[57]

Further, informal and context-specific practices such as the Quimsacocha consultation question the assumption that the state is the unique locus and guardian of democracy. Given the ever-present gap between democracy in its institutionalized form and transgressive aspirations for democratization of various realms of social, economic, and political life (democratization that may well entail rethinking the boundaries that divide these reified spheres of action), the question remains whether it is possible to more thoroughly democratize democracy, and through what means this might be achieved.[58] This question becomes particularly salient and strategically complex when social movements deploy existing democratic institutions (institutionalized forms of participation or codified rights, for example) in their effort to radically transform the practice and meaning of democracy. This strategic complexity is evident in the scholarly debate over both informal community consultations and state-sanctioned prior consultations. Some scholars see in such *consultas comunitarias* the bottom-up redeployment of the law as protest tactic; others worry about the encroachment of "judicialization" that converts substantive politics into procedure, and domesticates the radical potential of social movements.[59] With and against these readings, I concur with Bret Gustafson and Natalia Guzmán Solano that "it is within this strategic tension that the new tactics of community referenda—*consultas populares*—represent a novel space of struggle that combines direct action, the language of democratic participation, and a claim to popular rights."[60]

In the heat of political practice, neat distinctions between state and society, between demands for legal reforms and wholesale rejections of the state, and between constituent and constituted power, give way to the complex imbrication of resistance and rule. In the case of the community consultation I observed in Ecuador, UNAGUA, in an act of vernacular statecraft, both mimicked the conventions of official formality and challenged state authority; the state, meanwhile, claimed to represent both a monolithically conceived nation and the specific interests of those most immediately affected by extraction.[61] Ultimately, UNAGUA asserted their interpretive authority and, in the process, constituent power, a power not defined *against* the Constitution, but as its popular fulfillment. This social movement group redeployed constitutional articles as a protest tactic and interpreted the constitutional text in ways that exceeded the letter of the law. The technicalities of legal procedure, rather than neutralize and depoliticize, furnished the site for agonistic politics.[62] This was in keeping with a broader pattern in the conflict over extraction. As I argue in the next chapter, despite state and corporate attempts to declare mining a "technical" and not a "political" issue, the dream of conflict-free, technocratic administration of extraction remained elusive.

5   Governing the Future

"Information,"
Counter-Knowledge,
and the *Futuro Minero*

The preceding chapters depicted a self-identified leftist administration in political battle with indigenous peoples, campesinos, and radical environmentalists over extractive projects and the model of development. These disputes unfolded on a shared terrain of struggle, the topography of which had been shaped by a long history of social conflicts over the relationship between the state, its territory and natural resources, and the collective subject of democratic politics. This history was kept alive through its invocation in political practice, just as it was reconfigured through the articulation of a new problematic: *extractivismo*.

In contrast to previous chapters, here my point of departure is a state's-eye view of this terrain. I demonstrate how competing visions of transformation inflected the practice of governance and the forms of social resistance mobilized in response. State actors viewed their mission as the construction of a post-neoliberal state. They shared a narrative that defined neoliberalism as state absence (especially in the zones of resource extraction) and aspired to build a state that could expertly regulate economic activity. State actors, and their corporate counterparts in mining companies, saw the problem of post-neoliberal governance in epistemic terms. From their perspective, the challenges of governing a new extractive sector could be overcome by what they called "information." They figured the regulation of mining and the conflict surrounding it as eminently "technical" affairs, defined in explicit contrast to the political. Against this will to depoliticize, activists seeking to block mining projects refused the distinction between the technical and the political, and contested the state's claim to epistemic authority. In their fight against what they called the extractive model, they enlisted the territory itself as a political actor, and a site of valuable and popularly accessible knowledge. For both state and social movement actors, knowing the truth of science or nature was vital to their political projects.

Those seeking to advance mining and those in opposition to it focused their epistemic efforts on localized sites of extraction. In their attempt to promote a nascent and highly speculative extractive sector, state and industry actors sought to manage protest that could scare off investors and disrupt mining activity. From their point of view, communities oppose mining because they are "misinformed"; likewise, the provision of accurate "information" would produce compliant communities. They identified what they called "information" as a panacea for anti-mining protest: it was a means to convince the communities potentially affected by mining projects of the socioeconomic benefits, and minimal environmental impacts, of extraction. In these communities, as I was repeatedly told, information was "missing" (*falta información*), "misleading" (*desinformación*), or outright "false" (*información falsa*). Talk of information almost always figured its absence. But for state actors, it was not only local communities who lacked information. In a more reflexive register, they bemoaned their own lack of expertise, and even of basic knowledge about the territory and the resources it contained—a lack they saw as impeding their own governance efforts. Corporate personnel also saw the problem of community resistance in informational terms, but, in contrast to self-critical bureaucrats, they characterized themselves as better suited to provide this information than their state counterparts. Bureaucrats and corporate personnel alike complicated the narrative of a post-neoliberal transition: they both depicted a state that lacked the knowledge to exercise authority and therefore remained highly dependent on foreign firms, not only for investment, but for institutional capacity and expertise.

Information discourse in Ecuador may seem familiar: state, corporate, NGO, and international institutional actors across the globe have often mobilized claims to technical expertise in the justification, promotion, and execution of development projects.[1] James Ferguson argues that such technical language has a depoliticizing effect: he dubs the regime of development discourse an "anti-politics machine."[2] However, even though bureaucrats and President Correa himself repeatedly asserted that mining is a "technical issue" and not a "political" one, information discourse did not depoliticize mining.[3] Instead, claims to technical expertise became intensely politicized, fueling polemical distinctions between pro-mining bureaucrats and their more ambivalent colleagues, and raising questions about the state's capacity to govern. Further, in response to the consolidation of an alliance between state and industry with a shared technocratic narrative, anti-extractive activists challenged the epistemic authority of both the state and mining corporations. They engaged in the production of counter-knowledge that cast el territorio as not only a living ecological and cultural landscape, but a moral-political agent.[4] For these activists, to know this territory is to defend it and the forms of life it sustains from the encroachment of extractivism. Such "knowledges otherwise"—ways of knowing and relating that challenged the taken-for-granted understanding of the political as an arena exclusively populated by human actors—were, however, challenging to produce, disseminate, and politically mobilize.[5]

In what follows, I first analyze the problem of governing a new extractive sector from the perspective of state and corporate actors. I show how these actors understood their task of managing resistance in technical and informational terms. Next, I demonstrate how both the imbrication of state and corporate roles, and state actors' own doubts about their knowledge, complicated the image of a post-neoliberal administration. I then pivot to anti-mining activists. These activists also questioned the state's epistemic authority, but their critique cut deeper: for them, the solution was not more technical "information," but a fundamental reconfiguration of the relationship between humans and nature, and a different way of knowing el territorio.

Resistance as *Desinformación*

In October 2011, I spoke to Rosa Cecilia, the director of the "social dialogue" unit of the SPMSPC (Secretariat of Peoples, Social Movements, and Citizen Participation). The unit's mission is to work with the Ministry of Environment to "Increase the participation of communities in their processes of conflict management in the areas of influence of National Strategic Projects."[6] When I asked her why there was resistance to mining, she attributed it to two causes: affected communities' negative experiences with prior governments, and their lack of information.[7] These two were connected. The absence of the state, attributed to the legacy of neoliberal administrations, resulted in the absence of accurate information about public policies. As a result, she said, communities resist because of the "issue of information, there is a lack of information, and bad information." Consequently, the best state strategy to prevent conflict is "to go to the zone of influence and inform [them] about the new policies."

The terms and grammar of pro-mining information rhetoric in Ecuador can be traced to a global genealogy of development projects and "improvement schemes" designed by state and non-state actors, whether NGOs or international financial institutions.[8] As Ferguson writes, when villagers in the Thada-Tseka district in Lesotho resisted a Canadian aid-funded agricultural development project, project "officials almost invariably recorded this opposition as a lack of understanding. Time and again I was told by officials (whose own claims to power and authority, of course, rested on their education or technical expertise) that villagers who opposed their schemes lacked education, that they did not understand the proposals, that matters needed to be explained better."[9] In Ecuador, the claim that communities resist because they do not understand mining projects was not neutral: it constituted a polemical intervention in a field of polarized debate over resource extraction, wherein state actors promoted resource extraction in the guise of post-neoliberal, state-led development.[10] As opposed to understanding neoliberalism as the contemporary incarnation of capitalism or imperialism, these state actors defined it as the "weakness" of the state, its territorial "absence" (especially in the territories where new mining and oil projects were located), and its failure to "coordinate" the economy.[11] Overcoming neoliberalism meant constructing regulatory capacity, which entailed a particular type of relationship between the state, corporations, and citizens.

As stated in a lengthy report published by SPMSPC in April 2010, a recurrent pattern across the eighteen conflicts discussed was "a profound absence of the state apparatus, in regard to the regulation of extractive activities and a substitution of [state] roles by companies."[12] As the report also makes clear, this state absence has allowed not only for the outsized role of private companies, but also has allowed for the efforts of anti-mining activists, some of whom it presents as originating from outside affected communities (Quito-based or transnational environmentalist NGOs, for example).[13] Based on this understanding of the causes of contention around mining, state officials saw their role as mediating between communities and mining or oil corporations to communicate the costs and benefits (but mainly the benefits) of the project in question—a role they explicitly contrasted with the actions of past administrations. When I asked him about the most important changes in his ministry since Correa had been in power, Walter Garcia, a functionary in the Sub-Secretariat of Environmental Quality, noted "improved communication with the people."[14] Referring to the process of state *deconcentración* (deconcentration)—the redistribution of responsibilities to lower levels of government—he emphasized the "agility of the responses, not everything is centralized in Quito."[15] In contrast to an unspecified past, he told me, "Now you cannot hide information." In bureaucratic discourse, the image of a transparent state was a recurrent theme. In response to the community mining consultation in Victoria del Portete described in Chapter 4, Doris Solíz, then coordinating minister of public policy and a key figure in formulating official policy toward social movements, told a reporter, "Information has been distorted and the population has been lied to in the case of Quimsacocha." In contrast: "We want citizens to clear up their doubts. That it is the citizens that evaluate that information, that there is all the necessary oversight. We have nothing to hide."[16]

Bureaucrats repeatedly represented the state as providing neutral information to communities, in explicit contrast to actors with more partial interests. During our interview, Francisco Cevallos, a top mining adviser to both the Minister of Nonrenewable Resources and the vice-minister of mining, played the role of an imagined community member: "Finally, the state has come to inform us, not the environmentalists or the companies. A woman told me, 'One paints hell and the other heaven.'"[17] The "main source of resistance" is, again, "disinformation," which comes from "groups effectively organized to reach the people." In contrast to groups that "manipulate them," referring to communities, the state gives "objective and impartial information," as he had put it months earlier at the International Mining Fair in Zamora.[18] These claims on the part of officials described a state capable of providing information to those citizens potentially affected by strategic projects, a state with a kind of exclusive communicative authority.

Such a state would in turn require citizens that were capable of assimilating that information. But how would bureaucrats be able to distinguish between the innocent, if misguided, "community" and the manipulative "activists" that ostensibly misinformed them? This ambiguity troubled the state's attempt to reassert itself via the dissemination of information. Meanwhile, corporate actors saw themselves as inhabiting this very same role—and performing it more efficiently than the state. And, more fundamentally, actors within the state questioned their own access to the knowledge required to govern extraction.

When anti-mining protests occurred, state and corporate actors invariably interpreted them as caused by misinformation—and as best confronted with more or better information. Two weeks after the organized blockade that prevented functionaries from the Ministry of Environment and representatives of the Canadian junior mining company Cornerstone from entering Shaggly parish, I attended an event entitled "Conversation: Mining in Ecuador," organized by students in the Department of Engineering and Mining at the private University of Azuay in Cuenca.[19] At the front of the room was sociologist Gustavo Alvarez, a Cornerstone employee and among those forcibly prevented from entering Shaggly. For the first half hour, Alvarez presented a PowerPoint slideshow to the audience of students and professors, and made the relatively standard argument that mining is socially and environmentally sustainable, and that it would trigger the economic development that Shaggly, "one of the poorest of [Azuay's] 230 parishes," so desperately needed.

As his presentation progressed, Alvarez increasingly relied on a technocratic conception of information to define the cause of and solution to mining conflict. Referring to the organizers of the protest in Shaggly, he said: "The group did the same as us, disseminate. They used the radio to misinform (*desinformar*)." Alvarez suggested that both companies and activists are engaged in a war of information. But he was emphatic that the information the company provides is accurate, while that of their opponents is false. Alvarez then posed a broader question: Why do communities oppose mining? "There is complete disinformation, and they resist being informed." Here, as elsewhere in the presentation the "they" is ambiguous: it is unclear whether it refers to the activists mentioned shortly before, who supposedly come from "other places," or the "communities" that were the subject of the question. "They show videos from fifty years ago, of informal mining, not with mining under the new law": by invoking the past to portray the future and present, he accused anti-mining activists of misinforming communities.

During the question and answer session, Alvarez said that NGOs had sown "five years of disinformation. They do not allow us to inform. Community by community they do anti-mining presentations." In response, one student denounced the "disinformation" disseminated at a recent forum organized by anti-mining environmentalists. A second student read aloud a list he had composed during the forum in question, detailing the "points of the opposition" as follows: "the reserve is already a mine; we are going to eliminate the vegetation cover; all of the minerals go overseas; there will be no environmental remediation . . . the water will be used up; they will destroy the mountains." As he reenacted the scene, the student switched between "they" and "we," between statements told from the position of an "environmentalist" and that of a "miner," thus animating anti-mining discourses, making the opposition present, staging a debate. With an ironic tone and a distance effected by reporting the speech of another, each "view of the other side" was made to seem absurd (several members of the audience laughed out loud during the performance), a bunch of "nonsense" (*barbaridades*), as another student put it. This reenactment, in the context of the preceding invocations of the anti-mining movement, portrayed activists as fundamentally clueless about what the process of large-scale mineral extraction entails. For example, in claiming that mining will "destroy the mountains," "they" confuse the size of the concession with the geographic area of extraction.

During the Q&A, a professor in the audience suggested that the company should do a better job of explaining "why you are asking for so many hectares, in terms of the dispersion of minerals" as well as defining whether the mine will be underground or open-pit, otherwise "you give an opportunity to opponents." He argued that people oppose mining because "there is absolute ignorance, people have a high-school education" and therefore it is very important that a mining company's discourse be "more technical, not allow room for speculation." This professor underlined the political stakes of technical precision, but also pointed to the contradictions of a technocratic discourse that simultaneously paints its opponent as in need of technical information and as mentally deficient or even irrational, beyond the reach of reasonable dialogue.

The dynamics of such events reveal how discursive formations circulate, gain momentum, and shape the policy debate by providing ready-to-hand language. It was the proliferation of such fora—ranging from state- and corporate-sponsored mining conventions to NGO-organized mining "dialogues"—that accounted for the dissemination of particular ways of talking about mining among elite actors, and in turn shaped their policy interventions and modes of confronting resistance. The efficient dissemination of "information" talk resulted in a striking similarity between corporate and state discourses. Just a couple of days after the protest in Shaggly, the state-owned newspaper analyzed it as one of many instances of intentionally misinformed communities: "These communities, which live traditionally on agriculture and cattle farming, are constantly bombarded with false information, which seeks to convince them that mining will affect them terribly and will put an end to everything they love and protect . . . In the communities of Shaggly . . . the majority of those interviewed say that they have not participated in the protests against mining, since, well, they recognize that they do not have information on the issue."[20] In two swift rhetorical moves, coverage in the official media makes sense of local resistance at the same time that it claims that it is unlikely that any such local resistance occurred. If communities are "bombarded with false information," their rejection of large-scale mining is understandable. At the same time, the news article questions whether this resistance was local at all, since those interviewed purportedly professed to not have enough knowledge of the issue to protest the mining project. In the context of a post-neoliberal administration, the similarity between the language of Cornerstone personnel and publications in the state-owned media raised questions about the reassertion of state authority in a nationally strategic policy area.

The words of Leonardo Elizade, vice president of ECSA (the company with a contract to exploit the Mirador open-pit copper mine), were indistinguishable from that of a variety of state bureaucrats I spoke to. "I like the word information more than socialization, it is broader. It doesn't matter what you call it, it is to give information. Politicians like consultation because they like opposition. Participation? Once you have information, you can talk about the issue, participation without information is almost degrading. Everyone will say, 'No, that is not the process that the Constitution looks for.'"[21] He contrasted consultations—which he linked to opposition politicians, likely a reference to Pachakutik assembly member Lourdes Tibán's attendance at the 2011 community consultation in Victoria del Portete—to informed participation. According to Elizade, despite the constitutional requirement for state-led consultations ("the process the Constitution looks for"), the process has become politicized (even "degrading") and only unspecified "information" can guarantee substantive participation. As our conversation continued, he questioned the capacity of residents of a parish in the zone of influence of the Mirador project to participate without first receiving this "information": "in Tundayme, university education is 0 percent, illiteracy is 50 percent—they are not ready."

But beyond these striking similarities in state and corporate discourse, and the alliance they attest to, interviews with corporate personnel also painted a starkly different picture than bureaucrats' description of a state capable of providing information to communities. As Elizade continued, he related the direct role of ECSA in providing such vital information: "Socialization is permanent. Regulations have a beginning and an end, but the projects live with the people, beyond regulatory times (*tiempos normativos*). The way is to converse all of the time."[22] Elizade moved from defining socialization as information and questioning community members' capacity to participate without first being informed to stressing the company's ongoing role in providing information. He specifically contrasted this ongoing socialization with that required by the law, suggesting the insufficiency of existing regulatory frameworks for ensuring the dissemination of information. From this perspective, the company does what the state does not, and perhaps cannot, do: its permanent presence in the community both requires and allows for permanent communication ("converse all the time") with residents.

Corporate actors frequently emphasized their role in providing information to affected communities and often contrasted their constant presence to what they perceived as an absent or distant state. María Clara, director of corporate responsibility at the Canadian multinational mining company Kinross (then the concession holder for the Fruta del Norte gold project), detailed the firm's educational efforts at the community level, enthusiastically showing me a picture book written in Shuar, an indigenous Amazonian language, that they used to explain the large-scale mining process. The book emphasized the benefits of mining and the practices of environmental control and mitigation.[23] As she flipped through the pages, brightly colored and highly stylized Shuar community members extolled corporate social and environmental responsibility, their comic strip word bubbles illustrated by cartoonish mining machinery, water recycling plants, and a pristine if generic rainforest. Virtually repeating Elizade's narrative, she asserted: "There are so many processes around consultation and participation within the law. What is important is a fluid communication and constant information . . . The fundamental strategy is to look for the form of communication of the communities, to meet constantly with the communities, with the local authorities." Clara distinguished between legally mandated consultation processes and the "constant" work of the companies that is situated in local and specific communication styles, with the illustrated book in Shuar functioning as an example.

Carlos Alberto, who worked in community relations for the Canadian exploration company Lowell Minerals, captured the difficulty of delineating state and corporate responsibilities in the context of an emergent extractive sector: "Socialization is a complicated issue. It is a good ideal, to give information to the communities, balanced information. It remains under debate how balanced information can be. In accordance with the law, the companies can't socialize alone, put up an information center. It has to be the state that goes to the communities, but it would be impossible to present information without a role for the company, because the state does not have information, it requires information on the part of the company."[24] Alberto claimed that the state cannot act alone; it depends entirely on the corporation for the information it must provide to communities. Here, by questioning officials' own knowledge about the extractive activities the government promotes, he inadvertently voiced the concerns expressed by both social movement actors and critical bureaucrats. He continued, explaining the challenges faced by the state: "No project is the same as another. Each has its own specifications, in environmental and social terms, and what the companies have planned to do." Just as Elizade explicitly distinguished between regulatory temporality (*tiem-*

pos normativos) and ECSA's "constant" work, and Clara implicitly contrasted the official consultation apparatus with the company's locally situated communication practices, Alberto too mobilized a distinction between the state and mining firms. In his account, state actors relied on corporations for information because of the uniqueness of each project, which is in part a product of the relevant company's plans, suggesting that state knowledge was inescapably general while mining knowledge implied myriad "specifications."

These distinctions between state and corporation suggested a division of labor wherein the state produced regulations and provided the legally mandated minimum of information, while companies produced more detailed information and engaged in ongoing communication. The aforementioned SPMSPC report on socio-environmental conflict, a document otherwise committed to expanding the role of the state in the context of such conflicts, envisions just such an ongoing role for mining corporations. Citing the regulations that guide the implementation of the 2009 Mining Law, the report states, "Referring to the processes of citizen participation and consultation, the regulation establishes that the opinions issued by the community should be present in the environmental impact studies; and that there should be a permanent interaction between company and community by means of programs of information and diffusion."[25] The imbrication of state and private sector responsibilities generated ambiguity and problematized not only the delineation of tasks but the very boundary between public and private. While corporate representatives emphasize their uniquely local knowledge of both mining projects and their associated zones of influence, official actors too made claims about an agile and "deconcentrated" state, no longer centralized in Quito but efficiently dispersed throughout the territory of the nation.

Compliant Communities

When I asked Alberto why he had said that socializations for mining projects are "complicated," he responded: "The population is immersed in disinformation. Distorted (*tergiversada*) information is worse. The closer one gets to the projects, the more the information is distorted." But who exactly is the community, and why does its proximity to the site of extraction make it less knowledgeable rather than more? In the discourse of these state and corporate actors, the local community is an ambivalent figure: depending on the invocation, it is either passive (misinformed, manipulated, but also potentially well informed) or active (resisting when in opposition, participating when involved in state-led informational events). Distinguishing between senders and recipients of disinformation was key: if the community members *were* the activists, they may not be so receptive to information, and their opposition might have to be dealt with by other means, more forceful than persuasive. The concrete implications of information discourse thus hinged on whether anti-mining activists, and the communities they were presumed to influence, could be shown the error of their ways.

From the perspective of those promoting mining, the task of the state and mining corporations was to disseminate accurate information to the communities near projects. As for the activists seen to intentionally manipulate those communities, they were for all practical purposes unreachable via informational strategies. Their only modality of action was "political," understood as a realm of instrumental logic, force, and violence. As President Correa said in his weekly radio address a few days after the incident in Shaggly: "You realize the gang (*caterva*) of people we are dealing with, people who are not interested in dialogue, who are not interested in the common good, they are interested in electoral ends, this mayor of Santa Isabel . . . Here, it is a state of law, all of the rigor of the law will be applied, and see, afterward these charlatans always say that social protest is criminalized."[26] This "gang" believes "in violence, in roadblocks, in burning tires (*la quemellanta*), in rocks, in fighting, in aggression. Enough. We are not going to tolerate that, let's act with the law in our hand but with all of the strength (*con todo la firmeza*). They are cowards, controlled by that mayor of the MPD from Santa Isabel." If your opponents act beyond the pale of dialogue, the only way to counter the political violence of anti-mining resistance is with the force ("rigor" and "strength") of the law. Correa reproduced the distinction between the "good people" that reside in the "beautiful canton" of Santa Isabel and the "bad authorities" that incite "bullies" (*garroteros*) to violence. Information could reach the former but not the latter. The series of distinctions between *técnico* and *político*, between "the people" and "a certain part of the population," shaped the political limits of information as a strategy to manage conflict.

These distinctions, however, proved unstable. Other official interventions suggested that activists and communities are not the only ones who lack information. As the vice-minister of mines, Federico Auquilla, wrote in December 2011: "The absence of information at all levels of society about mining activity in Ecuador has been another consequence of the disarticulation of the mining sector. This has implied the lack of knowledge on the part of large sectors of Ecuadorians of the basic issues of the reality of mining, which has permitted that their opinion can be easily manipulated by different interests."[27] In addition to contrasting the "large sectors of Ecuadorians" and the "interests" that manipulate them, Auquilla states that another source of the "absence of information" is the "disarticulation"—the lack of coherent organization—of the mining sector itself. Inadvertently confirming critiques from within the state (discussed below), he suggested that, in the context of a sector under construction, disinformation is bound to proliferate.

The possibility that the state is also uninformed emerged in an interview on the evening news show *De frente* in late June 2012, in the midst of growing indigenous resistance to the Eleventh Round of Oil Tender. President Correa expressed his exasperation with opposition to mining and oil exploration: "Enough of the fundamentalism! There are people that oppose even mining exploration, oil exploration—even to know what we have. How can one make decisions without information? We have to explore our country. The southwest is totally unexplored in regard to oil, almost all the country is unexplored in regard to mining. It is necessary to explore. If they want we can debate exploitation afterward, but we have to have information."[28] Correa presented anti-extractive resistance as opposed not only to extraction, but even to the very gathering of information, information that is necessary for all involved in the debate. The stretch of discourse slipped between a plural we ("to know what we have"; "we have to explore"; "we have to have information") and a third person plural ("if they want, we can discuss"). Here, the "we" was left undefined, but by linking it to the national territory ("we have to explore our country"), Correa invoked a national collective subject juxtaposed with a "they" identified only in terms of their "fundamentalist" opposition to exploration and the information it generates. He deployed a familiar and locally salient trope of particularistic interests aligned against those of the nation, a nation that wants to explore its own territory and register its resources.[29] This us/them distinction is linked to another: between exploration and exploitation. This rhetorical strategy delinked the two phases and depoliticized exploration as a form of mere information gathering (as opposed to a necessary step for a corporation to negotiate an exploitation contract), asserting that it can be carried out without the implication that extraction will necessarily occur. Indeed, the information generated by exploration is necessary for both the "we" and the "they" to properly debate exploitation. For this reason, the subjectless imperative "it is necessary to explore" commanded supporters and opponents of extraction alike.

While Correa started off as vitriolic ("Enough of the fundamentalism!"), he concluded with the possibility that detractors will come to see exploration as necessary, if only to provide the requisite information to substantiate their position in the subsequent debate over extraction. But in this stretch of discourse, Correa inadvertently substantiated the concerns of the critical bureaucrats to whom I now turn: his assertion that "almost all the country is unexplored" implied that the state itself lacked the knowledge necessary to govern this new extractive sector.

We Confuse Ourselves

At an early morning meeting in an affluent neighborhood in north Quito, in an outdoor café with a view of the Parque Carolina and punctuated by the noise of rush-hour traffic, Mario Ruales drank *café con leche* and smoked interminable cigarettes.[30] He was distressed about information. Ruales, the environmental adviser at the Coordinating Ministry of Heritage, had told me about the ideological divides ("contradictions") within the Ecuadorian state before, but he now mapped them onto a complex of institutional alliances and antagonisms.[31] He asked me if I could help provide him with any information about the five strategic mining projects, since "the Ministry of Nonrenewable Resources and the Ministry of Environment do not give us information." Conflict over the extractive model reverberated within the state and inflected disagreements over the implementation of state policy in the communities affected by extraction. During our interview in the cramped office of the social dialogue unit of SPMSPC, Alicia Hidalgo criticized the accessibility and quality of state-provided information, and in turn identified the lack of information as a cause of social conflict: "Citizen participation is a strategy to manage conflict. The law says that information must be opportune, truthful, in their [the communities'] languages. But it doesn't always happen . . . The environmental impact reports are terrible. The people don't understand. We are trying to put ourselves higher up, to have influence in the Ministry of Environment, to improve the presentation of information, so that the people are informed, [so that] the conflict diminishes substantially."[32] Hidalgo reiterated the prevailing bureaucratic narrative that defined participation as information, and that it is the lack of information that caused conflict. She departed, however, with the discourse of the president and more consistently pro-mining bureaucrats in the ministries of Environment and of Nonrenewable Resources by placing the blame squarely on the state, and specifically on the Ministry of Environment, for producing "terrible" environmental impact assessments that are incomprehensible to their intended audience. Her comments were in line with the aforementioned 2010 report on socio-environmental conflict published by her agency, which states that the underlying cause of conflict over the Mirador project is that "there is no socialization or information toward the communities of the phases of the Mirador project" and therefore recommends an "information campaign on the radio about the mining issues, explaining in a transparent manner the benefits and possible damages that they would cause to the environment and the community" to be carried out by state institutions.[33]

Romulo Heredia, a bureaucrat in the same unit as Alicia, explained the problems with the current socialization process at length.[34] Explicitly criticizing the time frame dictated by Executive Decree 1040, Heredia told me, "The information processes should be much more before, not seven days like now," and should be "well supported."[35] Furthermore, "With all frankness, truly, they [the other ministries] offer a lot to the people, from there the problems are born . . . With something like this, one wouldn't need the consultation, using social pedagogy processes, the maternal language of the people . . . Speaking with frankness, other ministries confuse investment with what they are going to give out to the community. Also, they don't explain the phases. Wanting to rush ourselves, we confuse ourselves. The short time makes it so that it isn't done well."

Heredia mounted several critiques around what he calls "information processes." He started and ended with a rejection of the legally required time frame, which results in a poor-quality presentation. He asserted that in the rush to meet the mandated deadline, bureaucrats become "confused" and present erroneous information.[36] For Heredia, the type of disinformation generally ascribed to social movements and communities was in fact a product of a particular institutional dynamic. He contrasted this informational style with his preferred methods ("social pedagogy"), which are so effective that they would render the mandated "consultation" unnecessary, and invoked a sort of local knowledge ("the maternal language of the people")—albeit one that would improve rather than resist the state's technical apparatus. Heredia unintentionally echoed the corporate discourse described above, which juxtaposed the short time frame of state socialization with the "constant" work undertaken by mining firms. But the relevant contrast here was not between the public and private sectors, but within the state, between his agency and "other ministries." And he took a reflexive turn, as he moved from a "they" ("they offer"; "they don't explain"), indexically linked to those "other ministries," to a more inclusive "we" ("we confuse ourselves"). He slid from inhabiting the position of outsider critic to an insider, ambivalently accepting responsibility for both his own unit's failures *and* those of the state as a whole. Regardless of who was to blame, for Heredia, the consequences of failing to provide good quality information were great. As he put it, "the life of the community is in play."

Critical bureaucrats could be found in unexpected places, such as in the Ministry of Environment, an agency generally perceived by other state actors and anti-mining activists as collaborating with the Ministry of Nonrenewable Resources to advance extractive projects. When Pablo Mera, a bureaucrat in the state planning agency SENPLADES who previously worked in the Ministry of Environment, told me his theory of mining conflict, it resonated with Hidalgo's and Heredia's statements. As he explained: "If the people feel threatened by the lack of information, they will be afraid. None of the state entities say that 'we are going to have this project; it will cause this damage.' The government—everyone—says that there won't be damage. It is a lie. The people of the southern Amazon know what has happened, from their own family members, an accumulated experience from, for example, those who have migrated. None of them have participated in any round of negotiation of mining contracts or information about the contracts."[37] Mera claimed that both "the lack of information" and, worse, false information ("it is a lie") on the part of official actors are to blame for conflict. He also suggested that those affected by mining projects in the southern Amazon have access to alternative sources of information, which resonated with activists' claims to non-technical forms of knowledge. As he subsequently detailed, indigenous (Shuar and Kichwa) familial networks that stretch across the Amazon were a conduit to communicate experiences with oil extraction to those potentially affected by large-scale mining.

Intra-state disagreements over the issues of "information" and participation reflected deeper divisions between what was often described to me as the "two camps" within the Ecuadorian state.[38] The depth of these disagreements was evident in the similarity in the statements made by critical bureaucrats and former high-ranking officials who resigned in explicit protest over resource extraction and indigenous rights. Echoing Hidalgo, Heredia, and Mera, former cabinet member Monica Chuji blamed state informational practices for the social conflicts around extractive projects.[39] When I asked her why she thought bureaucrats do not provide adequate information to communities potentially affected by extractive projects (or, from her perspective, substantively implement prior consultation), she responded: "Why don't they comply? They are afraid to inform them the real things, to say the effects, how it will affect the territory, if it [the territory] needs to be expropriated, the royalties. This transparency of information, they don't want to give us. There would be fewer social conflicts, fewer problems, if they did it. The lack of consultation means many more conflicts." Against ministers' claims of transparency ("We have nothing to hide"), for Chuji, it was the state, not the movements, that intentionally misinformed, thus generating more conflict.

As one woman put it during a protest against the municipality of Cuenca for barring a scheduled anti-mining event in their building, "they are afraid of what the people will learn."[40] At the same time, Chuji also understood contention in informational terms, and suggested that if communities were better informed they might be less prone to resist mining projects.

The fact that Chuji, among other high-ranking state officials, ultimately left the regime due to political differences over resource extraction policy highlights the difficult position of bureaucrats who critiqued from within the state. Although their concerns at times overlapped with those of activists and opposition politicians, critical bureaucrats wary of mining aimed to improve rather than protest official policy; more explicit opposition or political activism would have cost them their jobs. Despite their relative political marginality, which they often bemoaned, critical bureaucrats were key actors in the political dispute over extraction. By contributing to the diversity of state discourse, they posed challenges for pro-mining officials and activists alike: they undermined the ideological unity prized by the former, and contributed to the ambiguity that complicated the latter's resistance. From an analytic perspective, attending to the "many voices" of the state multiplies the relevant sites of contestation.[41] "Resistance" is not confined to non-state actors such as social movements, but "may be found at the heart of the bureaucratic apparatus, where experts debate the merits of diverse plans or argue against excessive intervention in peoples' lives."[42] More fundamentally, the appearance of a unified state is just that: a potent claim enacted in the symbolic rituals of state-making that conceals the struggles and asymmetries that mark the bureaucratic field.[43]

A War of Information

Late in the afternoon of May 16, 2012, five of us sat around a table in Chela Calle's office. The topic of conversation was information, and it arose in the form of concern over the discrepancies between different measurements of the mining company Cornerstone's concessions in rural Azuay. Specifically, we discussed the confusing differences in the names used to designate projects and concessions, as well as the precise number of hectares they spanned. Based on our review of the company's website, and information I had collected in interviews, it was unclear how much land would be explored for gold.[44] The activists were particularly interested in this discrepancy since the figures on the Cornerstone website suggested that the company was in violation of the 2009 Mining Law, which stipulates a maximum of 5,000 hectares per concession and three concessions per project.[45] This possible violation would have constituted grounds for a legal claim against the mining company and the Ministry of Nonrenewable Resources. As the conversation continued, one of the group's newer activists asserted that confusion about where the concessions are, and what will be mined, served as an impediment to anti-mining mobilization. He suggested creating a website listing and mapping all mining projects in the province to serve as a mobilizational tool. But Chela Calle and Abel Arpi, long-time political organizers, pointed out that the campesinos directly affected by projects may not have regular access to the internet. In the course of the meeting, activists alternately invoked and called into question the power of "information."

When they talked about information, opponents of mining articulated a range of concerns. First, they criticized the difficulty of obtaining information from private firms and public institutions. Second, they claimed that state actors lack the information (particularly, environmental studies) they would need to design good mining policy. Finally, they questioned the quality of official information: it contained errors or is contradictory, and/or is supplied by corporations themselves and therefore presumed to be biased. When social movement actors decried their own lack of access to information, they in effect coincided with official claims that anti-mining groups are underinformed, and lent support to the prevailing official position that the role of the state is to provide information. In the second two claims, however, they turned official discourse on its head: it is not the opposition but the state that is misinformed. More radically, activists articulated alternative sources of information and, indeed, ways of knowing. When anti-mining activists pointed to their own knowledge of land and waterways, of particular ecosystems (*páramo, selva*) and the social groups (whether they identify as campesinos or *pueblos indígenas* or both) that have historically interacted with them, they invoked a kind of local authority and non-technical expertise grounded in the *territorios* beyond the reach of the Ecuadorian state.

Alicia Granda, a staff member of human rights organization CEDHU, started out our conversation on the subject of information in the form of a recent *informe* (report) the group had coauthored.[46] After articulating some of her main critiques of mining, she returned to the topic of information: "There is no information from the state. We ask for information from the Ministry of Nonrenewable Resources and of [the Ministry of] Environment. It's a big problem." She immediately, however, called into question the quality of state information, referring to it as "imprecise" and lacking detail, concluding that their information is very "deficient" and, even more drastically, "the state does not have information."

William Sacher and Alberto Acosta, who coauthored a book on large-scale mining, emphasized both the absence of "information" and its poor quality in their critique of mining policy.[47] Their book has an appendix entitled "Database: statistical elements of industrial mining in Ecuador," which contains a section entitled "Quality of information."[48] Sacher writes, "It is worth pointing out that, despite originating from official sources, the information gathered presents various limitations." He explains that the Ministry of Nonrenewable Resources' registry "does not permit the user to directly obtain a list of concessions and their petitioners." In a similar vein, Salvador Quishpe, the antimining prefect of Zamora Chinchipe, recounted to me his unsuccessful efforts to collect information from various ministries.[49] "We have requested information," but "the only thing they respond to us is, 'there are infantile environmentalists (ecologistas infantiles), they oppose development,'" mockingly voicing one of the oft-repeated epithets Correa used to insult those opposed to oil and mining extraction. He listed various dates on which he had requested meetings to obtain information—July 11, 2010; October 4, 2010; March 14, 2011—in total, "four years requesting a meeting" without a response from the relevant ministry. He walked over to a shelf in his office and took down a thick binder, turning to pages at random, showing me one letter after another, penned to various state agencies, as well as various notifications that he had received, stating that his request was being transferred to another ministry. I had the uncanny experience of observing a situated actor go through the same motions of my own research practices, attempting—often unsuccessfully—to obtain information from the nexus of ministries and secretariats involved in mining policymaking. Sacher, Acosta, and Quishpe mobilized a discourse of information to call into question Correa's Citizens' Revolution's avowed commitment to transparency.

In addition to claims regarding its inaccessibility, opponents of the administration's resource extraction policies also found fault with the quality of official data, which they often attributed to the fact that the government relies on mining corporations for information on mineral reserves, information that they claimed is systematically biased. As Sacher writes, "The information gathered from private mining companies is no better" than state information; due to their "economic interests," exploration companies "tend to inflate these figures (cifras) and take advantage of the ambiguities of the multiple terms used to describe these quantities."[50] He attributes the poor quality of information to the speculative nature of the mining industry—in part a product of the sector's financial structure—evident in the complex classification of resources (inferred, indicated, and measured) and reserves (probable and proven).[51] Sacher and Acosta articulated these informational concerns in a variety of public events. At the Second Social Forum on Mining, organized by opposition prefect Paúl Carrasco and held in Cuenca on March 1, 2012, Acosta argued, "there aren't reliable numbers (*cifras*), the government uses data from the companies."[52] A few months later, at an event in the political ecology series at the University of Cuenca, Acosta reiterated the point: "it is sad that the government takes on the numbers [of the companies] as their own."[53] Sacher and Acosta pointed to the irony that a self-identified post-neoliberal administration was dependent on foreign firms for basic knowledge about the resources contained in its territory.

Transparent Territories

Movement actors evinced an ambivalent stance on the question of information. On the one hand, they critiqued official information practices, thus holding pro-mining actors accountable to their own technical standards. On the other hand, activists refuted the argument that only *technical* knowledge is relevant, insofar as such knowledge is linked to a certain professional expertise as well as defined in opposition to the political. Although opponents of mining disparaged the lack of technical studies, they also asserted that such studies are not necessary to understand the environmental impact of mining. In our first of several meetings, Marcelo Quizhpe—who, unusually, was both a bureaucrat at Cuenca's water utility, ETAPA, and an anti-mining activist—captured this ambivalence.[54] Referring to the Yunacay watershed, he told me, "There isn't enough information about the quantity of water in the basin." Later in the conversation, regarding the "contamination of air and soil and water" that the Quimsacocha project would cause, he insisted, "you only need to look, you don't have to be a hydrologist or a geologist."[55]

Anti-mining activists directly contested the epistemic authority of the state and corporations. They claimed an intimate knowledge of the territories slated for mining projects. These claims drew on some activists' background in managing community water systems in rural areas, but they were also rooted in a more recent practice of organizing long walks (called *caminatas*) in the territories granted as mining concessions. Visits to mining concessions positioned local inhabitants as experts and figured the landscape (rivers, hills, mountains, soil, groundwater, grass, shrubs) as a transparent source of knowledge, self-evidently worth protecting. One month after the corporate presentation at the University of Azuay described above, I participated in a trip to the Cornerstone concession (see Figure 5.1). After a long hike, we reached the Carachula, a towering craggy rock formation that, according to local myth, becomes a city at night (see Figure 5.2). This rock formation and the accompanying myth was seen by anti-mining activists from the area, as well as those visiting from as far as Quito, as a testimony to both the landscape and the local cultural practices that would be threatened by the planned mining project. From this perspective, it was the territory itself that invalidated pro-mining information discourse. Insofar as their actions were grounded in a particular relationship with the land, anti-mining resistance could not be misinformed.

Recall that during the Cornerstone event I observed the month before, corporate representatives and students painted the activists as "outsiders" and the community as "manipulated." In contrast, in the practice of visiting concession sites, it is the activists that learned from local inhabitants, who themselves learned directly from the land. Meanwhile, for activists, it was the government and corporations who lacked this sort of knowledge, who did not see what is self-evident to anyone who looked. As Salvador Quishpe put it at a press conference in Cuenca during the March for Water, Life, and the Dignity of Peoples, in response to the minister of environment's claim that mining would not affect primary forest, "what a shame that she doesn't know the territory."

Such an understanding of territory also immediately implied a risk: that such territories would not be sufficiently known—not only by state officials but by potential allies—and thus would not be defended against the expanding extractive frontier. The political work required to organize and ensure the success of such visits belied the transparent availability of the "territory." And activists' pedagogical efforts were by no means uniformly successful. A case in point occurred during my second visit to Quimsacocha on May 12, 2012. Three buses transported around 120 participants from Cuenca to the Iamgold concession, which is a distance of 30 kilometers away, but can take anywhere from three to four hours to drive, depending on weather and road conditions. High-speed wind and torrential rain slowed down this particular trip to four hours on snaking roads with hairpin turns. We were a diverse group: members of the political ecology course at the University of Cuenca, for which the visit was originally organized; sociology and economics students with their professor; anthropology students from the Politécnica Salisenia, the main Catholic university of Quito; Cuenca-based anti-mining activists; two Colombian travelers researching social movements in Latin America; a Peruvian student;

Figure 5.1 Consulting a map of Cornerstone concessions.

Figure 5.2 The Carachula.

from Victoria del Portete, the parish president Federico Guzmán and resident Vinicio; and a family from Shaggly, invited in light of recent anti-mining mobilization there.

According to one of the organizers of the event, my close friend Kléver Calle, the intended purpose of the trip was to teach students the hydrological aspects of the highland wetland system (*páramo*) and the location of the deposits, and to introduce them to local social movement leaders. Guzmán gave a brief speech about his community's decade of resistance to mining, and, at one of the many spots where the application of even the slightest pressure sent water trickling upward, through myriad minuscule pathways in the mossy ground, Vinicio kneeled and pointed at the subterranean water, as physical evidence against Correa's assertion that since the three lakes are not part of the concession, the Iamgold project would not affect the water. There were several short speeches at lunch. Standing directly below a statue of the Virgin of Quimsacocha, which had been placed on a ledge in the boulder overlooking the lakes during a previous site visit, Chela Calle discussed the cultural value of the water around and below us. But the activists' nonhuman ally soon turned against them: the increasingly torrential rain made subsequent lessons practically impossible, and the visit became a "missed opportunity," according to Kléver Calle. Given the tremendous organizational work required to arrange such trips, it was also a less than fully capitalized political investment.

In the context of a debate where an uncertain future was at stake, much hinged on compellingly depicting a particular mining future, to "paint heaven or paint hell," as I was told in two different interviews.[56] In letting the land speak for itself, the anti-mining movement invited *caminata* participants to behold a future past, to experience a politically potent nostalgia for what they have not yet lost.[57] The political labor to disseminate a territorialized knowledge, as well as the accumulated experience of activism such a labor drew on and extended, constituted a rejection of the pro-mining claim that activists misinform "communities" or are themselves uninformed. Instead, in their rhetoric, it is those without direct contact with the "territories," in ministry buildings in Quito or the far-flung corporate headquarters of multinational mining corporations, who lacked the knowledge and experience that ought to ground mining politics. In the debate over extraction in Ecuador, despite (and in part because of) attempts to distinguish the technical from the political, information was politically salient and highly contested; to talk of who knows or does not know about mining was to make a claim about its desirability.

At a workshop during the national convention of the recently formed Plurinational Assembly on May 19, 2012, in Quito, we reflected upon the achievements of the two-week long March for Water, Life, and the Dignity of Peoples, and the challenges that lay ahead. In the midst of this conversation, Abel Arpi stated, "there is a psychological war of information, on the part of the government and on the part of ourselves." Pro-mining official and corporate actors mobilized information talk to delegitimize anti-mining movements and distinguish them from innocent if passive "communities," while at the same time offering a vision of participation-as-information to address critiques of national policy. Meanwhile, social movement actors deployed a variety of information discourses that alternately valorized their own knowledge as grounded in an interwoven accumulation of political experiences and natural encounters, and called into question official and corporate information. As the Argentinian anti-mining activist Marta Antonelli stated during the Second Social Forum on Mining in Cuenca, when governments promote large-scale mining, "the state becomes more opaque" with regard to "information" (*datos*) on concessions. The visits to potential sites of the *futuro minero*—Quimsacocha,

Vetas Grandes—suggested that according to these activists, while the state may be opaque, the territory is transparent.[58]

Conclusion

"The territory is an actor," María Belen told me. "Above all in Ecuador," she continued, where nature is the subject of constitutional rights.[59] Despite the multiple resonances—the simultaneous echo with actor-network theory's expansion of the concept of actor to encompass the nonhuman, and with activists' counter-knowledge practices that figured the territory as a central protagonist in the resistance to extractive projects—María Belen was a bureaucrat reflecting on her own situated practice of the complexities of governance.[60] For Belen, then posted to the Sub-Secretariat of Decentralized Planning at SEN-PLADES, the territory was neither as transparent as it was regarded by activists, nor as amenable to state authority as many of her colleagues assumed. "Forty years of concessions," the legal vestiges of prior models of governance, impeded the territorial knowledge required to build a post-neoliberal state. She continued, "We haven't recuperated control over our territory. We don't know to whom we have given the concessions . . . We don't know where the resources they've extracted have gone. We don't have any idea of the wealth that we have. As a state, in regard to the strategic mining sector, we haven't totally achieved the exercise of sovereignty. We don't know what is happening here because we don't have the capacity to regulate. Private entities are the ones regulating. But we ourselves do not know what is happening."

This was not just a historical narrative. Or rather, like all such narratives, it was shot through with the concerns of the present. The aspiration of a post-neoliberal transition was belied by troublesome continuities in the relationship between the state and foreign capital. The legacy of neoliberalism did not endure by inertia but was rather reproduced in the ongoing imbrication of state and corporate roles in producing technical information about extractive projects, the very subsoil wealth that state actors saw as the medium of national sovereignty, and disseminating it to communities with the aim of ensuring their quiescence. As quoted above, Correa asserted, "the southwest is totally unexplored in regard to oil, almost all the country is unexplored in regard to mining." The state did not know its own territory. Critical bureaucrats worried that this undermined regulatory capacity and triggered mining conflict. Meanwhile, corporate actors situated at the sites of potential extraction claimed to be in "constant" and "fluid" communication with communities, outside of "regulatory time."

Even if state and corporate roles could be disambiguated, and the authority of the former deployed to regulate the activities of the latter, the ambivalent status of local communities unsettled the prevailing understanding of information as panacea. This understanding relied on a distinction between "communities" (innocent, passive, and misinformed) and anti-mining activists (political, even conspiratorial, and beyond dialogue). But anti-mining activists hailed from locales both affected and unaffected by mining projects, forging alliances within and across zones of influence. In this context, the distinction between "community" and "activist" proved unstable and inconsistently drawn, leaving it unclear whether information constituted a viable strategy to mitigate resistance.

Anti-mining activists explicitly targeted the state's informational apparatus, which they saw as not only a thinly veiled attempt to present pro-mining propaganda to communities but as in and of itself a form of territorial invasion. For state and corporate actors, such episodes suggested that affected communities were not passive, and that their lack of information was not innocent, but rather the result of a willful and obstinate resistance to learning the truth of "responsible mining." But the prescription did not change: in their imaginary, mining was so thoroughly beneficial that only a fool would advocate remaining "beggars sitting on a sack of gold."[61] In official and corporate actors' understanding, if citizens are not informed, they are liable to resist, and therefore the persistence of protest did not prompt pro-mining officials to reconsider prevailing resource policy but only signaled the need for more information. This self-corroborating logic of information discourse in part accounted for its crystallization. As an explanation of resistance and a prescription for state action, it could not be proven wrong. Ongoing contestation was only proof of the continued need for information, while the diminution of anti-mining activity would indicate its successful application.

The abiding appeal of "information" lay in its promise to excise resource extraction from the domain of politics. In the words of Federico Auquilla, the vice-minister of mining, anti-mining activists were "extremists who have taken advantage (*han aprovechado*) by politicizing an issue that is eminently technical."[62] This fantasy of depoliticization seduced both avidly pro-mining and more critical bureaucrats; the latter's situated critiques only reinscribed the desideratum of technocratic administration. These self-identified *técnicos* understood neoliberalism as the interconnected absence of state control and absence of state knowledge; as a corollary, post-neoliberalism entailed the technocratic administration of socioeconomic life grounded in state expertise.[63] This rendering of post-neoliberalism, divorced from a critique of capitalism, ironically revealed a deep affinity with neoliberal governance: both seek to disembed the economic from the social and political, and in the process reify them as distinct spheres of social life.[64]

While elites envisioned a regime of technical information capable of both mitigating mining conflict and reasserting state authority, activists rejected the opposition between the technical and the political, just as they opened up the category of political action to include *el territorio* as a sentient socio-natural landscape. For Marisol de la Cadena, such acts constitute an "epistemic rupture" with the foundational opposition between "Humanity" and "Nature."[65] But the expansion of the political cuts both ways: if these activists inserted nature into politics, they also revealed the eminently political conditions of nature's agency. These conditions were both proximate and historical. Proximately, enlisting *el territorio* as a protagonist in the battle against extraction required an organizational infrastructure capable of bringing together rural and urban residents on logistically complicated excursions, and enfolding such encounters in a cumulative process of resistance. Thus, contra James Scott, local knowledge does not flow immediately from situated experience, but is instead a representative practice equally subject to failure as the "generic knowledge" entailed in state-led modernizing projects.[66] Historically, as de la Cadena emphasizes, what is new is not the imbrication of the human and the nonhuman—the conceptual architecture of modernity might deny such entanglements but has never eliminated them—but the public visibility of such hybrid "earth-beings."[67] Although she does not specify exactly what it is about the contemporary conjuncture that has rendered such beings politically visible, she suggests the importance of the expansion of the extractive frontier to regions previously deemed "remote, unproductive, or even empty."[68] She recapitulates the Polanyian "double movement" of the territorial expansion of commodification and accumulation, and localized social resistance.[69] In Ecuador, however, the development of a new extractive sector did not single-handedly expand the scope of the political: such resistance practices can only be understood as a moment in a trajectory of struggle over the territory and its resources, a struggle that has encompassed diverse objectives, strategies, and visions of radical transformation. From petro-nationalism to post-extractivism, in Ecuador the subsoil has long constituted the fertile ground and historically specific horizon of radical politics.

The Dilemmas of the Pink Tide

On December 14, 2016, President Rafael Correa declared a state of emergency in the Amazonian province of Morona Santiago and deployed hundreds of troops and national police.[1] This marked the culmination of years of clashes at the site of an open-pit copper mine in the area of San Carlos that indigenous Shuar activists had occupied in protest against the expansion of mining and the threat it posed to their territory and livelihoods. Between 2009 and 2015, state forces killed three Shuar, either while they were protesting mining or defending their water rights. The months leading up to the 2016 state of emergency saw military raids and the destruction of Shuar villages, homes, tools, and agricultural plots. In mid-December, the conflict reached its peak in a fight that left a policeman dead, prompting Correa to call in the military. The state of emergency officially lasted three months, but as of late 2017 there were ongoing reports of checkpoints, harassment, and criminalization, and the mining camp was still a militarized zone. Correa continued to verbally attack the Shuar in his weekly public addresses, and Shuar communities continued to protest.

This episode was not an isolated event. It epitomized a decades-long regional conjuncture of intensified extraction and related social conflict. With the implementation of neoliberal reforms, investment in mining exploration in Latin America soared, growing by 400 percent compared to 90 percent globally between 1990 and 1997.[2] During the commodity boom that lasted from 2000 to 2014, the region remained one of the world's top destinations for mining investment.[3] Latin America has likewise stood out in terms of local contention around interrelated extractive, energy, and infrastructure projects.[4] And these conflicts were often violent: in 2017 alone, 197 "land and environment defenders" were killed across the globe.[5] Some 60 percent of these murders occurred in Latin America, making it the world's deadliest region for activists resisting mining, oil, agribusiness, and similar projects. The pattern of protest in Ecuador was in keeping with these regional dynamics, both in terms of frequency and intensity, and in terms of its historical arc. Conflict in response to "accumulation by dispossession" (whether open-pit mining, oil exploration, or shrimp farming) that began during the neoliberal period continued and intensified under Correa's post-neoliberal government.[6]

In addition to causing social conflict, the expansion of the extractive frontier also deepened the region's economic dependency. Projects were in large part financed through foreign capital, and extractive sectors' export-orientation left economies and states vulnerable to the volatile prices of raw materials. The commodity boom and subsequent bust represented the opportunities and perils of this mode of integration into global capitalism. For many of the region's inhabitants, these turbulent years unfolded in the context of a historic wave of leftist governments. These Pink Tide administrations were committed to not only reducing poverty and inequality but also to transforming the economic model, democratizing the state, and attaining sovereignty. Whether or not these lofty goals were achieved, the combination of export-led economic growth and redistributive policies pulled tens of millions of people out of poverty and mitigated inequality in the most unequal region of the world.

The combination of dramatic improvements in material well-being, renewed dependency, and contentious politics amid an unprecedented political mandate for the electoral Left occasioned a profound debate over development.[7] In this debate, elected leaders and activists invoked—and contested—the historical paradigms of resource nationalism, dependency theory, and endogenous development.[8] They also articulated new visions of regional integration, neo-developmentalism, post-extractivism, *sumak kawsay/buen vivir*, and eco-socialism.[9] These concepts, and the social practices they indexed and imagined, served as an inspiration to activists and progressive policymakers in the United States, Canada, and Europe.

But such aspirations for a region transformed would soon implode. In 2013, Hugo Chávez, the first president elected in what would later be named the Pink Tide, died of cancer. The next year, the commodity boom came to a decisive end with a precipitous drop in oil prices, and recessions followed. In quick succession, these dramatic events were followed by the election of the conservative president Mauricio Macri in Argentina, the parliamentary coup that removed Dilma Rousseff from power in Brazil, Bolivian voters' rejection in a popular referendum of Evo Morales's attempt to run for a fourth term (a rejection subsequently overruled by the country's Constitutional Court), Venezuela's descent into seemingly intractable political-economic crisis, and, finally, the 2018 defeat of the Brazilian Workers' Party presidential candidate Fernando Haddad by Jair Bolsonaro, an open admirer of the military dictatorship that ruled that country from 1964 to 1985. The Left was in retreat and right-wing politics ascendant. Only Mexico, where the leftist candidate Andrés Manuel López Obrador was elected president in a landslide victory, bucked the trend. What went wrong?

As is the case with any attempt to specify a moment of rupture, the exercise of dating the end of the Pink Tide inevitably slips into the infinitely recursive dialectic of the period and the break.[10] When, precisely, did the "retreat" begin? In 2014, with the end of the cycle of export-led economic growth? In 2012, when the "delayed reverberation of the global crisis" first began to perturb the economic underpinnings of a "'mutually' beneficial relationship between capital and labor"?[11] Or was it an earlier shift in the broader ecosystem of the Left in Latin America, away from rebellious street protests and popular assemblies and toward elections, campaigns, and parties, with all their connotations of political moderation, leader-centric personalism, and organizational hierarchy? Or had the Pink Tide been doomed from the start? Was the aspiration to capture state institutions, democratize them, and redeploy them to serve the interests of the oppressed ultimately a quixotic project, always already fated to fail, whether by the iron law of oligarchy, the disciplining effects of the iron cage of state bureaucracy, or the assured reaction of the ruling class?[12] Or perhaps the ebb of the tide was not so much a result of the ascent to state power but rather a product of social movements' lack of structural leverage, in turn a product of a prior era of neoliberal reforms that deprived the working class of the conditions of cohesive, and threatening, political organization?[13] Either way, the search for the beginning of the end ultimately ends up back at the beginning—or before it.

As Fredric Jameson declared, we cannot *not* periodize. Without narratives, history amounts to an "endless series of sheer facts" or, in Walter Benjamin's oft-quoted phrasing, "one single catastrophe which keeps piling wreckage and hurls it in front of his feet."[14] Each of these narratives offers a valuable perspective on what is inevitably an overdetermined process.[15] Drawing on their insights, I focus my analysis specifically on the period in which leftist governments were in power. This is not to downplay the ways that prior decades of neoliberalism had structured the political terrain, or the fact that antineoliberal movements were the condition of possibility of the Pink Tide, but rather to zoom in on the relationship between leftist governments and leftist movements. This relationship is marked by a dialectic of governance and resistance—and disputes between political forces with shared experiences in struggle and intellectual formations.

During the Pink Tide, leftist governments and leftist movements faced vexing dilemmas with broader lessons for processes of radical transformation across the globe. From the position of the government, how do you achieve economic equality without deepening economic dependency? How do you democratize the state while also strengthening it against global capital and domestic elites? From the position of social movements, how do you protest against the state when the government's avowed goals align with your long-standing demands from below? And, given the political economy described in this book, how do you organize around territorial dispossession and socio-environmental harm, as well as build a mass coalition that includes those who economically benefit from resource-funded welfare?

Pink Tide governments inherited, and intensified, a model of accumulation based on the extraction and export of natural resources. This model enabled important forms of socioeconomic inclusion and political empowerment for the masses, while simultaneously undermining more radical transformations. Reactions from the domestic right and transnational capital also imposed a serious constraint on leftist governance. This is the case for the Left anywhere in the world. But in Latin America, and the Global South more broadly, this constraint binds more tightly due to the conditions of dependency and deep inequality.

Anti-extractive movements faced challenges as well. On the one hand, they demonstrated the capacity to stall or disrupt both oil and mining projects at the local level. On the other hand, directly affected communities and allied environmental activists had difficulty assembling a popular sector coalition at the national scale with the power to articulate and enact an alternative to the extractive model.

In a warming world riven by inequality, it is more vital than ever to understand the accomplishments and the shortcomings of both of these leftist orientations to extraction. In what follows, I will reflect on the Left-in-power and then on the Left-in-resistance. While most of this book has featured the voices and actions of situated actors directly involved in governance and resistance, and has especially highlighted discursive innovations on the part of anti-extractive protesters, in this concluding chapter I also attend to the contributions of regional critical intellectuals as well as their interlocutors in the United States and Europe. Most of these intellectuals have themselves been involved in processes of social mobilization, and in some cases have held office in leftist administrations. Their appraisals of Pink Tide governments and anti-extractive resistance, and their proposals for a post-extractive future, represent the most important contributions of contemporary Latin American critical thought to leftist politics around the world.

A brief clarification before moving forward. Dilemmas are not "failings." They are the challenging choices and situations that any attempt to transform the world encounters. They are constituted by the entanglement of radical potentialities, concrete achievements, and disappointing limitations. In that spirit, I will close this conclusion on a note of generosity to the Left-in-power and the Left-in-resistance. Both forms of leftism are urgently essential to address the planetary crisis in its ecological and political dimensions.

Dilemmas of the Left-in-Power

For the Left-in-power, hydrocarbon and mineral resources provide crucial revenues to fund social spending and public infrastructure. In a deeply unequal society, such policies directly benefit the majority of the population and consolidate the electoral Left's political support. For the Left in Latin America, equally important is the ideological resonance of resource nationalism: if a country is rich in natural resources, the benefits should flow to the people in the broadest sense, not just to the rich and foreign corporations. In this section, I evaluate leftist governments' achievements and shortcomings with regard to two key goals: sovereignty and equality.

In Ecuador, a long history of popular demands for nationalization, rooted not only in militancy amongst oil workers but also in the indigenous movements that would go on to reject extractivism *tout court*, framed natural resources as the collective property of the sovereign people. Here, sovereignty means the opposite of dependency, a condition with dimensions that are at once local (the disarticulation of enclaves from the national economy), national (the political alliance of domestic elites and foreign investors), regional (economic competition with neighboring countries), and global (the role of international capital and vulnerability to commodity prices).

However, it is precisely the goal of sovereignty that the reliance on primary commodity exports renders elusive. Instead, this reliance has implicated Latin American countries in new forms of dependency—especially vis-à-vis an ascendant China—and exposed them to the boom-and-bust cycles of global commodity markets. Despite important innovations in the contract model for oil and mining concessions that increased the state's take, the extent of classic nationalizations via wholesale expropriation has been quite limited. Rather, forced divestments, majority equity stakes, and joint ventures predominate.[16] Thus, foreign firms retain significant influence over the extractive process, the territories in which it unfolds, and the very state agencies ostensibly tasked with its regulation. It is thus perhaps in extractive sectors that we see some of the clearest continuities across neoliberal and avowedly post-neoliberal reforms. More fundamentally, if in the midcentury variant of developmentalism the goal was rapid industrialization, which would progressively reduce the share of the economy occupied by extraction while climbing the ladder of economic sophistication, the "neo-developmentalism" of the Pink Tide made peace with service sector-dominated labor markets and prioritized extraction over manufacturing.[17] And exporting countries, rather than coordinating to protect prices, enforce standards for revenue sharing, or jointly adopt labor and environmental regulations, have competed for investment. They thus betrayed promises of regional integration and mutually reinforced their peripheral status.[18]

The dilemmas of national sovereignty also raise the question: Who is "the nation" presumed to be the owner of resource wealth?[19] This national subject already had a long and multivalent history. In Ecuador, it had been first articulated from above, by a developmentalist military government intent on asserting state control over the oil sector, and then, decades later, from below, by a rebellious popular sector coalition that claimed popular sovereignty over subsoil resources. The further problematization of this identity was also the product of multiple developments. Across decades of conflicts with the state and extractive firms, indigenous groups have defined themselves as "nations" and "peoples," and claimed sovereignty and territorial self-determination.[20] These claims were bolstered by the 2008 Constitution, which defined Ecuador as a plurinational state and stipulated a slate of new collective rights for indigenous, Afro-Ecuadorian, and Montubian communities. Meanwhile, with the election of a leftist president, the anti-neoliberal grassroots coalition, which the national and regional indigenous federations historically played a vital role in coordinating, lost its oppositional force and organizational unity. By pitting indigenous and environmentalist activists against the beneficiaries of state spending, Correa contributed to this dynamic. His administration's vilification and criminalization of anti-extractive protesters exacerbated the fragmentation of the "social bloc of the oppressed" that had spearheaded anti-neoliberal protest.[21] The "nation" to which Correa continued to appeal—the "nation" first articulated by the popular sector coalition that had brought him to power years before—was thus increasingly unmoored from its historical conditions of articulation: meetings, assemblies, protests, and the shared discursive repertoire woven through these actions. It became an ideological resource for commodity-fueled, top-down leftist populism rather than a reflexively mediated collective subjectivity.

In addition to the challenge of asserting sovereignty, the reliance on resource rents presented dilemmas for the core leftist goal of equality. In boom times, resource rents enable material benefits for the least well-off precisely because they do not require income redistribution, let alone expropriation. Echoing the postwar social-democratic bargain in core capitalist states, itself enabled by abundant cheap energy, commodity export-led growth is a positive-sum game: governments can boost the incomes of the poor without reducing the wealth of the rich, thus ensuring the political support of the former without provoking the reaction of the latter. Furthermore, the "compensatory state" helps mitigate the social conflict around extraction: for a democratically elected, leftist government, responding to anti-extractive resistance with repression alone is not politically viable.[22] Whence the contractual innovations and legislative reforms that channel resource revenues to directly affected communities.[23]

Under Correa's decade in power, the combination of sustained growth, increased state revenues, and redistributive social spending (which doubled as a percentage of GDP) made a significant impact: poverty plummeted from 37.6 to 22.5 percent.[24] The improvement in material well-being of the poor, working class, and lower-middle classes has been argued to represent a "second incorporation," comparable to the region's midcentury official recognition of unions, codification of collective bargaining rights, and increases in welfare spending.[25] It is also important to note that, in some cases, this incorporation went beyond welfare payments and involved substantive, grassroots empowerment—even if in a tense relationship to simultaneous efforts to secure top-down control. In Venezuela under Chávez, for example, there were experiments in involving the poor as protagonists in the participatory planning of municipal budgets, land use, water management, and even economic production (via technical boards, land committees, communal councils, and communes).[26] In the case of Bolivia, social movements achieved significant influence within Morales's Movement for Socialism party, over both candidate selection and policy orientation.[27]

Increasing popular sector income, while a good in and of itself, also expanded domestic markets for consumer goods. In the absence of state regulation, this in turn encouraged firm consolidation and the increasing concentration of capital. Healthcare is a case in point. Universalizing access to healthcare and offering as many free services as possible was a major priority for the Correa administration. This was also a boon to private firms.[28] As the state did not build the capacity to directly provide all health services, the sector depended on public-private partnerships that transformed state spending into private profit. In addition, since the state-owned pharmaceutical company produced a tiny portion of prescription drugs (0.04 percent) and there was little regulation of the pharmaceutical market, the increased spending on healthcare (both by the state and by consumers) proved a windfall for the top two pharmaceutical companies, which soon controlled virtually the entire drug market. A similar dynamic held in the exploding construction sector. As these sectors grew, so did the political influence of their leading businesses, rendering it less and less likely that the state would strengthen regulations (as exemplified by the ongoing fallout from the region-wide Odebrecht corruption scheme).[29] Changes in class structure compounded these market dynamics: with more discretionary income, new consumer habits reshaped the political subjectivity of leftist governments' popular sector constituency. Even if economically precarious, an emergent "middle-class" identity was politically mobilized by centrist and right-wing political forces.[30] Meanwhile, when the commodity bust slashed state revenues in 2014, even avowedly leftist governments resorted to austerity measures—thus weakening their political support.

This volatile pattern of state spending maps onto boom-and-bust cycles. For states that depend on resource rents for their fiscal base, global market conditions are an important constraint on budgets, especially if they have low rates of domestic taxation. And oil prices function as a particularly tight constraint for Ecuador, which is a "price-taker," and which, additionally, uses the US dollar as its currency and is thus deprived of the tool of expansionary monetary policy.[31] But contra conventional depictions of "rentier states," which predict that governments will distribute windfall revenues to appease rival elites and mass constituencies (while repressing dissidents), price cycles alone cannot explain the content or targets of expenditures.[32] The specific forms state spending took under the Correa administration—monthly cash transfer programs, health services and education, public infrastructure (especially highways), and targeted investments in communities directly affected by oil and mining projects—were shaped by longer trajectories of state-formation and social conflict, and inflected by the particular understanding of post-neoliberalism that circulated among state actors. The monthly cash transfer program (*Bono de desarrollo humano*) and expanded social services were a response to long-standing social movement demands for the redistribution of resource wealth to the popular sectors—and a way to pay off the "social debt" accrued under neoliberalism and deepened by the 1998–1999 financial crisis.

Meanwhile, in a state historically characterized by territorially uneven capacity, new public infrastructure facilitated political incorporation and market integration, and served as a potent display of state presence (reinforced by the billboards that accompanied all new public works projects, proclaiming the "Citizens' Revolution" and stating the precise amount spent).[33] The fact that state actors tended to define neoliberalism as the absence of the state and, as a corollary, defined post-neoliberalism as its assertive presence only further encouraged this highly visible form of public intervention in socioeconomic life.[34] Lastly, the history of intense, localized conflict around extractive projects—conflicts that only increased in frequency and militancy during Correa's years in office—incentivized state planners and bureaucrats to channel resource revenues to directly affected communities.

These interwoven trajectories shaped spending decisions and their political, economic, social, and symbolic consequences. Against simplistic versions of the "resource curse" framework, commodity booms (or busts) do not tell us much about the specific content of state policy. Indeed, defying the stereotypes of the rentier state, during the boom the Correa administration made important progress in expanding direct taxation and, with new taxes on large properties and capital exports, in making fiscal policy more progressive.[35] Spending, however, outpaced both resource rents and new taxes, and Ecuador became increasingly indebted to China as well as to regional development banks. Further, the reliance on resource rents for both broad redistribution and targeted spending on the directly affected only reinforced the extractive imperative, which, as Eduardo Gudynas argues, in turn "create[s] new social and environmental impacts that will require new compensations."[36] When anti-extractive activists mobilized against these intensified socio-environmental impacts, state actors invoked redistribution and compensation policies to legitimize the expansion of the extractive frontier.[37] The tendency to ratchet up social spending evidences the provisionality of any "political settlement" in extractive economies, and the mutually reinforcing and ideologically mediated dynamic of broad redistribution, localized compensation, and extractive development.[38]

Across the region, declining commodity prices—beginning in 2012 for agricultural exports, and then for oil in 2014, decisively ending the boom—destabilized the balance of class forces that had provided leftist governments with a modicum of protection from conservative reaction. As Jeffery Webber writes, despite benefiting from the years of sustained export-led growth over which leftist governments presided, economic elites were ultimately not loyal: "during a drop in profitability and increasing political instability, capitalists returned to their natural home of old or new-right configurations."[39] Meanwhile, the characteristics of the model of accumulation and accompanying state-society relations described above—popular incorporation via welfare programs and compensations for directly affected communities, both paid for by windfall resource rents, and the fragmentation of the grassroots coalition that had protested neoliberalism—limited leftist governments' options once revenues shrank. From Venezuela to Brazil to Ecuador, austerity measures undermined grassroots support at the same time that elites defected and, in some cases, turned to extra-electoral means to remove the Left from power.

For a time, Bolivia was the semi-exception that proved the rule: its gas exports depend more on regional than global demand and were therefore less affected by China's slowing growth rates. This, in combination with prudent macroeconomic planning, dampened the effects of the commodity bust.[40] But even there, all aspects of the changing conjuncture eventually applied. Voters' rejection of Evo Morales's bid to change the constitution in order to run for a fourth term reflected declining popularity and the disaffection of parts of his base. In the fall of 2019, protests swept the country. The unrest hinged on allegations of fraud in the October 20 elections and mobilized large numbers of urban middle classes. The contention was quickly channeled by elite reactionary forces, causing Morales to flee the country after the military "suggested" he resign.[41] As I write these final pages, a conservative interim government has taken power, police and military are violently repressing dissent, and the outcome is far from certain.

It was in this evolving regional context that in 2017 Alianza País faced its most competitive national election since Correa took power, with Lenín Moreno barely defeating wealthy banker Guillermo Lasso in the second round of the presidential elections.[42] In Ecuador, as elsewhere on the continent, the retreat of the Left-in-power was overdetermined.

For the decade and a half of the Pink Tide, leftist governments did not monopolize leftist politics. In collaboration and conflict with these administrations was the Left-in-resistance: social movements employed extra-electoral means of mobilization and protest, and pushed political parties and elected officials to enact the sweeping transformations promised in campaign platforms, inauguration speeches, and opening ceremonies of constituent assemblies. The relationship between state officials and social movement activists varied across national contexts and evolved over time. And, as argued throughout this book, "the state" is not a monolithic entity, but rather a variegated terrain shot through with internal disputes, asymmetric power relations, and a range of institutional spaces that are more or less open to activist pressure (or, conversely, to alliances with economic elites). Despite this diversity and site-specific nuance, in all cases Pink Tide governments neither fully implemented grassroots demands nor fully co-opted, demobilized, or repressed social movements. Unaddressed grievances combined with continued bottom-up capacity meant that intra-leftist contention was an ongoing feature of the Left-in-power. In this regional setting, Ecuador stands out as evincing especially agonistic confrontations between a leftist national government and the social movements and radical intellectuals that originally supported its leader's rise to power, and from the ranks of which some of his top bureaucrats were appointed. Once extractivism crystallized as the crux of dispute, a polarized dynamic ensued, diminishing possibilities for collaboration.

Dilemmas of the Left-in-Resistance

In Ecuador and elsewhere, just as the Left-in-power was caught by a series of dilemmas, so too was the Left-in-resistance. Just as the former's achievements were limited by the contradictions of a political-economic model that it in part inherited and in part newly constructed, the latter came up against the contradictions of a critique and strategy centered on mobilizing those directly affected against extractive development. Anti-extractive movements can claim impressive accomplishments: they stalled specific extractive projects and reshaped the broader debate over resource extraction, forcing state actors and firms to respond to a new set of grievances and demands. However, to date, anti-extractive activists have not mobilized a mass movement of the scale and strength of the anti-neoliberal popular sector coalition that swept the leftist governments into office in the first place. To understand this set of achievements and limits, it is worth reflecting on three distinct sets of dilemmas of the resource radicalism of the Left-in-resistance: first, the dilemmas of *extractivismo* as critique; second, the dilemmas of post-extractivism as positive vision; and third, the dilemmas of anti-extractivism as political strategy. I explore each in turn.

First, the dilemmas of *extractivismo* as critique. Extractivism is the central term of a critical discourse that recombines preexisting strains of Latin American thought with more recent discourses around the environment and indigeneity. It constitutes a critique of the social formation it calls extractivism, into which it folds the traditional Left, seeing in both capitalism and state socialism a wanton disregard for socio-natural harmony.

This critique is indebted to dependency theory, expanding on the latter's evaluation of economies organized around the export of primary commodities.[43]

It shares with this school of thought a narrative that begins with the violence of colonial encounter and traces its enduring effects in neocolonial patterns of "plunder, accumulation, concentration, and devastation."[44] Like its progenitors, the framework of *extractivismo* attends to the constitutive territorial unevenness of global capitalism, and, more specifically, to the fractal structure of cores and peripheries, a structure relentlessly reproduced via the ever-expanding extractive frontier. In this sense, both Pink Tide governments' renewed resource nationalism and anti-extractivism drew on the repertoire of dependency theory. The former saw underdevelopment as rooted in the historic absence of national sovereignty and as a corollary regarded state-directed extraction as a route to equitable development; the latter focused on the pathologies of the "super-exploitation" of natural resources for export.[45]

The critical discourse of *extractivismo* also deviates from leftist tradition. Dependency theorists contemplated routes out of the situation of dependency. Indeed, theorists were sharply divided over nationalist-developmentalist versus revolutionary paths to development.[46] The first hoped for an alliance of the state and national capital, whereas the second hoped to overthrow both dependency and capital at once. In contrast, *extractivismo* discourse not only rejects "development" as a goal but regards the extractive model as deeply embedded in social structure, ideology, and even subjectivity, thus troubling the very possibility of revolutionary transformation.

As discussed in Chapter 2, the framework of *extractivismo* combines a *longue durée* timescale (from colonial conquest to the present) with attention to the expansionary territorial dynamic of extraction. According to Gudynas, the pathologies of extractivism travel far beyond the sites of extraction.[47] In order to advance a specific extractive project, governments might dismantle environmental and labor protections, or adopt an investor-friendly contract model. But the "spill-over effects" of these policy reforms facilitate extractive projects more generally.[48] The transportation infrastructure that accompanies extractive projects also triggers a domino effect of territorial reorganization, as new roads attract human settlement, expand the agricultural frontier, and lead to further deforestation.[49] From the perspective of *extractivismo* as critique, the ideological spillover effects are even more pervasive. In this rendering, extractivism becomes hegemonic common sense, what Maristella Svampa refers to as "the commodities consensus," which structures the parameters of politics and operates on an affective register to bind subjects to the logic of extractive capital.[50] Employing a telling biological metaphor, Alberto Acosta refers to "extractivist DNA entrenched (*enquistado*) in our societies" and a sort of extractivist cunning that "traps" even critics of capitalism in its nefarious tentacles.[51] In short, by shaping subjectivity, extractivism "builds culture."[52]

The flipside of the breadth, depth, and coherence of this critique is a twofold challenge. First, given this depiction of extractivism, it is difficult to account for the emergence, circulation, and political impact of the critical discourse of *extractivismo*. Analysts of extractivism tend not to reconcile their assertion of its hegemonic status with their discussion of the contention over the extractive model of development. Second, and perhaps more importantly, is the implied difficulty of articulating a post-extractive vision and an anti-extractive strategy. If extractivism is a total, ideologically closed system with a variety of internal mechanisms ensuring its reproduction and expansion, it would appear to foreclose the possibility of transformation, short of an exogenous shock. Whence the problem of envisioning how a post-extractive society could be built starting from the extractive society that currently exists. Relatedly, there are the challenges of anti-extractivism as political strategy. Namely, who is the imagined collective subject leading this transformative process? How is this subject composed, and by what means could it dismantle extractivism and assemble a post-extractive society in its place? In what follows, I attend to each of these sets of difficult tasks: post-extractivism as positive vision and anti-extractivism as political strategy.

Chronologically prior to a post-extractive society would be post-extractive transition. Or, at least, a concerted effort to wind down extractive projects, secure alternative sources of state revenue, and remediate social and environmental harm. In embarking on such a concerted effort, there would be the immediate obstacle of capital's disciplinary power: revoking concessions or modifying contractual conditions inevitably provokes foreign firms to appeal to investor arbitration tribunals. Recently in Ecuador, four oil firms have appealed to such tribunals, resulting in awards of nearly $2 billion to three of them, and the reversal of a $9.5 billion dollar ruling in Ecuador's favor.[53] (This is one domain where anti-extractive activists could learn from their resource nationalist opponents, given the latter's experience in implementing expropriations, forced contract renegotiations, and loan defaults—all of which can result in legal actions from investors or creditors.)

This hurdle aside, there is the question of the complex temporality of a post-extractive transition. While anti-extractive activists demanded an immediate cessation of oil and mining projects in the heat of political struggle, allied radical intellectuals and policy researchers have theorized a "planned decrease" that would phase out extraction while still channeling extractive rents to address social needs until, first, new economic sectors are developed, and second, state taxation capacity is consolidated.[54] Such plans must avoid the trap of an ever-deferred post-extractive future. To wit, even the critical bureaucrats I spoke with invoked the impossibility of an "overnight" (*de la noche a la mañana*) transition in order to justify the expansion of extraction.[55] In this way, as Webber writes, increasing popular sector "consumptive capacities" became an end in itself, "rather than the basis for more audacious structural ruptures with the existing order."[56] Directly addressing this pitfall, Miriam Lang distinguishes between the pace and the direction of change, arguing for prioritizing the latter in evaluating the process of creating a post-extractive society.[57] Gudynas conceives of this directionality in terms of an initial shift from the reigning "predatory" model of extractivism to "sensible" extractivism—wherein socio-environmental regulations are strengthened and enforced, which itself would necessitate a simultaneous increase in state capacity and reduction in current levels of extractive activity—followed by a shift to "indispensable" extractivism, which is the minimum resource extraction necessary to "ensure people's quality of life under the field of sustainability" and within the parameters of national and regional supply chains.[58] Regional coordination is not only key to reorient production and consumption toward satisfying human needs while maintaining ecological balance, but also to avoid the race-to-the-bottom competitive dynamic that undermines regulatory capacities.[59]

If transitioning away from the extractive model raises the challenges associated with any lengthy policy process unfolding over time, there is the further dilemma of articulating a positive vision for a new type of society. *Sumak kawsay/buen vivir* ("living well") aims to offer precisely that. In the broader activist and academic conversation around alternative models of development, *sumak kawsay/buen vivir* is an adjacent discourse to that of post-extractivism. It imagines a society that would be founded on the principle of harmony between individuals, communities, and nature, governed by social relations rooted in reciprocity and solidarity, and that would prioritize "the reproduction of life"—broadly understood to encompass nonhuman nature—"not of capital."[60] Though often framed in terms of indigenous "cosmovisions" and livelihoods, and inflected by collective memory, *sumak kawsay/buen vivir* is both a recent discourse, emerging at the turn of the millennium, and oriented toward the future, envisioned as "Andean and Amazonian utopias."[61] But the concept's ambiguity unsettles its own utopian vision. This is in part due to the versatility of the Quechua word *kawsay*, a portmanteau dating to early colonial Peru, the meanings of which have "ranged from basic connotations of existence and subsistence to appraisals of health and well-being."[62] Moreover, it reflects the distinct and even mutually opposed political projects to which the concept has been attached. Existing in the "'cultural borderlands' between indigeneity and dominant capitalist society," *sumak kawsay/buen vivir* echoes both mainstream and more radical discourses around environmental sustainability and indigenous rights.[63] Across the region, critics of extractivism use the concept in a critical and utopian register to critique what exists from the standpoint of a desired future. But it also appears in the preamble of Ecuador's 2008 Constitution (as well as framing multiple sections of the text), emblazons official documents, and constituted a key term in official discourse.[64] In addition, state actors have used the concept to promote new frontiers of commodification and accumulation, such as the bio-knowledge sector.[65] These ambiguities in the meaning of *sumak kawsay/buen vivir* shape and are shaped by its contours of circulation. In my fieldwork experience, compared to the key terms I have focused on in this book—extractivism, territory, prior consultation, community, water—*sumak kawsay/buen vivir* circulated less frequently among anti-extractive activists. This may seem surprising, given the attention this paradigm has received among scholars of the region. It is difficult to interpret a silence, but my sense was that Ecuadorian activists saw this concept as tainted by its use in official discourse and specifically by the glaring contradiction, in their view, between the state's avowed commitment to *sumak kawsay/buen vivir* and policies that promoted extraction.

In addition to these conceptual ambiguities, post-extractive utopian visions such as *sumak kawsay/buen vivir* face the dilemma of territorial scale.[66] Whether the focus is on sustainable agriculture, artisanal production, governing the commons of water, land, and other shared resources, or cultural practices that would re-embed social life in nature, the recurrent point of departure for these visions is a small, rural—and usually indigenous—community. The focus on this particular socio-spatial context raises at least two challenges related to scale: first, the challenge of scaling "up" from the local community to increasingly more encompassing orders of social life; and second, the challenge of scaling "out" from the rural to the urban. One key means of addressing the first challenge is creation of national policies that encourage local-level experimentation and provide resources to replicate and scale up viable initiatives. Such an approach, sometimes referred to as a "solidarity economy," would require complementary policies of land and water redistribution, and local participation in territorial planning and budget allocation.[67] The implementation of such policies would in turn be more likely in a political setting in which social movements had the leverage to demand their adoption and/or were more substantively represented in state institutions.[68] Addressing the second scalar challenge would require movement linkages and policy diffusion between anti-extractive activism and urban movements for public housing, mass transit, and green spaces—all of which are essential components of a non-extractive, low-carbon vision of living well.[69]

The challenge of territorial scale is closely linked to the third and final set of challenges facing the Left-in-resistance: those related to political strategy. There are myriad dimensions to social movement strategy, but here, I focus on the *collective subject* of resistance, understood as the protagonist and the emergent outcome of processes of social mobilization. As discussed throughout this book, anti-extractivism centers on the directly affected community. Such communities, located in the immediate zones of extraction, are at once the collective subject and geographical site of protest against oil and mining development. The local territorialization of resistance is a strength and a limit. On the one hand, community-level mobilization can obstruct a crucial choke-point in the political economy of extraction and, by slowing or stalling specific projects, shape the global contours of the extractive frontier.[70] On the other hand, this form of mobilization faces the difficulty of assembling a broader popular sector coalition with the capacity to take political power and transform the model of accumulation.

Across the region, scholars have noted an increase in resource-related conflict, especially in the expanding mining sector—a pattern that holds true for Ecuador.[71] This conflict has increasingly taken the form of local opposition to extractive projects and/or demands for greater compensation, pitting directly affected communities against firms and, often, the state agencies that promote or oversee the extractive process. Several factors account for this proliferation of local protest. The uneven territoriality of extraction, and more importantly its socio-environmental impacts, is key among them. Geography, however, is not destiny. Rather, the relationship between local communities—starting with their very self-identification as "directly affected"—is highly mediated by contextually specific social, economic, and political conditions, resulting in varying levels of opposition across zones of extraction. Militant opposition to oil and mining projects is more likely in cases of new projects (especially in areas without a prior history of extraction) that threaten preexisting economic livelihoods, disrupt collective consumption or social reproduction, or conflict with place-based cultural practices.[72] Project type, scale, and ownership also matter: in the mining sector, foreign-owned, large-scale, open-pit mines are particularly contentious.[73] In addition, legal norms and community-level political organization shape the form resistance takes. The salience of the "directly affected community" is in part a product of the availability of international and national legal instruments such as the *consulta* and the writ of *amparo* (also referred to as a *tutela* in Colombia), which aim to protect human rights from their violation by states or corporations. These instruments recognize the local community as a subject of particular rights and provide an institutional venue to contest projects, whether local consultations, social participation in environmental impact assessments, or domestic and regional courts.[74] And communities that are already politically organized (for example, via neighborhood associations, water committees, indigenous organizations) and allied with movements at other scales are more equipped to deploy such instruments in political battle with firms and states.[75]

Under these specific conditions, local communities are a powerful geographical site and collective protagonist of protest. Given their spatial proximity to a key node of the extractive process, they have the capacity to stall and disrupt projects. And, when communities join together in broader alliances, such protests can potentially shape policies beyond the local level. However, an anti-extractive strategy that centers on directly affected communities is also by its nature a limited one: the legal and moral force of their grievances and demands is rooted in claims of spatial proximity and, often, particular rights linked to that proximity (and/or to ethnic status). Even though this strategy has proven effective at contesting specific projects, it is thus contained by the fragmented and uneven territoriality of extraction.[76] Moreover, as illustrated in the opening vignette to this conclusion, in the absence of strong alliances and organized solidarity, the territorial isolation of directly affected communities can leave them vulnerable to state repression.[77]

In order to shift from a defensive position of resistance to an offensive position of political hegemony, anti-extractivism would need to join forces with a broader coalition of rural and urban popular sectors. Such a coalition would include not only those who are not immediately harmed by extraction, but also those who stand to benefit from the social programs and public infrastructure currently funded by resource rents. This is a population that, under prevailing conceptions of the "directly affected," is much larger than frontline communities.

Recent contention in Ecuador brings into relief the challenges of assembling such a coalition under the banner of anti-extractivism. On October 1, 2019, President Lenín Moreno—Correa's successor and erstwhile political ally—implemented a series of austerity measures as part of an agreement with the International Monetary Fund. Among these measures was the elimination of a long-standing subsidy for gasoline and diesel. Immediately, a coalition comprising the national labor federation (FUT), the national student union (FEUE), and CONAIE announced protests. Ten days later, after massive demonstrations filled the streets of Quito, briefly occupied the National Assembly as well as multiple oil fields in the Amazon, and ultimately forced the government to temporarily relocate to Guayaquil, the Moreno administration agreed to negotiate with CONAIE. As a result of their dialogue, protesters achieved their primary demand of the reinstatement of fuel subsidies, as well as an official investigation into state repression that resulted in nine deaths, over one thousand injured, and over one thousand arrests.[78]

Among the most remarkable aspects of this episode of contention was the re-articulation of a popular sector coalition—labor, youth, and indigenous; rural and urban; sierra and Amazon—with CONAIE playing a key leadership role. The resonance with the mid-1990s was striking. And, crucially, this provisional alliance was not anti-extractivist in orientation; it was, if anything, radical resource nationalist. Despite the fact that fuel subsidies are regressive (the rich use more fuel than the poor), for those living at the margins of their income in a petro-state, such subsidies are an important form of social welfare and a powerful symbol of petro-nationalism. How might anti-extractivism transform to encompass a similarly territorially diverse bloc of the oppressed?

The articulation of the directly affected as protagonist and site of anti-extractive resistance is neither natural nor inevitable, but itself a product of political scale-making.[79] And as a corollary, identities and interests can be rescaled. Indeed, "scale shifting" is a central component of successful social movements. Through alliances and solidarity, movements can expand their mobilizational capacity beyond those most immediately or severely impacted by a given form of oppression, and, by linking overlapping grievances and demands, expand their collective identity and interests.[80] Across the Americas, there are inspiring examples of such coalitions. In 2018 in El Salvador, an alliance of anti-mining groups, progressive Catholic leaders, and national environmental NGOs pressured the government to adopt the world's first national ban on mining for metals. For this movement, the defense of water was a central concern.[81] Activism against large-scale mining first scaled up to the national level in 2005, in response to neoliberal policies that courted private investment in the sector. But as Rose Spalding has shown, anti-mining activism in El Salvador is rooted in community organizations that date to the late stages of the country's civil war, which ended in the early 1990s. Refugees who had fled massacres returned to villages that had largely been abandoned by the state and turned to collective self-governance as a form of survival. The result was a dense network of rural communities linked together in an umbrella organization—a powerful front of resistance when large-scale mining reached the extraction permit stage in 2004. In direct response to the national anti-mining movement's demands, deputies of the left-wing FMLN introduced a bill to ban large-scale mining in 2006. Eleven years later, the law was adopted unanimously by El Salvador's legislature. A number of factors account for this success: dense organizational structures linking affected communities together; the movement's ability to frame the national conversation around impacts on the country's vulnerable water system; the innovative use of municipal *consultas* on mining (all of which registered community opposition); and the strong support of progressive Catholic bishops as well as FMLN deputies in congress. This dynamic, involving both the anti-mining movement and a political party, built on long-standing ties between rural community movements and the FMLN, was essential to channeling popular power into policy change.

Coda: A Note of Generosity

In the preceding pages, I surveyed the dilemmas confronting the Left-in-power and the Left-in-resistance in the context of an extractive model of accumulation and a state positioned on the periphery of the global economy. In Ecuador, these two forms of leftism confronted one another in a dispute that became so polarized that each saw in the other a political enemy more dangerous than neoliberalism. Lost in this internecine dispute was the radical promise of "twenty-first-century socialism": collective, democratic control over the conditions of socio-natural existence. Such a program could have coherently demanded *both* the redistribution of oil and mining revenues *and* a transition away from the extractive model of accumulation that generates those revenues. Just such a vision inflected CONAIE's 1994 political program, published amidst massive mobilizations against neoliberal land reforms, that called for a "planned ecological communitarian economy."[82] Yet two decades later, "socialism" and "anti-extractivism" had come to name two counterposed political projects. Socialism in Correa's usage meant state investment and spending in the pursuit of national development without transforming the model of accumulation or the class relations that it generates. Anti-extractivism referred to the militant defense of communities and ecosystems against the threat of oil extraction and mining without mobilizing the majority not immediately affected by social and environmental destruction.

As I write, in winter 2020, a resurgent right-wing threatens both of these leftist projects. Exacerbating the effects of the commodity bust and ensuing recession, austerity measures are reversing the socioeconomic gains of the previous decade. Investor-friendly reforms in the oil and mining sectors are already expanding extraction, devastating ecosystems, displacing indigenous populations, and contributing to climate change.[83] These trends are starkly apparent in the ostensibly leftist administration of President Moreno, which abandoned even Correa's minimal definition of socialism and changed the oil contract model to court foreign firms.[84] At the same time, the regional turn to the right, in both its conventionally neoliberal and more fascistic guises, is already facing challenges from the left and from below: the election of López Obrador in Mexico and of Alberto Fernández in Argentina, and the massive, militant protests against austerity policies in both Ecuador and Chile—which resulted in policy concessions from the Moreno and Piñera governments, respectively.

At this juncture, it is worth highlighting the urgent necessity of both the Left-in-power and the Left-in-resistance. For the foreseeable future, achieving socioeconomic equality on a livable planet constitutes the key political task for the hemisphere—and the globe. For all the limitations and contradictions of the Pink Tide, without the Left in power, political, social, and economic inequalities mutually reinforce one another, denying a dignified life to the vast majority of the population, and protecting the privileges of the few against the democratic will of the many.[85] For all of the challenges of building an anti-extractive mass movement, resistance against oil, coal, natural gas, and large-scale mining projects is absolutely vital if we are to avert the worst of climate chaos. Despite the potential for conflict between them, these two projects are fundamentally intertwined. Global warming deepens inequality within and between countries, undermining a core goal of leftist governments. And wresting political power from fossil capital and democratizing state institutions is a prerequisite for meaningful action on climate change and other forms of environmental devastation.[86]

What is the possibility of Latin American leftists reconstructing a viable political project that can weave together egalitarian and ecological demands? The future is, more than ever, uncertain and unpredictable. But if the past three decades of contentious politics in the region offer any indication, a neoliberal turn in governance combined with the ongoing intensification of resource extraction will transform the terrain of policymaking and protest. In this transformed context, we can expect militant activists to refashion their critiques, revise their strategies, and assemble new resource radicalisms.

Introduction: Resource Radicalisms

Epigraph: In this context, peoples (*los pueblos*) refers to indigenous peoples.

1   "Manifiesto del encuentro de movimentos sociales del Ecuador por la democracia y la vida," August 9, 2011 (http://www.inesc.org.br/noticias-es/2011/agosto/manifiesto-del-encuentro-de-movimentos-sociales-del-ecuador-por-la-democracia-y-la-vida).

2   Activists and allied public intellectuals use this term interchangeably with "the extractive model." For definitions, see Albuja and Dávalos, "Extractivismo y posneoliberalismo, 89–98; Chavez, "El estado del debate sobre desarrollo, extractivismo, y acumulación en el Ecuador," 10; Gudynas, "Diez tesis urgentes sobre el nuevo extractivismo," 188; Svampa, *Debates latinoamericanos*, 372.

3   Francisca Cabieses Martinez, "Revolución ciudadana, el camino del Ecuador," *Punto Final*, May 25, 2012 (http://www.puntofinal.cl/758/rafael758.php).

4   Correa, "Ecuador's Path."

5   For paradigmatic examples, see Karl, *The Paradox of Plenty*; Ross, "Does Oil Hinder Democracy?" and *The Oil Curse*; and Weyland, "The Rise of Latin America's Two Lefts." For the earlier rentier state literature that the resource curse concept draws upon, see Beblawi, "The Rentier State in the Arab World"; Mahdavy, "The Patterns and Problems of Economic Development in Rentier States."

6   For the phrase "rentier mentality," see Beblawi, "Rentier State."

7   As Michael Watts argues, the notion that primary commodities, abstracted from social relations, possess special economic or political powers is a form of "commodity determinism" (Watts, "Righteous Oil?"). See also, Huber, *Lifeblood*, 116.

8   For the proliferation of resource-related conflict in a warming world, see Parenti, *Tropic of Chaos* and Welzer, *Climate Wars*.

9   Bebbington et al., "Political Settlements and the Governance of Extractive Industry," 6–8; Bridge, "Contested Terrain"; Bridge and Le Billon, *Oil*, esp. 40–76; Perreault, "Political Contradictions of Extractive Development."

10 Bebbington et al., "Political Settlements," 6.

11 For the term "Global South," see Garland Mahler, "What/Where Is the Global South?" (https://globalsouthstudies.as.virginia.edu/what-is-global-south, accessed December 8, 2018). As she writes, while the term originated as a "post-cold war alternative to 'Third World' . . . in recent years and within a variety of fields, the Global South is employed in a post-national sense to address spaces and peoples negatively impacted by contemporary capitalist globalization." While the countries to which I refer to here are located within the term's earlier, and narrower,

geographic contours, I concur with the post-national expansion of the concept, as it better captures the territorial pattern of uneven capitalist development (and accords with the fractal structure of core/periphery and satellite/metropole in world systems theory).

12 Karl, *Paradox of Plenty*; Smith, *Hard Times in the Lands of Plenty*.

13 Bebbington et al., "Political Settlements," 8–10, 16; Kohl and Farthing, "Material Constraints to Popular Imaginaries"; Perreault and Valdivia, "Hydrocarbons, Protest, and National Imaginaries."

14 For seminal analyses of this relationship, see Frank, *Lumpen-Bourgeoisie and Lumpen-Development*; Prebisch, "Crecimiento Desequilibrio y Disparidades." For the notion of unequal ecological exchange, see Ciplet and Roberts, "Splintering the South." For an excellent overview of classical dependency theory, as well as its recent reformulations in the context of the Pink Tide, see Svampa, *Debates latinoamericanos*, Part I, Chapter 2 and Part II, Chapter 2.

15 Dependency theorists use the term "underdevelopment" to describe the result of the incorporation of Latin American countries into global capitalism, first through imperial conquest and then through forms of neo-colonialism. The extraction of raw materials and the exploitation of enslaved (and otherwise extra-economically coerced) labor produced "development" for the core capitalist powers and "underdevelopment" for the periphery. Thus these theorists refute the notion that Latin America or other countries in the Global South are simply "undeveloped" or "backward"; rather, the Global North (in collusion with domestic elites) has actively "underdeveloped" the periphery via relations of domination and the extraction of surplus value. See Frank, *Lumpen-Bourgeoisie*; Stern, "Feudalism, Capitalism, and the World-System in the Perspective of Latin America and the Caribbean." For a definition of developmentalism, see the contributions to Woo-Cumings, *The Developmental State*.

16 Escobar, "Latin America at a Crossroads," 1.

17 Levitsky and Roberts, "Introduction: Latin America's 'Left Turn,'" 1.

18 For the term "decolonial," see Mignolo, *The Darker Side of Western Modernity*.

19 The term *ecologismo popular* was developed by Joan Martínez Alier, and refers to territorialized conflicts that arise in response to the detrimental socio-environmental effects of economic growth; these effects threaten local means of subsistence and thus provoke social conflict. The actors that mobilize in such conflicts may or may not explicitly invoke environmental discourse. See Martínez Alier, "El ecologismo popular"; Latorre, "El ecologismo popular en el Ecuador."

20 The concept circulates in scholarly work (e.g., Svampa, "Commodities Consensus"; Webber, "Revolution against 'Progress'"; Veltmeyer and Petras, *The New Extractivism*), and in more popular genres (e.g., Klein, *This Changes Everything*). For further analysis of Ecuador as a particularly emblematic case of contention over extraction, see Escobar, "Latin America at a Crossroads"; Svampa, "Commodities Consensus."

21 In Latin American scholarship and in everyday political discourse, the phrase "popular sectors" (*sectores populares*) refers to the set of social groups who have

historically been exploited or excluded, whether due to their class, race, or ethnicity (or, more commonly, some combination thereof): peasant, working class, rural and urban poor, indigenous, and Afro-descendent.

22 Perreault, "Tendencies in Tension," 19.

23 These paradigms center on the governance of oil and, more recently, large-scale mining. Ecuador has also historically depended on the export of primary agricultural resources and other food commodities: cacao, banana, shrimp, and cut flowers. See Larrea and North, "Ecuador," 915–21; Latorre, Farrell, and Martínez-Alier, "The Commodification of Nature and Socio-Environmental Resistance in Ecuador."

24 There is a large scholarship on the causes of the Pink Tide. Specific case studies are cited elsewhere in this introduction and in the chapters that follow. This paragraph, which focuses on region-wide causes of the electoral shift to the Left, draws on the work of Arditi, "Arguments about the Left Turns in Latin America"; Cameron, "Latin America's Left Turns"; Levitsky and Roberts, "Latin America's 'Left Turn'"; Silva, *Challenging Neoliberalism in Latin America*.

25 On the commodity boom, see CEPAL, *Panorama de la inserción internacional de América Latina y el Caribe*; Cypher, "South America's Commodities Boom"; Cypher and Wilson, "China and Latin America"; Ruiz Acosta and Iturralde, *La alquimía de la riqueza*; Sinnot, Nash, and de la Torre, *Natural Resources in Latin America and the Caribbean*.

26 Perreault, "Tendencies in Tension," 19.

27 Perreault, "Tendencies in Tension," 19.

28 In addition, the law outlined plans (eventually realized by the Rodríguez Lara government) for a national oil company, Corporación Estatal Petrolera Ecuatoriana (CEPE), later renamed Petroecuador. See Martz, *Politics and Petroleum in Ecuador*, 55–61.

29 Garavini, "Completing Decolonization," 479.

30 Garavini, "Completing Decolonization," 478–83.

31 Prices spiked in 1973 when the Arab–Israeli War disrupted Middle East supplies and OPEC decided to increase the price per barrel (Martz, *Politics and Petroleum*, 116). See the following for historical accounts of nationalist oil policies among Third World countries during this time period: Dietrich, *Oil Revolution*; Garavini, "Completing Decolonization."

32 Martz, *Politics and Petroleum*, 103–13.

33 These policies, and their limitations, are discussed at more length in Chapter 1.

34 Conaghan, Malloy, and Abugattas, "Business and the 'Boys,'" 6–7; Hey and Klak, "From Protectionism to Neoliberalism"; Martz, *Politics and Petroleum*, 105–6, 125–7; Sawyer, *Crude Chronicles*, Chapters 3, 4.

35 Specifically, Ecuador's five principal exports (oil, bananas, shrimp, flowers, prepared/canned fish) accounted for on average 74.8 percent of total exports (Ruiz Acosta and Iturralde, *La alquimía de la riqueza*, 29).

36 Banco Central del Ecuador, "Información estadística mensual," December 2012; Banco Central del Ecuador, "Información estadística mensual," April 2014.

37 Gallagher, Irwin, and Koleski, "New Banks in Town," 6–10; Joshua Schneyer and Nicolas Medina Mora Perez, "Special Report: How China took control of an OPEC country's oil," *Reuters*, November 26, 2013 (https://www.reuters.com/article /us-china-ecuador-oil-special-report/special-report-how-china-took-control-of-an -opec-countrys-oil-idUSBRE9AP0HX20131126).

38 Petroecuador was founded in 1989 and is the successor to CEPE. For this figure, see the China-Latin America Finance Database (http://www.thedialogue.org/map _list/).

39 For attempts to construct a large-scale mining sector in Ecuador, and the resistance they occasioned, see the following accounts of the plans to develop the Junín Mine in the Intag Valley: Bebbington et al., "The Glocalization of Environmental Governance"; Cisneros, *¿Cómo se construye la sustentabilidad ambiental?*; Kuecker, "Fighting for the Forests Revisited"; Carlos Zorrilla, "The Struggle to Save Intag's Forests and Communities from Mitsubishi," June 21, 1999 (http:// www.hartford-hwp.com/archives/41/103.html).

40 Berrios, Marak, and Morgenstern, "Explaining Hydrocarbon Nationalization in Latin America"; Haslam and Heidrich, "From Neoliberalism to Resource Nationalism." Although my focus here is on leftist governments, Berrios, Marak, and Morgenstern show that during the boom, center and right-of-center governments have also increased the regulation of extractive sectors and the state "take" in terms of taxes and royalties.

41 Berrios, Marak, and Morgenstern, "Explaining Hydrocarbon Nationalization"; Haslam and Heidrich, "From Neoliberalism to Resource Nationalism"; Kaup, "A Neoliberal Nationalization?"; Kohl and Farthing, "Material Constraints."

42 As discussed in more depth in Chapter 1, in 2006, under pressure from protests, the Palacio administration terminated the contract with Occidental Petroleum for contract violations, but this was not a nationalization (despite how it has sometimes been portrayed in the literature and news reports). For changes to oil contract model, see Ghandi and Lin, "Oil and Gas Service Contracts around the World"; Mateo and García, "El sector petrolero en Ecuador, 2000–2010."

43 Poverty declined from 37 percent to 23 percent. Income inequality, measured by the Gini coefficient, declined from 0.55 to 0.47. See Larrea and Greene, "De la lucha contra la probreza a la superación de la codicia"; Ordóñez et al., "Sharing the Fruits of Progress"; Weisbrot, Johnston, and Merling, "Decade of Reform."

44 Amarante and Brun, "Cash Transfers in Latin America." See also CEPAL, "Base de datos de programas de protección social no contributiva" (https://dds.cepal.org /bpsnc/ptc, accessed January 7, 2019).

45 Amarante and Brun, "Cash Transfers."

46 Larrea and Greene, "De la lucha contra la probreza a la superación de la codicia"; Iturralde, *El negocio invisible de la salud*; Ponce and Vos, "Redistribution without Structural Change in Ecuador." It is worth noting that Ponce and Vos show that a significant portion of the reduction in income inequality was due to the recovery from the 1998–1999 economic crisis, but that this positive effect was amplified by the Correa administration's economic and fiscal policies.

47 Author's calculation based on the data provided in CEPAL, "Base de datos."

48 Ponce and Vos, "Redistribution without Structural Change."

49 I return to the topic of political retreat in the Conclusion.

50 For an in-depth analysis of this dynamic in Bolivia, see Kaup, "A Neoliberal Nationalization?"

51 For a helpful explanation of the various direct and indirect pressures investors exert on the state, see Block, "The Ruling Class Does Not Rule."

52 "Ecuador Pushing Ahead with Reforms to Lure Mining Investors," *Reuters*, May 6, 2013 (http://articles.chicagotribune.com/2013-05-16/news/sns-rt-ecuador -mining12nodx2h8-20130516_1_mining-law-mining-bill-mining-industry).

53 "Canadian Gold Giant Kinross Pulls Out of Ecuador Mine Project, Will China Take Its Place?" *International Business Times*, June 6, 2013 (http://www.ibtimes.com /canadian-gold-giant-kinross-pulls-out-ecuador-mine-project-will-china-take-its -place-1305761).

54 As discussed in Chapter 5, these continuities with neoliberalism were also evident at the level of ideology, especially bureaucrats' and corporate actors' emphasis on technocratic solutions to political problems.

55 Rafael Correa Delgado, Decreto ejecutivo n. 870, September 5, 2011.

56 Asamblea Nacional, Ley de Minería, art. 89.

57 Harvey, *A Brief History of Neoliberalism*, 159–65; Latorre, Farrell, and Martínez-Alier, "Commodification of Nature."

58 Cisneros, "Corporate Social Responsibility and Mining Policy in Ecuador."

59 Hogenboom, "Depoliticized and Repoliticized Minerals in Latin America," 151–2.

60 By "emic," I refer to the contextually specific discursive categories employed by the actors situated in the conflict under study, and through which they under-stand and ascribe meaning to their social world.

61 For a similar analysis of the relationship between critique and justification, see Boltanski and Chiapello, *The New Spirit of Capitalism*.

62 For example, as described in Chapters 2 and 5, the Correa administration em-braced a variant of resource nationalism that was devoid of much of its radical content (for example, no nationalizations or expropriations) and ideologically repurposed it to delegitimize anti-extractive resistance and promote extraction at all cost.

63 Kohl and Farthing, "Material Constraints"; Gledhill, "The Persistent Imaginary of 'the People's Oil'"; Nem Singh, "Who Owns the Minerals?"; Shever, *Resources for Reform*; Perreault and Valdivia, "Hydrocarbons." For an example of radical resource politics from earlier in the century, see Nash, *We Eat the Mines and the Mines Eat Us*.

64 Kohl and Farthing analyze this imaginary in relation to Bolivia's history of a militant miners' union that played a key role in the 1952 national revolution, and the eruption of protests against water and gas privatization in the early 2000s. See Kohl and Farthing, "Material Constraints," 229.

65 Kohl and Farthing, "Material Constraints," 229.

66 In Escobar's terms, Ecuador exemplified the conflict between "neo-developmentalism and post-development" (Escobar, "Latin America at a Crossroads," 20). See also Gudynas, "Value, Growth, Development"; the contributions to Munck and Delgado Wise (eds.), *Reframing Latin American Development* ; Svampa, *Debates latinoamericanos*, Part II, Chapter 2.

67 For existing scholarship, see Acosta, *La maldicion de la abundancia*; Albuja and Dávalos, "Extractivismo y posneoliberalismo"; Bebbington and Bebbington, "An Andean Avatar"; Burchardt and Dietz, "(Neo-)Extractivism"; Gudynas, "Diez tesis"; Gudynas, "Extractivisms"; Gustafson and Guzmán Solano, "Mining Movements and Political Horizons in the Andes"; Veltmeyer, "The Political Economy of Natural Resource Extraction"; Veltmeyer and Petras, *The New Extractivism*; Webber, "Revolution against 'Progress.'" Burchardt and Dietz do initially treat "(neo)-extractivism" as a concept that emerged in critical response to Pink Tide governments, but they proceed to employ it as an analytic and descriptive label. Lastly, Svampa takes an approach closer to mine, although her focus is primarily on professional intellectuals rather than activists: she defines the concept of extractivism and situates it within a dynamic field of debate over the model of development (Svampa, *Debates latinoamericanos*, Part II, Chapter 2).

68 Similarly, throughout the text I use Spanish words when their meaning is context-specific and/or not directly synonymous with English words. I define such terms in English whenever I use them.

69 Foucault, "Politics and the Study of Discourse," 60.

70 Foucault, "The Order of Discourse" and "Politics and the Study of Discourse."

71 Glaeser, *Political Epistemics*, 12–13.

72 Glaeser, *Political Epistemics,* 12–13.

73 For a discussion of shifts in the logic of action as the redeployment of existing techniques in new combinations, see Foucault, *Security, Territory, Population*, 22–4.

74 Boltanski and Chiapello, *New Spirit of Capitalism*; Wuthnow, *Communities of Discourse*.

75 Although, as I discuss below, no resource radicalism is wholly "new" (in that it involves the recombination or resignification of existing elements) and there is a temporal lag between the shift in governance and the modification or transformation of critique.

76 Bowen, "Multicultural Market Democracy."

77 The phrase "sociotechnical means" comes from Glaeser, *Political Epistemics*, 30: "Effects can flow from one person's action to be picked up by another without there being any reverse flow. In fact, the actions can be spatiotemporally separated, and actor and reactor need not—and very often and in highly complex societies typically do not—know each other. What makes this possible are sociotechnical means of projectively articulating actions across space and time through mediating communication, transportation, and storage." Timothy Mitchell refers to a similar set of material relationships that enable the diffusion of apparently disembodied "ideas" with the phrase "the acoustic machinery of their circulation" (Mitchell, *Carbon Democracy*, 69).

78 Agha, *Language and Social Relations*, 3.

79 Nakassis, "Materiality, Materialization," 403, original emphasis.

80 Nakassis, "Materiality, Materialization," 402, original emphasis.

81 As Marx writes, "The production of ideas, of conceptions, of consciousness, is at first directly interwoven with the material activity and the material intercourse of men, the language of real life" (*The German Ideology*, 47).

82 For regimes of discourse, see Foucault, "The Order of Discourse"; Foucault, "Politics and the Study of Discourse." For problematics, see Althusser, *For Marx*, 49–86. For an analysis of discursive regimes that draws on Foucault, see Ferguson, *The Anti-Politics Machine*.

83 One way to conceptualize this capacity is as performativity: under certain felicitous conditions—statements such as "I now pronounce you man and wife" or "I nominate you candidate"—the act of utterance calls into being the reality that it describes. See Austin, *How to Do Things with Words*; see also Agha, *Language and Social Relations*, 55–60; Searle, *Speech Acts*; Silverstein, "Metapragmatic Discourse and Metapragmatic Function," 45–8. Performativity also encompasses semiotic activity that is nonlinguistic and does not explicitly describe its social effects. See, e.g., Butler's analysis of the performance of gender: Butler, "Performative Acts and Gender Constitution"; Butler, *Gender Trouble*.

84 My use of the concept "problematic" draws on Althusser, albeit with a few substantial modifications (Althusser, *For Marx*, 49–86). He defines a problematic as the system of internal reference, the "principle of intelligibility," that unifies an ideology. It is "the system of *questions* commanding the *answers* given by the ideology" (67, original emphasis). Disagreements take place, and are intelligible within, the shared ground of a given problematic. Althusser further argues that the analyst's interpretation of a problematic must take into account "the existing *ideological field* and . . . the *social problems and social structure* which sustain the ideology and are reflected in it" (66, original emphasis). For Althusser, the locus of change between problematics cannot be found within a given problematic but must be located in the given conjuncture of social forces. He asserts that ideologies do not transform because of their own internal contradictions, or through progress to more rational systems of thought, but rather as a result of changes in their socio-historical conditions of possibility. In contrast to Althusser, however, I do not sharply distinguish between "ideology" (or, the term I use more often, "discourse") and the "objective problems" that actors confront. In line with Wedeen's work on political domination in Syria and democratic publics in Yemen (Wedeen, *Ambiguities of Domination* and *Peripheral Visions*), I argue instead that there is a mutually determining relationship between how we talk about social life and the social structures that constrain and enable certain forms of political action. The task of analysis is therefore to determine under what conditions changes in public discourse alter patterns of political action, and, conversely, transformations in forms of political action reconfigure the terms of debate. Finally, I am also explicitly interested in the piecemeal ways that actors respond to new historical circumstances by retooling their political visions and identities,

and, relatedly, how new problematics almost always involve recontextualized redeployments of discursive elements from earlier periods. Thus, what follows is not a stadial or epochal history of a transition between two hermetically sealed resource radicalisms, but rather a temporally complex narrative of the shift between salient modes of understanding and enacting politics in which actors often intermingle discursive strategies that index both past and current political conjunctures.

85 In other words, this ideological disagreement was oriented toward some shared concern and a degree of mutual recognition (Agha, *Language and Social Relations*, 172–3, 305; Boltanski and Thévenot, *On Justification*; Rancière, *Disagreement*). Or, in Mouffe's terms, the dispute over extractivism was "agonistic"—fought within a shared symbolic space—rather than "antagonistic" (Mouffe, *The Democratic Paradox*, 13).

86 Steinberg, "The Talk and Back Talk of Collective Action," 769.

87 For Bourdieu, a social field is a "configuration" of positions that stand in "objective" relationship to one another, in the sense that (borrowing from Marx) "they exist independently of individual consciousness or will" (Bourdieu, *The Logic of Practice*, 66–7; see also Bourdieu and Wacquant, *An Invitation to Reflexive Sociology*, 97–105). Bourdieu's conceptualization of social fields has important drawbacks, namely his emphasis on individual (rather than collective) actors, and his difficulty accounting for change (Fligstein and McAdam, "Toward a General Theory of Strategic Action Fields," 19–20). For my usage of the word "terrain," see Gramsci, *The Prison Notebooks*, 172, 180–5.

88 See Warner's explanation of the distinction between a "targeted public" and the actual empirical circulation of discourse in Warner, *Publics and Counterpublics*, 72–4.

89 For animation and reanimation, see Goffman, *Forms of Talk*, 131–4, 144–5; Warner, *Publics and Counterpublics*, 87–9.

90 Warner, *Publics and Counterpublics*, 74.

91 See Arendt's analysis of the "frustration" of political action and speech in Arendt, *The Human Condition*, 220.

92 Nelson, *The Argonauts*, 29.

93 Bakhtin, *The Dialogic Imagination*, 293–4.

94 This draws on a central insight of historical institutionalist theory, and one I argue applies to crystallized discourses, which I consider to be "institutions" in their own right. See Riofrancos, "Discursive Institutionalization."

95 Benjamin, *Illuminations*, 253–64.

96 Benjamin, *Illuminations*, 261.

97 For the phrase "repoliticized" see Hogenboom, "Depoliticized and Repoliticized Minerals." For examples of recent scholarly work on the topic, see Arce, *Resource Extraction and Protest in Peru*; Bebbington and Bury, *Subterranean Struggles*; Deonandan and Dougherty, *Mining in Latin America*; Haslam and Heidrich, *The Political Economy of Natural Resources and Development*; Haslam and Tanimoune, "The Determinants of Social Conflict in the Latin American Mining Sector"; Hindery,

From Enron to Evo; Humphreys Bebbington, "Consultation, Compensation and Conflict"; Mähler and Pierskallar, "Indigenous Identity, Natural Resources, and Contentious Politics in Bolivia"; Rosales, "Going Underground"; Svampa, "Commodities Consensus"; Tockman and Cameron, "Indigenous Autonomy and the Contradictions of Plurinationalism in Bolivia."

98   Karl, *Paradox of Plenty*; Ross, "Does Oil Hinder Democracy?" and *Oil Curse*; Weyland, "The Rise of Latin America's Two Lefts." For the earlier rentier state literature that the resource curse concept draws upon, see Beblawi, "Rentier State"; Mahdavy, "Patterns and Problems."

99   For a discussion of the contrasting treatment of the state in the oil curse literature, see Smith, "Resource Wealth and Political Regimes" and *Hard Times*, Chapters 1, 2.

100 Haber and Menaldo, "Do Natural Resources Fuel Authoritarianism?"; Kurtz, "The Social Foundations of Institutional Order"; Luong and Weinthal, "Rethinking the Resource Curse" and *Oil Is Not a Curse*; Smith, *Hard Times*.

101 Smith, *Hard Times*, 7.

102 Dunning, *Crude Democracy*.

103 Mitchell, *Carbon Democracy*.

104 Mitchell, *Carbon Democracy*. For Mitchell's argument that coal extraction—and, specifically, militant coal-worker organization—enabled democratization, see *Carbon Democracy*, 12–42.

105 Bebbington and Bury, *Subterranean Struggles*; Bebbington et al., "Political Settlements"; Golub, *Leviathans at the Gold Mine*; Hindery, *From Enron to Evo*; Kohl and Farthing, "Material Constraints"; Latorre, Farrell, and Martínez-Alier, "Commodification of Nature"; Li, *Unearthing Conflict*; Perreault, "Tendencies in Tension"; Perreault and Valdivia, "Hydrocarbons"; Sawyer, *Crude Chronicles*; Shever, *Resources for Reform*; Watts, "Resource Curse?"

106 Most seminally, see Castañeda, "Latin America's Left Turn," but see also Flores-Macías, "Statist vs. Pro-Market," and Weyland, "The Rise of Latin America's Two Lefts."

107 For reflections on ethnographic approaches to the study of politics and power, see Auyero and Joseph, "Introduction"; Comaroff and Comaroff, "Ethnography on an Awkward Scale"; Ferguson and Gupta, "Spatializing States"; Glaeser, "An Ontology for the Ethnographic Analysis of Social Processes"; Schatz (ed.), *Political Ethnography*; Wedeen, "Reflections on Ethnographic Work in Political Science."

Chapter 1: From *Neoliberalismo* to *Extractivismo*

1   Interview with the author, July 12, 2010.

2   As described in more detail below, in the 1960s and 1970s, military governments made tracts of land in the Amazon available to migrants from the highlands for human settlement and agriculture colonization. From the perspective of preexisting indigenous communities, this wave of colonization threatened their territorial autonomy, and led to conflicts between Amazonian indigenous groups and *colonos* (some of whom were members of highland indigenous communities).

3   Interview with the author, July 20, 2010.

4   *Buen vivir*, a central concept in the 2008 Constitution and the government's development plan discussed below, recurred frequently in both the critical discourse of *extractivismo* as well as the justification of development policy on the part of state actors. For further reading, see Caria and Dominguez, "Ecuador's Buen Vivir"; Escobar, "Latin America at a Crossroads"; Svampa, "Commodities Consensus."

5   Chavez, "El estado del debate," 10. For a more multidimensional definition, see Albuja and Dávalos, "Extractivismo y posneoliberalismo," 84–5. For a longer discussion of approaches to defining extractivism, see the Introduction.

6   Foucault, "Nietzsche, Genealogy, History," 147.

7   For a discussion of my approach to analyzing critique as a material and historically situated practice, see the Introduction.

8   Silva, *Challenging Neoliberalism*, 147–94; Yashar, *Contesting Citizenship in Latin America*, 144–51.

9   Becker, *Indians and Leftists in the Making of Ecuador's Modern Indigenous Movements*, 17–76.

10   Becker, *Indians and Leftists*, 77–104; Yashar, *Contesting Citizenship*, 101–2.

11   Becker, *Indians and Leftists*, 96. There is a historiographical debate over the degree to which the FEI represented the "imposition" of class identity over ethnic identity (see Yashar, note 10), but Becker presents compelling archival documentation of the use of ethnic discourse among FEI leaders and members, although the relative weight of class and ethnic identification shifted over time in response to determinate circumstances, and the FEI was ultimately unable to survive the turn toward indigeneity. It was, in some senses, the victim of its own success.

12   Following scholarly practice, I refer to it as the *Ley de comunas* for short. Becker, *Indians and Leftists*, 50–72; Colloredo-Mansfeld, *Fighting Like a Community*, 17; Lucero "Locating the 'Indian Problem,'" 27–31; Yashar, *Contesting Citizenship*, 88–90.

13   As Clark discusses, the 1918 reform, among others, was a product of liberal, coastal elites' ongoing attempt to attract labor to export-oriented cocoa production. See Clark, "Ecuadorian Indians, the Nation, and Class in Historical Perspective." From their perspective, highland elites used extra-economic means to keep laborers on their haciendas, who would otherwise migrate if they could (Clark, "Ecuadorian Indians," 55–6). For discussion of the 1964 law, see Becker, *Indians and Leftists*, 137–9; Yashar, *Contesting Citizenship*, 92–7. Both authors agree that the total amount redistributed was quite small, and that the more important legacy of this law was the elimination of the *huasipungo* system.

14   It is worth noting that the extent of redistribution was limited by the reaction of landed elites (Martz, *Politics and Petroleum*, 119–22). Rodríguez Lara's oil policies are discussed in more detail below, as well as in the Introduction. After Rodríguez Lara resigned and was replaced by a different military junta (1976–1979), Ecuador underwent transition from a military dictatorship to a democratic regime.

15   Colloredo-Mansfeld, *Fighting Like a Community*, 17–19; Lucero, "Locating the 'Indian Problem,'" 27–9; Yashar, *Contesting Citizenship*, 90–91. For a discussion of

similar unintended reappropriation of official legal categories by indigenous actors in Bolivia, see Gotkowitz, "Under the Dominion of the Indian."

16   Becker, *Indians and Leftists*, 72, 147.

17   Clark, "Ecuadorian Indians," 60. See also Becker, *Indians and Leftists*, 145–6.

18   Kichwa is an indigenous language spoken in Ecuador, Colombia, and parts of Peru. Kichwa belongs to the broader Quechua language family. For the history of Ecuarunari, see Fontaine, *El precio del petróleo*, 208–10; Yashar, *Contesting Citizenship*, 102–6.

19   Yashar, *Contesting Citizenship*, 113.

20   The Rodríguez Lara government's policies are described at more length in the Introduction.

21   According to Sawyer, by 1992, OPIP "represented the majority of indigenous peoples of Pastaza and was arguably the most active indigenous organization in lowland Ecuador" (Sawyer, *Crude Chronicles*, 43).

22   Fontaine, *El precio del petróleo*; Sawyer, *Crude Chronicles*, 43.

23   Leaders from both organizations formed a national organization in 1980, which was subsequently replaced by CONAIE (Yashar, *Contesting Citizenship*, 130–3). In addition, CONAIE soon encompassed three regional federations, the third being the coastal organization CONAICE (Coordinadora de Organizaciones Indígenas y Negras de la Costa Ecuatoriana), which CONAIE played a role in establishing (Yashar, *Contesting Citizenship*, 87).

24   I say initial because, after peaking in the mid- to late 1990s, CONAIE's political capacity subsequently declined, though not monotonically (as described below).

25   For a discussion of internal decision-making structures, see Colloredo-Mansfeld, *Fighting Like a Community*. For an in-depth analysis of Ecuarunari's communicational infrastructure (which is arguably more developed and effective than that of CONAIE as a whole), see Green-Barber, "The Ecuadorian State and ICTs."

26   For discussion of CONAIE's coalition work, see Silva, *Challenging Neoliberalism*, 158–61; Yashar, *Contesting Citizenship*, 85–154.

27   Becker, *Indians and Leftists*, 170–75; Bowen, "Multicultural Market Democracy"; Clark, "Ecuadorian Indians."

28   This was the first demand of their "16 points" presented in the 1990 uprising. "Los 16 puntos" (https://www.yachana.org/earchivo/conaie/hoy.php, accessed September 25, 2017). See also CONAIE, "Proyecto político de la CONAIE"; CONAIE, "Proyecto de constitución del estado plurinacional del Ecuador"; and Sawyer, *Crude Chronicles*, 83–4. As an ideology, *mestizaje* refers to the valorization of ethno-racial intermixing between populations of European, indigenous, and African descent to produce a homogeneous, if multi-lineal, national race. Since this ideology promotes linguistic and cultural assimilationism, and justifies the ethno-racial superiority of *mestizos* at the same time that it denies the existence of racial hierarchy, it has been an object of critique on the part of indigenous and Afro-descendent social movements.

29   Lucero, "Locating the 'Indian Problem,'" 32.

30   For the Marxist roots of the concept of indigenous nationality, see Lucero, "Locating the 'Indian Problem,'" 34; Becker, *Indians and Leftists*, 81, 173–4. For the

internal organizational dynamics, see Lucero, "Locating the 'Indian Problem,'" 32–40. It is worth noting that Marxist analysis of "the nationalities problem" in fact predates the Russian Revolution and can be traced to the writings of Austro-Marxists Karl Renner and Otto Bauer. See Löwy, "Marxists and the National Question."

31 The differences between the two regions became particularly acute during the restructuring of the ministry-level agency of indigenous affairs in 1998 under President Jamil Mahuad (1998–2000), and the twin notions of *"pueblo"* and *"nacionalidad"* managed to roughly equalize representation on the ministry's executive board (Lucero, "Locating the 'Indian Problem,'" 32–40).

32 In comparison to the indigenous organizations it succeeded, or with which it competed and/or allied (Lucero, "Locating the 'Indian Problem,'" 32, 34).

33 Sawyer, *Crude Chronicles*; Yashar, *Contesting Citizenship*, 109–30.

34 Yashar, *Contesting Citizenship*, 132.

35 "Los 16 puntos."

36 That "land" refers to land being granted to highland indigenous communities and "territories" to the legal recognition of the land as Amazonian indigenous territory is implied, not explicit. The demand reads, *Entrega de tierras y legalización de territorial de las nacionalidades.*

37 These demands had been articulated during CONAIE's Fifth National Congress, in Pujilí, Cotopaxi, in April 1990. For the full list see, "Pliego de reivindicaciones" (http://www.yachana.org/earchivo/conaie/pujili.php, accessed January 11, 2019).

38 Silva, *Challenging Neoliberalism*, 158–61; Yashar, *Contesting Citizenship*, 85–154.

39 For a similar treatment of *neoliberalismo* that attends to its specific emic resonances in the form of locally situated critique, see Shever, *Resources for Reform*, 11.

40 For a canonical definition of neoliberalism, see Harvey, *Neoliberalism*, 2. For useful overviews of the range of definitional approaches I refer to, see Ferguson, "The Uses of Neoliberalism" and Flew, "Six Theories of Neoliberalism." Finally, for two examples of the last approach I mention (a focus on social relations and subjectivities), both in the context of Argentina, see Gago, *Neoliberalism from Below*; Shever, *Resources for Reform*.

41 Bowen, "Multicultural Market Democracy," 455; Conaghan, Malloy, and Abugattas, "Business and the 'Boys,'" 15; Hey and Klak, "From Protectionism to Neoliberalism," 68.

42 CONAIE, "Proyecto político"; Silva, *Challenging Neoliberalism*, 161–88.

43 For additional scholarship on resource nationalism in Ecuador, see Silva, *Challenging Neoliberalism*, 158–61; Slack, "Digging Out from Neoliberalism"; Valdivia, "Governing Relations between People and Things." For similar framings of Bolivian resource politics, see Albro, "The Water Is Ours, Carajo!"; Kohl and Farthing, "Material Constraints"; Perreault, "Assessing the Limits of Neoliberal Environmental Governance in Bolivia."

44 Hurtado had served as vice-president to President Jaime Roldós and succeeded him after Roldós died in a plane accident in May 1981.

45 Brogan, "The Retreat from Oil Nationalism in Ecuador," 29–30; Hey and Klak, "From Protectionism to Neoliberalism," 70–71.

46 Brogan, "Retreat from Oil Nationalism," 29–31.

47 Brogan, "Retreat from Oil Nationalism," 30–33.

48 Brogan, "Retreat from Oil Nationalism," 30–33; Hey and Klak, "From Protectionism to Neoliberalism," 71.

49 Sawyer, *Crude Chronicles*, 27–46, 81–105. According to Sawyer, by 1992, OPIP "was arguably the most active indigenous organization in lowland Ecuador" (*Crude Chronicles*, 43).

50 The Borja administration partially met OPIP's demands: it recognized 55 percent of the land they claimed, granting land titles to indigenous communities. But, this land was not subdivided following OPIP's understandings of nationality and traditional use, but rather using the logic of the 1937 *Ley de comunas*, which resulted in nineteen blocs that did not correspond to existing patterns of land use. Furthermore, *colonos* retained their property rights and the state its claim over subsoil (oil) resources. See Sawyer, *Crude Chronicles*, 50–52; Yashar, *Contesting Citizenship*, 126–8.

51 Sawyer, *Crude Chronicles*, 81.

52 Sawyer, *Crude Chronicles*, 97–8.

53 Alier, "El ecologismo popular."

54 Polanyi, *The Great Transformation*, 136–8; Silva, "Exchange Rising?"

55 The administration lacked the congressional support for reforms such as financial sector liberalization and major privatizations (Hey and Klak, "From Protectionism to Neoliberalism," 80; Silva, *Challenging Neoliberalism*, 161–3). On the labor movement in Ecuador, see Spronk and León Trujillo, "Socialism without Workers?," 132–3.

56 Silva, *Challenging Neoliberalism*, 161–3; Hey and Klak, "From Protectionism to Neoliberalism," 80.

57 Labor unions had protested neoliberal policies from the early 1980s, with political strikes and work stoppages (peaking at 167 in 1989). They were, however, unable to stop the onslaught of neoliberal restructuring and were increasingly met with state repression. Hey and Klack, "From Protectionism to Neoliberalism," 72, 88; Spronk and León Trujillo, "Socialism without Workers?," 137–40.

58 Quoted in Silva, *Challenging Neoliberalism*, 164.

59 Fontaine, *Petróleo y desarrollo sostenible en Ecuador*, 101; Sawyer, *Crude Chronicles*, 95–6.

60 Silva, *Challenging Neoliberalism*, 165–7; Sawyer, *Crude Chronicles*, 149–50.

61 CONAIE, "Proyecto político."

62 CONAIE, "Proyecto político," 1.

63 For the term "social bloc of the oppressed," see Dussel, *Twenty Theses on Politics*, 75–7. See also Collins, "New Left Experiences in Bolivia and Ecuador and the Challenge to Theories of Populism," 72–4; Sawyer, *Crude Chronicles*, 158, 165–7, 175.

64 Sawyer, *Crude Chronicles*, 168.

65 Sawyer, *Crude Chronicles*, 170.

66 Sawyer, *Crude Chronicles*, 1, 30, 54. This platform reappeared in CONAIE's 1997 constitutional proposal, which stipulated that "nonrenewable resources" would be exclusively owned and managed by the state (CONAIE, "Proyecto de constitución," art. 129–30).

67 Andolina, "The Sovereign and Its Shadow," 730–31.

68 Andolina, "Sovereign," 736.

69 These rights included, inter alia, the right to prior consultation, discussed in Chapters 3 and 4.

70 Bowen, "Multicultural Market Democracy," 466–7. I should note that his category of "multicultural market democracy" is meant to comprise a hegemonic strain of Ecuadorian elite discourse from roughly 1990 up to and including the Correa administration. I argue here that there have been significant changes in official discourses under the Correa government (discussed at more length in Chapter 2).

71 Bowen, "Multicultural Market Democracy," 455.

72 Silva, *Challenging Neoliberalism*, 190.

73 Chuji, Berraondo, and Dávalos, *Derechos colectivos de los pueblos y nacionalidades*, 62.

74 Chuji, Berraondo, and Dávalos, *Derechos colectivos*, 62; Conaghan, "Correa's Plebiscitary Presidency," 49; Ramírez Gallegos, "Fragmentación, reflujo y desconcierto," 27–9.

75 Ramírez Gallegos, "Fragmentación," 27–9.

76 Widener, "Global Links and Environmental Flows," 36–7, 40–42. There were also protests along other points of the pipeline's route.

77 Perreault and Valdivia, "Hydrocarbons," 693–4.

78 Valdivia, "Governing Relations," 467.

79 Interview with the author, June 14, 2016.

80 The observation that privatization was rhetorically framed as the corporate colonization of the body is indebted to conversations with Laura Finch.

81 Valdivia, "Governing Relations," 467. See also "Apoyo y solidaridad con los petroleros de Ecuador," July 12, 2003 (http://www.nodo50.org/derechosparatodos/Areas/AreaEcuador13.htm).

82 Perreault and Valdivia, "Hydrocarbons," 694.

83 "Poder y crudo dividen a Confeniae," *Hoy*, January 10, 2005.

84 "El petróleo 'rompe' a la Confeniae," *Hoy*, January 10, 2005.

85 "El petróleo 'rompe' a la Confeniae," *Hoy*, January 10, 2005.

86 "El petróleo 'rompe' a la Confeniae," *Hoy*, January 10, 2005.

87 "Los Shuar se declaran en emergencia antipetrolera," *El Comercio*, April 21, 2005.

88 Comité de Paro, "Boletin de prensa: contra las empresas petroleras paro biprovincial Sucumbíos y Orellana," August 16, 2005 (http://ecuador.indymedia.org/es/2005/08/10810.shtml).

89 Tai-Heng Cheng and Lucas Bento, "ICSID's Largest Award in History: An Overview of Occidental Petroleum Corporation v the Republic of Ecuador," Kluwer Arbitration Blog, December 19, 2012 (http://kluwerarbitrationblog.com

/2012/12/19/icsids-largest-award-in-history-an-overview-of-occidental-petroleum
-corporation-v-the-republic-of-ecuador/).

90   The strike resulted in $570 million in economic losses, $300 millions of which
      would have been state revenues. President Palacio declared a state of siege
      on August 17; confrontations with the military resulted in one death and
      at least 11 injuries. "570 milliones de pérdidas por paro Amazónico," *Ecuador
      Inmediato*, August 19, 2005 (http://ecuadorinmediato.com/index.php?module
      =Noticias&func=news_user_view&id=19156&umt=570_millones_perdidas_por
      _paro_amazonico); "Ecuador: An Oil Strike's Present and Future Consequences,"
      Stratfor, August 23, 2005 (https://www.stratfor.com/analysis/ecuador-oil-strikes
      -present-and-future-consequences).

91   Valdivia, "Governing Relations," 465.

92   Comité de Paro, "Boletin de prensa."

93   Comité de Paro, "Boletin de prensa."

94   As discussed below, the Occidental contract was terminated in May 2006.

95   "Un 12 de octubre contra las petroleras y el TLC," *El Comercio*, October 13, 2005;
      "Movilizaciones en america latina en el 12 de octubre," *Indymedia Ecuador*, Octo-
      ber 12, 2005, accessed January 11, 2019 (https://www.nadir.org/nadir/initiativ
      /agp/free/imf/ecuador/txt/2005/1012movilizaciones.htm); "12 de octubre 2005: Un
      repudio atravesó América," October 3, 2005 (http://cuasran.blogspot.com/2007/10
      /12-de-octubre-2005-un-repudio-atraves.html 3/10/07).

96   "Fuera Oxy y No el TLC Ecuador: marchas por la constituyente y nacionalización
      de petróleo," *Minga Informativa*, October 12, 2005 (http://movimientos.org/node
      /5496?key=5496).

97   "Fuera Oxy y No el TLC Ecuador," *Minga Informativa*, October 12, 2005.

98   Frente Patriótico por la Soberanía Petrolera (http://soberaniapetrolera.blogspot
      .com/).

99   "Movilización amazónica en Quito contra Oxy y el TLC," *El Universo*, May 8,
      2006; "Pachakutik se une a las marchas contra la Oxy," *El Universo*, May 9,
      2006.

100   Occidental pursued legal action against Ecuador via the International Center for
      Settlement of Investment Disputes (ICSID). In 2012 the ICSID ruled that Ecuador
      pay Occidental $1.77 billion in damages; Ecuador negotiated the amount down
      to $1 billion. See "Ecuador to pay $980 million to Occidental for asset seizure,"
      Reuters, January 13, 2006 (http://www.reuters.com/article/ecuador-occidental
      -idUSL2N14X0U420160113).

101   "Pachakutik va en alianza: Rafael Correa es su primera opción," *El Comercio*,
      April 29, 2006; "Pachakutik no logra consenso para definir candidature," *El
      Universo*, April 29, 2006; "Vientos de division soplan en Pachakutik," *El Comercio*,
      May 4, 2006; "Ecuarunari tendra su candidato," *El Comercio*, May 21, 2006; "La
      Ecuarunari irá con un candidato propio a comicios," *El Universo*, May 22, 2006.

102   "Ecuarunari condiciona a Correa para alianza," *El Universo*, May 23, 2006; "Pacha-
      kutik propone la 'Vice' a Correa," *El Comercio*, June 17, 2006.

103   "Rafael Correa dice no a las primarias," *El Comercio*, June 15, 2006.

104 Luis Macas came in seventh out of thirteen candidates, with just over 2 percent of the vote.

105 In addition, the administration promoted new oil projects in the untapped reserves of the southern Amazon.

106 For a longer discussion of the 2007–2008 Constituent Assembly and the 2008 Constitution, see Chapter 3.

107 Assembly President Alberto Acosta (AP) had a history of critically analyzing resource extraction. He co-edited a volume with Esperanza Martínez (a founder of Acción Ecológia), critiquing oil-dependency and envisioning a "post-oil" future: *Ecuador Post-Petrolero*. A month before the assembly finished its work, he resigned from the administration and became a key intellectual and political ally of anti-extractive activists.

108 Asamblea Constituyente, Acta 37 (April 18, 2008), pp. 13, 40. For more discussion of this framing of neoliberalism by state actors in the Correa administration, see Chapters 2 and 5.

109 Asamblea Constituyente, Acta 37, pp. 23–5. See also the intervention of Diana Acosta, pp. 29–34.

110 The Mining Mandate was a legislative act; the Constituent Assembly had "full powers."

111 Constituent Mandate Number Six, art. 1–5.

112 Constituent Mandate Number Six, art. 6, 8, 11.

113 It is worth noting that although absent from public political debate, this position on extraction would subsequently resurface in my interviews with some bureaucrats (between 2010 and 2016). I refer to bureaucrats who are critical of but not opposed to mining and new oil extraction as "critical bureaucrats," actors which I discuss at more length in Chapters 2 and 5.

114 "Sobre el mandato minero," Acción Ecológica, April 2, 2008 (https://www.alainet .org/es/active/23237).

115 Ironically redeploying Correa's pronouncement that he would transcend "the long night of neoliberalism" (Correa, "Discurso del Presidente Rafel Correa al presentar la comisión del CONESUP para codificar la propuesta para la Asamblea Constituyente," speech delivered in Quito, February 28. https://www.presidencia .gob.ec/wp-content/uploads/downloads/2012/10/28-02-07Discurso_codificar _propuesta_para_Asamblea.pdf.).

116 CONAIE, "Resoluciones de la Asamblea Extraordinaria de Las Nacionalidades y Pueblos Indígenas del Ecuador."

117 Asamblea Constituyente, Acta 37, p. 50.

118 It is worth pointing out that at the time of this statement there were no large-scale mines in operation in Ecuador, although projects in the exploration phase had provoked protest, along with violent repression from state and corporate actors. See Cyril Mychalejko, "Canadian Mining Project in Ecuador Tainted by Human Rights Abuses," *Upside Down World*, September 25, 2006 (http:// upsidedownworld.org/archives/ecuador/canadian-mining-project-in-ecuador -tainted-by-human-rights-abuses/).

119 Asamblea Constituyente, Acta 37, p. 56.

120 Asamblea Constituyente, Acta 40 (April 29, 2008), p. 11.

121 Asamblea Constituyente, Acta 40, pp. 12, 16. *Extractivismo* discourse also circulated via the roundtable meeting "Hydrocarbons, Mining and Sustainable Development," featuring Uruguayan researcher Eduardo Gudynas, a key architect of the concept, and public fora such as "Mining and the Extractive Model." Informe de Actividades, March 25, 2008, memo no. 14-MCH-ANC-2008; Caprio to Chuji (correspondence), March 20, 2008. For Gudynas's work, see the Bibliography.

122 "Ecuador: 20 de enero, Movilización Nacional por Agua, Tierra, Vida y Soberanía Alimentaria," *Servindi*, January 8, 2009 (https://www.servindi.org/node/38246).

123 *Enlace ciudadano* no. 103, January 10, 2009.

124 "Congresillo aprobó la nueva Ley Minera," *Hoy*, January 13, 2009.

125 "Protesta contra ley minera deja 6 policías heridos en Ecuador," *El Economista*, January 20, 2009 (http://eleconomista.com.mx/internacional/2009/01/20/protesta-contra-ley-minera-deja-6-policias-heridos-ecuador); "Ecuador: gran movilización nacional contra la ley minera. Represión y al menos 11 detenidos," *Indymedia Ecuador*, January 21, 2009 (http://www.lahaine.org/index.php?p=189); "Movilización antiminera, Ecuador, 20 de Enero 2009," *Abya Yala*, January 20, 2009 (http://www.abyayalacolectivo.com/web/compartir/noticia/movilizacion-antiminera-ecuador-20-de-enero-2009); and Jennifer Moore, "Ecuador: Mining Protests Marginalized, but Growing," *Upside Down World*, January 21, 2009 (http://upsidedownworld.org/main/content/view/1673/1/).

126 For a longer discussion of the law's alleged violation of the Constitution, and the 2010 court case regarding its constitutionality, see Chapter 3.

127 Ecuarunari, "Movilización por defensa de la vida y la Pachamama," press release, January 20, 2009 (http://www.llacta.org/organiz/coms/2009/com0011.htm).

128 For example, CONAIE, "El consejo de gobierno de CONAIE evaluó como positiva la jornada de movilizaciones en el país," press release, January 21, 2009 (http://www.llacta.org/organiz/coms/2009/com0017.htm).

129 Both UNAGUA and Acción Ecológica were parties to the case, further cementing the anti-extractive coalition.

130 Thea Riofrancos, "Ecuador: Indigenous Confederation Inaugurates New President and Announces National Mobilization," *Upside Down World*, February 6, 2008 (http://upsidedownworld.org/main/ecuador-archives-49/1120-ecuador-indigenous-confederation-inaugurates-new-president-and-announces-national-mobilization).

131 "Dirección bajo 4 Amazonicos," *Hoy*, November 14, 2004.

132 The oil concession was originally granted in 1996. The Sarayaku first brought their case before the court in 2003, alleging the failure of the Ecuadorian state to consult them prior to exploration of their territory by the oil company CGC. In July 2012, the Inter-American Court of Human Rights ruled in favor of the Sarayaku.

133 Also important was the Water Law in May 2010, in which CONAIE claimed victory when the legislature was forced to shelve the bill as a direct result of their

mobilization. "Indígenas de Ecuador proclaman 'victoria' ante no aprobación de Ley de Recursos Hidrícos," *El Tiempo*, May 13, 2010 (http://www.eltiempo.com /archivo/documento/CMS-7708489).

134 Interview with the author, November 28, 2011.

Chapter 2: *Extractivismo* as Grand Narrative of Resistance

1 Latour, *Reassembling the Social*, 22.

2 As explained by Edgar Isch at the Second Social Forum on Mining in Cuenca, March 1, 2012. As discussed in Chapter 1, Isch served as Gutiérrez's minister of environment, and was a participant in the 2006 "Oil and Sovereignty" meeting.

3 Gudynas and Acosta distinguish between "traditional" and "neo-" extractivism, increasing analytic precision but forsaking the concept's compelling simplicity (Gudynas, "Si eres tan progresista"; Alberto Acosta, interview with the author, December 2, 2011).

4 Albuja and Dávalos, "Extractivismo y posneoliberalismo," 89–98.

5 The marchers that I spoke with viewed the timing of the contract as an intentional decision on the part of the Correa administration to present mining as a fait accompli to the public, and thus blunt the march's political impact.

6 "Súmate a esta convocatoria," Minería Muerte, February 6, 2012 (https:// mineriamuerte.wordpress.com/).

7 The first example is discussed in Chapter 4; the last example is discussed in Chapter 3.

8 For the term bureaucratic field, see Bourdieu, "Rethinking the State."

9 Schmidt, "Discursive Institutionalism," 14. For further discussion of how language (and semiotic activity more broadly) gives humans the capacity to hold action at a distance, to reflect and intervene, see Glaeser, *Political Epistemics*, 12–13.

10 Ferguson, *Anti-Politics Machine*, 28, 74. See also Li, "Beyond 'the State' and Failed Schemes," 386.

11 Foucault, *Security, Territory, Population*, 356–7.

12 For a longer discussion of the social science literature on resource extraction, see the Introduction.

13 For a critique of this understanding of neoliberalism, see Dávalos, "Extractivismo y teoría de las instituciones" and Gago, "Financialization of Popular Life and the Extractive Operations of Capital."

14 Interview with the author, January 27, 2012.

15 For these more critical understandings of neoliberalism, see Chapter 1, n. 40. For analyses of the ways in which neoliberal policies have been accompanied by an augmentation of state power, especially in its repressive or carceral capacity, see Camp, *Incarcerating the Crisis*, and Wacquant, *Punishing the Poor*. For the argument that neoliberalism redeploys rather than reduces state power, see Slobodian, *Globalists*.

16 Interview with the author, September 22, 2011.

17 SENPLADES, "El plan nacional de buen vivir 2009–2013."

18   SENPLADES, "Plan nacional," 31.

19   I return to the influence of dependency theory on both anti-extractive activists and the Correa government in the Conclusion.

20   SENPLADES, "Plan nacional," 95–7.

21   Interview with the author, May 9, 2012.

22   For the canonical analysis of the enclave form, see Cardoso and Falleto, *Dependency and Development in Latin America*, 69–73.

23   Interviews with the author, December 1, 2011, and April 4, 2012, respectively.

24   Interview with the author, December 1, 2011.

25   Interview with the author, January 24, 2012.

26   Interview with the author, July 10, 2012.

27   Correa, interview, Gama TV [state-owned TV station], "De Frente," hosted by Jorge Gestoso, June 27, 2012. The implied characterization of anti-extractive activists as irrational is discussed at length in Chapter 5.

28   Ministerio de Recursos Norenovables. "Plan nacional de desarrollo del sector minero, 2011–2015."

29   "Consulta previa a la comunidad no es sinónimo de consulta popular," *El Comercio*, April 8, 2012 (http://elcomercio.com/politica/Consulta-comunidad-sinonimo -consulta-popular_0_677932294.html).

30   Correa, "Ecuador's Path," 95.

31   I reflect upon this challenge at more length in the Conclusion.

32   Correa, *Enlace ciudadano* (Saturday address) no. 351, Zámbiza, December 7, 2013.

33   Álvaro García Linera, "Geopolitics of the Amazon: Landed-Hereditary Power and Capitalist Accumulation."

34   The main difference is that, unlike Correa, García Linera considers himself an anti-capitalist. He thus argues that overcoming extractivism is insufficient to overcome capitalism, and that a future, noncapitalist society would necessarily involve some form of resource extraction. Although he recognizes the detrimental effects of resource dependency, especially as a position in the world system, his analysis instead centers on the capitalist model of accumulation.

35   See Correa, *Enlace ciudadano* no. 294, October 20, 2012.

36   As García Linera puts it: "While in the first world countries NGOs exist as part of civil society—in most cases funded by transnational enterprises—in the third world, as in the case of Bolivia, various NGOs are not really NON Governmental Organizations but Organizations of Other Governments on Bolivian territory; they are a replacement for the state in the areas in which the neoliberalism of the past initiated its exit . . . In fact, some NGOs in the country have been the vehicle for introducing a type of colonial environmentalism that relegates the indigenous peoples to the role of caretakers of the Amazon jungle (considered extraterritorial property of foreign governments and corporations), creating de facto a new relationship of privatization and alienation of the national parks and Communitarian Lands (TCOs) over which the state itself has lost custody and control" (García Linera, "Geopolitics," 9–10).

37   Cited in García Linera, "Geopolitics," 38–44.

38 I heard this modified version in an interview with Carlos Alberto Cordova, representative of Lowell Mining Corporation in the office of Community Relations (June 28, 2012), as well as during a pro-mining event at the University of Azuay (May 15, 2012).

39 It also reanimated a conservative elite discourse that was particularly salient during the 1990s, which accused the then ascendant CONAIE of cultural "inauthenticity" due to its foreign alliances. See Bowen, "Multicultural Market Democracy," 472–3, 481.

40 The ministry relied on Article 26 of Executive Decree 16, June 2013, which states that among the reasons for the dissolution of an NGO are its "Deviation from the ends and objectives for which it was constituted" and "interference in public policies that threatens the internal or external security of the state, or that affects public peace" ("Ministerio del Ambiente disolvió ONG por actos vandálicos," *El Ciudadano*, December 4, 2013). For Acción Ecológica, see "Acción Ecológica rechaza disolución," *El Universo*, December 22, 2016. For the 2009 and 2016 cases of Acción Ecológica, see Daniel Denvir, "Ecuadorian Government Shuts Down Leading Environmental Group," *Grist*, March 17, 2009 (https://grist.org/article /ecuadorian-government-shuts-down-leading/); "Acción Ecológica Finally Regained its Legal Status," Acción Ecológica, September 7, 2009 (http://www .accionecologica.org/boletines-de-prensa-sobre-la-clausura/1162-accion-ecologica -finally-regained-its-legal-status); "Ecuador Moves to Close Leading Environmental Organization as Part of Crackdown on Civil Society," Amazon Watch, press release, December 21, 2016 (https://amazonwatch.org/news/2016/1221-ecuador -moves-to-close-leading-environmental-organization-as-part-of-crackdown-on -civil-society).

41 For the case of Fundación Pachamama, see "Ecuador cierra una ONG que respaldaba la lucha antipetrolera en el Amazonas," *El País*, December 11, 2013; "Ecuador: Rights Group Shut Down," Human Rights Watch, December 6, 2013 (https://www.hrw.org/news/2013/12/06/ecuador-rights-group-shut-down).

42 "Los 'ideólogos' de Pachamama son estadounidenses," *El Telégrafo*, December 17, 2013.

43 "El Código Penal tipifica nuevos delitos politicos," *El Comercio*, September 3, 2013 (http://www.elcomercio.com/actualidad/codigo-penal-tipifica-nuevos-delitos .html); "Ecuador: Authorities Misuse Judicial System to Stop Protests," Amnesty International, July 17, 2012 (http://www.amnesty.org/en/news/ecuador-authorities -misuse-judicial-system-stop-protests-2012-07-17).

44 I return to this incident in the Conclusion. See Carmen Martínez Novo, "La minería amenaza a los indígenas shuar en Ecuador," *New York Times*, March 27, 2017 (https://www.nytimes.com/es/2017/03/27/la-mineria-amenaza-a-los-indigenas -shuar-en-ecuador/?smid=fb-share-es); Verónica Calvopiña, "¿Qué le hemos hecho presidente Correa? Mujeres shuar rompen el cerco del Estado de excepción en Ecuador," *Des Informemonos*, February 23, 2017 (https://desinformemonos.org /le-hecho-presidente-correa-mujeres-shuar-rompen-cerco-del-estado-excepcion -ecuador/).

45 See the YASunídos website (http://sitio.yasunidos.org/es/) (see http://sitio
    .yasunidos.org/en for English-language version, accessed January 12, 2019).
46 YASunídos collected 756,291 signatures for a national referendum on whether
    to extract oil in the park. The National Electoral Commission controversially
    rejected the petition. See John Vidal, "Yasuni Campaigners Claim Oil Drilling
    Petition Results Are Being Manipulated," *Guardian*, April 30, 2014 (http://www
    .theguardian.com/environment/2014/apr/30/yasuni-campaigners-oil-drilling
    -petition-results-referendum.

Chapter 3: *Consulta Previa*

1 For an analysis of constitutions (including Ecuador's 2008 Constitution) as open-
   ended, unfinished, and uncertain texts, see Bernal, *Beyond Origins*.
2 For the phrase "language of contention," see Roseberry, "Hegemony and the
   Language of Contention."
3 Kalyvas, "Popular Sovereignty, Democracy, and the Constituent Power," 238.
   Although Kalyvas interprets "civil disobedience, irregular and informal movements, insurgencies, and revolutionary upheavals" as enactments of "the irreducible outside" of constituent power (230), he also emphasizes the "extraordinary
   and exceptional" nature of constitution-making (237). I agree that formal processes of constitution-making are rare events that puncture the institutionalized
   rhythm of everyday politics (although, perhaps relatively less rare in Ecuador,
   which has been governed under four distinct constitutions over the past fifty
   years). As Jason Frank points out, however, the focus on "epochal constitutional
   shifts" neglects the myriad "small dramas of [democratic] self-authorization" that
   unfold in "the informal political contexts of crowd actions, political oratory, and
   literature" (*Constituent Moments*, 33). Similarly, I would argue that analytically
   limiting the assertion of constituent power to "exceptional" moments obscures
   the ongoing political work required to render a constitutional text relevant to
   political life—work which, in this case, was undertaken by popular movements in
   their battle with state authorities. For another critique of the division of politics
   into "exceptional" and "normal" moments, see Bernal, *Beyond Origins*, 143–4. And
   for another treatment of protests as more "ordinary" constitutional moments, see
   Zaiden Benvindo, "The Seeds of Change."
4 For a detailed account of Constituent Assembly debates over the rights of nature,
   see Akchurin, "Constructing the Rights of Nature." For an account of the various
   debates that pervaded the assembly, see Bernal, *Beyond Origins*, Chapter 5.
5 I list these collective actors (indigenous, environmental, anti-mining, and anti-oil
   activists, and allied intellectuals) separately despite overlap at the level of individual biography and identity, since there are distinct organizational trajectories
   and political agendas at play (see Chapter 1). Despite these diverse trajectories,
   there was, however, substantial convergence in their interpretation of the
   Constitution.
6 For "constituent power," see Ciccariello-Maher, "Constituent Moments, Constitutional Processes," 126–9; Dussel, *Twenty Theses*, 21–3, 51–2; Kalyvas, "Popular

Sovereignty," 229–30. It is worth noting that CONAIE and other social movement groups who demanded a constituent assembly explicitly framed their demand in the language of constituent power (Bernal, *Beyond Origins*, 149).

7 For the quote "strategies without a strategist," see Foucault, "Politics and the Study of Discourse," 60; Wedeen, *Ambiguities of Domination*, 153. For a longer discussion of the debate over extraction as a social terrain or field, see the Introduction.

8 Constitutional legal scholarship in the vein of popular or political constitutionalism also traces constitutional interpretation outside its official institutional site of the courtroom. For example, see Kramer, *The People Themselves* on the history of the political struggle between popular practices of constitutional interpretation and its professionalization in the form of judicial review in the eighteenth- and nineteenth-century American context. See also Zeisberg, *War Powers* for an account of how branches of government become sites of interpretive activity and develop distinct modes of constitutional interpretation.

9 For constituent power, see n. 6, as well as Bernal, "The Meaning and Perils of Presidential Refounding in Latin America," Cameron and Sharpe, "Andean Left Turns," and Frank, *Constituent Moments*. Note, however, that Frank distinguishes his approach from those that figure constituent power as the irreducible outside of constituted power (*Constituent Moments*, 7–9 and 257, fn. 32). For an emblematic example of the law-and-society approach, see Sarat and Kearn, "Beyond the Great Divide."

10 See Bernal, "Meaning and Perils"; Bernal, *Beyond Origins*, Chapter 5; Cameron and Sharpe, "Andean Left Turns"; Ciccariello-Maher, "Constituent Moments"; Escobar, "Latin America at a Crossroads."

11 Bernal, *Beyond Origins*, 134–8; Perez Ordoñez, "El Presidente Rafael Correa y su política de redención."

12 Some scholars have called this legal regime "post-liberal" for its emphasis on collective rights (and de-emphasizing individual rights); see Arditi, "Arguments"; Wolff, "Towards Post-Liberal Democracy in Latin America?"

13 Scheppele, "Constitutional Ethnography," 391, original emphasis. See also De, *A People's Constitution*.

14 Baxsi, "'Outline of a Theory of Practice' of Indian Constitutionalism," 96–8, 111.

15 Hetherington, *Guerrilla Auditors*.

16 Hetherington, *Guerrilla Auditors*, 90, emphasis added.

17 These events are detailed in Chapter 1.

18 Bernal, "Meaning and Perils"; Chuji, Berraondo, and Dávalos, *Derechos colectivos*; Ramírez Gallegos, "Fragmentación."

19 Andolina, "Sovereign"; Chuji, Berraondo, and Dávalos, *Derechos colectivos*, 55.

20 Namely, as previously discussed, his participation in the *forajido* movement and his brief tenure as minister of the economy, which earned him a reputation as a strong critic of neoliberal policies.

21 The original six-month timeline was extended by two months.

22 Library-Archive of the National Assembly (Archivo-biblioteca de la Asamblea Nacional), Quito, Constituent Assembly (Asamblea Constituyente), Mesa 5, December 7, 2007 to May 20, 2008 (for more information on the archive, see http://www.asambleanacional.gov.ec/archivo-biblioteca.html). For example, Esperanza Martinez, the director of radical environmentalist group Acción Ecológica, acted as an adviser to the Constituent Assembly president, Alberto Acosta.

23 Andolina, "Sovereign"; Chuji, Berraondo, and Dávalos, *Derechos colectivos*, 48; CONAIE, "Proyecto politico," 17–20; Sawyer, *Crude Chronicles*; Yashar, *Contesting Citizenship*, 144–6. See the previous chapter for a more detailed discussion of these political programs.

24 Bernal, "Meaning and Perils."

25 Indeed, one of the explicit aims of Correa's project is to remodel the relationship between state and citizen such that it is no longer mediated by "corporate" actors, a term that comprises both oligarchic political parties and social movement organizations. See Conaghan, "Correa's Plebiscitary Presidency"; Ospina Peralta, "Corporativismo, estado y revolución ciudadana"; Latorre and Santillana, "Capitalismo estatal o convergencias populares."

26 Correa, "Discurso de posesión," speech delivered in Quito, August 10 (https://www.voltairenet.org/article161992.html).

27 On increased taxation, see Bowen, "Rethinking Democratic Governance," 97–8.

28 Constitution of Ecuador, 2008, art. 71–4, 317, 318, 400, 407, 408; see also Bernal, "Meaning and Perils."

29 For an analysis and critique of a state-centric conceptualization of neoliberalism, see Gago, "Financialization."

30 Indigenous and Tribal Peoples Convention (ILO Convention 169), 1989, art. 6, 7, 15. These articles specifically focus on development projects or displacement processes that could negatively impact indigenous peoples' access to or use of their lands and territories.

31 Constitution of Ecuador, 1998, art. 84, 88. For an account of the historical conditions of the inclusion of these rights in the 1998 Constitution and the ratification of ILO Convention 169, which are both closely linked to the rising political power of the indigenous movement as well as the increase in oil-related conflict in the Amazon, see Falleti and Riofrancos, "Endogenous Participation." See also Andolina, "Sovereign," 731–6, 739; CONAIE, "Proyecto político"; Mijeski and Beck, *Pachakutik and the Rise and Decline of the Ecuadorian Indigenous Movement*, 48; Van Cott, "Ecuador Ratifies ILO Convention 169."

32 Before being elected to the Constituent Assembly on the president's party's (Alianza País) ticket, Monica Chuji served as the administration's secretary of communication. A few months after the assembly voted on the final text of the Constitution, she resigned from the administration due to differences on issues such as resource extraction, indigenous rights, and the growing polarization between the party and social movements. Regarding the uneven implementation of *consulta previa* in Ecuador, on July 25, 2012, the Inter-American Court of Human Rights issued its decision on the case of Sarayaku v. Ecuador, ruling in favor of

the Amazonian Kichwa community regarding the Ecuadorian state's failure to consult them prior to the Argentinian company CGC carrying out oil exploration on their territory. The oil concession was originally granted in 1996, and the Sarayaku first brought their case before the court in 2003. See Chavez, "Consulta previa"; Potes, "Al abrigo de los ponchos y las plumas."

33 Library-Archive of the National Assembly (Archivo-biblioteca de la Asamblea Nacional), Quito, Constituent Assembly (Asamblea Constituyente), Plenary debate minutes, April 29, 2008.

34 Plenary debate minutes, April 29, 2008.

35 In his 2009 national address, Correa referred to critics of mining as "fundamentalists" and "infantile environmentalists" who undermined the "common good" (Correa, "Informe a la nación en el inicio del tercer año de Revolución Ciudadana," 5).

36 Andolina, "Sovereign."

37 Andolina, "Sovereign," 740–41.

38 As discussed at length in Chapter 1.

39 Media coverage of the debate—cast in terms of "internal divisions" within the president's party—lends credence to this assertion. For example, the following article discusses multiple meetings between Correa and the committee, with Correa actively intervening in favor of consultation. See "Convicciones ambientalistas dividen a Acuerdo País," La Hora, April 23, 2008 (http://www.lahora.com.ec/index.php/noticias/show/711427/-1/Convicciones_ambientalistas_dividen_a_Acuerdo_Pa%C3%ADs.html#.UQWDvUpU4z5).

40 Library-Archive of the National Assembly (Archivo-biblioteca de la Asamblea Nacional), Quito, Constituent Assembly (Asamblea Constituyente), Mesa 5, Minority report, April 24, 2008.

41 Minority report, April 24, 2008.

42 Library-Archive of the National Assembly (Archivo-biblioteca de la Asamblea Nacional), Quito, Constituent Assembly (Asamblea Constituyente), video, plenary debate, April 29, 2008.

43 Plenary debate minutes, April 29, 2008. It is worth noting that the Partido Sociedad Patriotica is a personalist party formed around the figure of Lucio Gutiérrez, the former president discussed in Chapter 1.

44 Constitution, 2008, art. 57.

45 Chuji, Berraondo, and Dávalos, Derechos colectivos, 128.

46 Constitution, 2008, art. 398.

47 In the case of resource extraction, the relevant authority would be the Ministry of Environment and/or the Ministry of Nonrenewable Resources. Article 398 was eventually addressed in the April 2010 Organic Law of Citizen Participation, but very little new content was added (art. 82, 83). Indeed, it is almost a "literal copy" of the article in the Constitution (Potes, "Al abrigo de los ponchos y las plumas").

48 Constitution, 2008, art. 417.

49 United Nations Declaration on the Rights of Indigenous Peoples (UNDRIP), 2007, art. 19, emphasis added.

5050 Rancière, "Who Is the Subject of the Rights of Man?", 303.

51 It is worth noting that, as activists will point out, the Constitution establishes that all international instruments (a broad term that encompasses treaties, conventions, and declarations) regarding human rights and ratified by Ecuador must be fully respected ("direct applicability") according to the principle of "no restriction of rights" (Constitution, 2008, art. 417). Ratified by Ecuador in 1998, ILO Convention 169 is an international instrument that addresses human rights, and it stipulates "the objective of reaching agreement or consent to the proposed measures" (art. 6.2). Anti-mining activists have interpreted this as a guarantee to prior consent, although the convention does not state that consent is a binding requirement. As discussed above, consent is, however, required by UNDRIP, to which Ecuador is a signatory.

52 The assembly was held on May 13, 2008.

53 CONAIE, "Resoluciones de la Asamblea Extraordinaria."

54 For media coverage at the time, see Marc Becker, "Indigenous Organizations to Support Ecuador's Constitution," *Upside Down World,* July 31, 2008 (http:// upsidedownworld.org/main/ecuador-archives-49/1404-indigenous-organizations -to-support-ecuadors-constitution); "Indígenas de Ecuador apoyan con un sí crítico al proyecto constitucional," *Hoy,* September 4, 2008. For scholarly analysis, see Bernal, *Beyond Origins,* Chapter 5.

55 The term "lawpersons" is from Baxsi, "'Outline of a Theory," 97.

56 "Queremos ser constructores de alternativas. Entrevista a Humberto Cholango, Presidente de la CONAIE," *ALAI,* April 19, 2012 (http://www.alainet.org/active /54175).

57 Delfín Tenesaca, interview with the author, March 7, 2013.

58 A coalition of indigenous, environmental, labor, and other social movement organizations had formed a coalition that nominated Alberto Acosta as their presidential candidate; he received less than 3 percent of the vote, significantly lower than the 8 to 10 percent that had been forecasted. For analysis, see Pablo Ospina Peralta, "Primeras reflexiones sobre una derrota," *La Linea de Fuego,* February 20, 2013 (https://lalineadefuego.info/2013/02/20/primeras-reflexiones -sobre-una-derrota-por-pablo-ospina-peralta/?fbclid=IwAR2p3RxDK2HctBerkM5 RcjBPzwsDLLB6kYpXs3WS0jGXp341ONb5TVda_js).

59 Constitution, 2008, art. 57.17. This chapter does not primarily focus on the right to pre-legislative consultation, though I will discuss it in more length in the next section.

60 Monica Chuji, interview with the author, June 27, 2012.

61 Salvador Quishpe, interview with the author, October 4, 2011.

62 Alicia Granda, interview with the author, September 19, 2011.

63 As stated in the Constitution of Ecuador, 2008, art. 1: *La soberanía radica en el pueblo, cuya voluntad es el fundamento de la autoridad, y se ejerce a través de los órganos del poder público y de las formas de participación directa previstas en la Constitución.*

64 As discussed above, during the assembly debates, Correa held meetings with delegates to advocate for prior consultation over prior consent. This was part

of a pattern of his involvement in the planning, executing, and ratification of the Constituent Assembly and the 2008 Constitution, respectively. See Bernal, *Beyond Origins*, Chapter 5.

65 This point is inspired by Derrida's elaboration of the logic of the supplement, which adds only to replace. See Derrida, *Of Grammatology*.

66 This is particularly notable since *consulta previa* is recognized in the 1998 Constitution, and the 1999 Law of Environmental Management establishes consultation as a mechanism of participation in the same article the decree cites.

67 Rafael Correa, Executive Decree 1040, Quito, April 2008, art. 15.

68 Constitution, 2008, art. 57.7, 398.

69 This order of presentation—the interpretation of official text followed by a demonstration of its circulation in discourse and of its fraught and contentious application in practice—was inspired by Ferguson's analysis of the "discursive-practical apparatus of development" in Lesotho. See Ferguson, *Anti-Politics Machine*.

70 Executive Decree 1040, art. 1.

71 In the case of all large-scale mining projects, "socialization" processes were initiated after the concession had already been granted. While this had been the case for oil as well, in the 2012 round of tenders for new oil projects (that is, formal offerings for potential investors), the government carried out consultations prior to granting rights to companies (using the framework of Executive Decree 1247, July 2012). However, indigenous organizations criticized the consultations for being inadequately substantive. See, "Boletín de prensa CONAIE—CONFENIAE: Indígenas amazónicos se oponen a la XI Ronda Petrolera. No vale la pena y debe suspenderse de inmediato," November 28, 2012 (http://pachamama.org.ec/?p=4603).

72 Executive Decree 1040, art. 1.

73 Executive Decree 1040, art. 4.

74 Executive Decree 1040, art. 9.

75 Executive Decree 1040, art. 19.

76 Executive Decree 1040, art. 22.

77 These protests are discussed in Chapter 1.

78 Mining Law (*Ley Orgánica de Minería*), 2009, art. 83. *Precautelar* literally means to prevent risk or harm.

79 As discussed above, CONAIE articulated a range of demands and critiques of the Correa administration during its May 13, 2008 extraordinary assembly. CONAIE, "Resoluciones de la Asamblea Extraordinaria."

80 The point is stated in CONAIE's demand of unconstitutionality, submitted to the Constitutional Court, Quito, March 17, 2009, pp. 2–3 (for online access, see http://www.environmental-laws.net/Derecho/Documentacion/Demanda-Ley-Mineria-CONAIE.html). The Constitution recognizes the right to pre-legislative consultation in Article 57.17. Specifically, CONAIE claimed that the law affects the collective rights of indigenous peoples because the concessions are located within indigenous territories, and because the law regulates prior consultation, itself a collective right.

81 As discussed above, the 2008 Constitution guarantees the full implementation of all international instruments that expand human rights (art. 417), including UNDRIP, to which Ecuador is a signatory, which stipulates "good faith" consultations with the goal of obtaining consent.

82 I return to the tension between these competing claims to authority in Chapter 4.

83 Indeed, CONAIE's initial petition to the Constitutional Court devotes almost nine of twenty pages to the "Violation of the Right to Territory of Indigenous Nationalities" (CONAIE 2009, 4–14; see n. 80). For more on the concept of "territory" in Amazonian indigenous discourse, see Sawyer, *Crude Chronicles*, 83–4.

84 Mining Law, 2009, art. 28, 87–91, respectively. The argument points out that indigenous communities are only guaranteed consultation upon the granting of a concession: "Following the text of the Mining Law, the Ecuadorian State has the power to . . . concession this same [indigenous] territory to another person or company without the ancestral inhabitants having knowledge nor having been consulted" (CONAIE 2009, 18).

85 As stated in CONAIE's demand of unconstitutionality (CONAIE 2009, 16–17). The Mining Law explicitly excludes several territorial categories from the freedom of prospecting (protected areas, existing mineral concessions, urban areas, towns [*centros poblados*], and archaeological areas), but does not exclude indigenous territories (Mining Law, 2009, art. 25).

86 As I discuss in Chapter 4, in the dispute over *consulta previa*, state officials argued that indigenous and environmental activists have no constitutional authority over resource extraction and that the demand for that authority poses a threat to democracy itself.

87 Constitutional Court (*Corte Constitucional*), sentence no. 001-10-SIN-CC, 10, case nos. 008-09-IN and 011-09-IN, March 18, 2010.

88 Constitutional Court, sentence no. 001-10-SIN-CC, 12, March 18, 2010. According to the documentation that the administration representatives presented to the court, between February and December 2008, indigenous leaders communicated their concerns regarding the yet to be approved Mining Law. On February 22, 2008, two days after the promulgation of the new Constitution, the minister of mining and oil, Alfredo Palacio, presented the Mining Law to the assembly and requested the opinion (via e-mail or in person at the ministry) of government officials and "citizens in general, and among them, Marlon Santi," then president of CONAIE (Constitutional Court, sentence no. 001-10-SIN-CC, 12, March 18, 2010, 34–5).

89 Constitutional Court, sentence no. 001-10-SIN-CC, 12, March 18, 2010, 16.

90 The Court ruled that although the pre-legislative consultation of the Mining Law did not follow the letter of Article 57.17 of the Constitution, which states that the National Assembly (the body with "the legal authority to adopt legislative measures") carries out pre-legislative consultation, it *was* in line with both ILO Convention 169 and Constitutional Article 398 of the Constitution, neither of which specify legislative bodies as the consulting subject. Ultimately, since the

representatives of indigenous communities themselves "decided to participate and present their arguments" before the Committee of Economic Development and Production regarding the alleged unconstitutionality of the law, there was "a clear demonstration of a process of information and participation," and therefore "a direct application of the Constitutional precept . . . that guarantees pre-legislative consultation" (Constitutional Court, sentence no. 001-10-SIN-CC, 12, March 18, 2010, 37).

91 These instructions define, among other aspects of the consultation process, who is to be consulted and by whom, and the sequence of the process (Constitutional Court, sentence no. 001-10-SIN-CC, 12, March 18, 2010, 39–43). Furthermore, they include many mechanisms not carried out for the Mining Law, including some originally demanded in the CONAIE communication the court itself presented as evidence of participation, such as "the installation of a roundtable (*mesa de dialogo*)" made up of indigenous representatives and members of the assembly (42).

92 A canton is a geographic-administrative unit, smaller than a province and larger than a parish.

93 As stated in the report, "depending on whether the question is technical, environmental, social or legal," the consultant, company representatives or authorities present "absolve the concerns raised" (ECSA and Ministry of Environment [*Ministerio del Ambiente*], *Informe de Proceso de Participación Ciudadana del Estudio del Impacto Ambiental del Proyecto Minero Mirador para la Fase de Beneficio*, 15).

94 Potes, "Al abrigo de los ponchos y las plumas."

95 ECSA and Ministry of Environment (*Ministerio del Ambiente*), *Informe de Proceso de Participación Ciudadana del Estudio del Impacto Ambiental del Proyecto Minero Mirador para la Fase de Beneficio*, 21–27.

96 "Ecuador: Piden nulidad para Audiencia minera de ECSA," December 3, 2010, (http://cordilleracondor.wordpress.com/2010/12/03/piden-nulidad-para-audiencia -minera-de-ecsa/); William Sacher, "Socialización del estudio de impacto ambiental de Mirador: la necesidad de un proceso de consulta transparente y democrático," *Boletín ICCI-ARY Rimay*, no. 138, September 2010 (http://icci .nativeweb.org/boletin/138/sacher.html).

97 Diego Arcos, interview with the author, February 8, 2012.

98 Wilton Guaranda Mendoza, interview with the author, September 19, 2011.

99 This debate was held on June 19, 2012.

100 Chapter 5 shows how this technocratic discourse of "information" has circulated widely among state and corporate actors as an explanation *and* solution for mining-related conflict, and that anti-mining activists have articulated their own counter-discourse of information.

101 Federico Auquilla Terán, interview with the author, February 7, 2012.

102 For this formulation of the logic of the supplement, see Derrida, *Of Grammatology*.

103 Esteban Torracchi, interview with the author, June 6, 2012.

104 There are multiple spellings for the parish. I use this version unless I am directly quoting a source with a different spelling.

105 The video was then distributed via YouTube (and e-mail): http://www.youtube .com/watch?v=-wnTCq3SqQg&feature=youtu.be (accessed May 6, 2013).

106 The quote is from an e-mail, subject heading "The 17 Criminalized in Shaglly [*sic*], Ecuador," circulated by various activist groups on December 3, 2012.

107 This is one instance of a common trope, characterizing the protesters as violent and aggressive, contrasted with the peaceful, dialogue-oriented officials. "La próxima vez no salen con vida," *El Ciudadano,* May 5, 2012 (http://www .elciudadano.gov.ec/index.php?option=com_content&view=article&id=32331:la -proxima-vez-no-salen-con-vida&catid=40:actualidad&Itemid=63).

108 These modes of participation are among the permitted "participation mechanisms" listed in Executive Decree 1040, art. 8.

109 Wilton Guaranda Mendoza, interview with the author, September 19, 2011.

110 Alicia Hidalgo, interview with the author, July 25, 2012.

111 Romulo Heredia, interview with the author, May 29, 2012.

112 For a longer discussion of the Mining Mandate, see Chapter 1.

113 Federico Auquilla Terán, interview with the author, February 7, 2012.

114 "En Ecuador sí hubo consulta previa en torno a la explotación minera," *El Ciudadano*, March 23, 2012 (http://www.elciudadano.gov.ec/index.php?option=com _content&view=article&id=31507:en-ecuador-si-hubo-consulta-previa-en-torno-a -la-explotacion-minera&catid=40:actualidad&Itemid=63).

115 "En Ecuador sí hubo consulta previa en torno a la explotación minera," *El Ciudadano*, March 23, 2012.

116 "Consulta previa a la comunidad no es sinónimo de consulta popular," *El Comercio,* April 8, 2012 (http://elcomercio.com/politica/Consulta-comunidad-sinonimo -consulta-popular_0_677932294.html).

117 See the Introduction.

Chapter 4: The *Demos* in Dispute

1 The first documented community consultation took place in Peru in 2002, and communities in Argentina and Mexico have employed consultations as a tool of self-governance and anti-mining resistance. See Costanza, "Indigenous Peoples' Right to Prior Consultation"; McGee, "Community Referendum"; Walter and Urkidi, "Community Mining Consultations in Latin America (2002–2012)."

2 It is also recognized in the UN Declaration of the Rights of Indigenous Peoples, 2007.

3 As described in Chapter 3, during the 2007–2008 Constituent Assembly, delegates debated prior consultation versus prior consent. Consultation (which Correa supported) won. See also Falleti and Riofrancos, "Endogenous Participation."

4 Costanza, "Indigenous Peoples' Right to Prior Consultation," 276–7.

5 Arce, *Resource Extraction*; Walter and Urkidi, "Community Mining Consultations," 270–2, 275.

6 Rodríguez-Garavito, "Ethnicity.Gov," 293–7.

7 Tockman and Cameron, "Indigenous Autonomy," 70.

8   Christel and Torunczyk, "The Cycle of Socio-Environmental Mobilization Against Transnational Mining in Argentina"; Walter and Urkidi, "Community Mining Consultations," 273.

9   "Rechazan decreto que promueve minería a gran escala en el Orinoco," *Servindi*, April 10, 2016 (https://www.servindi.org/noticias/01/04/2016/rechazan-decreto -que-promueve-mineria-gran-escala-en-el-orinoco).

10   Dussel, *Twenty Theses*; Unger, *Democracy Realized*; Wolin, "Fugitive Democracy."

11   Wolin, "Fugitive Democracy," 17.

12   Dussel, *Twenty Theses*, 51.

13   Despite its name—Unión de Sistemas Comunitarios de Agua de Azuay—the organization does not represent the entire province of Azuay, only the canton of Cuenca. This paragraph and the next draws on Cisneros, *¿Cómo se construye la sustentabilidad ambiental?*, 214–25; Moore and Velásquez, "Water for Gold," 127–8.

14   Moore and Velásquez, "Water for Gold," 119–124.

15   For more on the political party Pachakutik, see pp. 44–50. For a detailed discussion of Tibán's political history, see Daniela Montalvo, "¿Quién es Lourdes Tibán?," *GK* (http://contexto.gk.city/ficheros/lourdes-tiban-lidereza-indigena -pachakutik/quien-es-lourdes-tiban, accessed January 12, 2019).

16   The name of the mine in corporate and state documents is Quimsacocha, while activists often use the spelling Kimsacocha. Both 'k' and 'qu' are used to transliterate the same Kichwa phoneme. In Kichwa, *quimsa* means "three" and *cocha* means "lake," referring to the three high-altitude lakes within the concession.

17   Colloredo-Mansfeld, *Fighting Like a Community*, 6–7.

18   Lucero, "Locating the 'Indian Problem.'"

19   The words are from the speeches of Cesar Padilla (director of the Latin American Observatory of Mining Conflicts) and Delfín Tenesaca (president of Ecuarunari).

20   The claim to ancestral rights was made by Carlos Pérez at a binational forum on consultation in Ecuador and Peru, held in Cuenca on February 28, 2012.

21   Carlos Pérez, interview with the author, November 19, 2011.

22   As of 2017, Carlos Pérez now goes by Yaku Sacha Pérez.

23   Radio Ciudadano, October 2, 2011. The acronym SENAGUA is that of the national water ministry.

24   I am indebted to Osman Balkan for this point.

25   The descriptions are from the speeches of Lizardo Zhagui (Ecuarunari and UNAGUA member), Cesar Padilla, and Delfín Tenesaca.

26   Carlos Pérez, interview with the author, November 19, 2011.

27   A transcript of this speech was acquired from Alberto Acosta, interview with the author, December 12, 2011. See also, "Ministra de la Política: hay tergiversación y mentira en el caso Quimsacocha," *Andes*, October 24, 2011.

28   For *consultas* modeled on Quimsacocha, see "La recolección de firmas para plantear la consulta popular en Quimsacocha finaliza en Girón," *El Comercio*, July 26, 2015; "Se plantea una Consulta Comunitaria para decir no a la minería en Pacto, Ecuador," Yes to Life, No to Mining (http://www.yestolifenotomining.org

/se-plantea-una-consulta-comunitaria-para-decir-la-mineria-en-pacto-ecuador/,
accessed January 12, 2019).

29   Anonymous flyer, emphasis in original.

30   Correa, *Enlace ciudadano* (Saturday address) no. 241, Chanduy, Ecuador, October 8, 2011.

31   Correa, *Enlace ciudadano* no. 241.

32   *Sarayaku v. Ecuador*, Inter-American Court of Human Rights, June 27, 2012. In June 2012 the court ruled that the Ecuadorian state had failed to consult Sarayaku indigenous people prior to oil exploration.

33   Correa, *Enlace ciudadano* no. 269, Cascales, Ecuador, April 28, 2012.

34   Executive Decree 1040, April 2008, establishes guidelines for "socializations." As discussed in Chapter 3, the term is associated with the corporate sector but also common in bureaucratic, NGO and, less frequently, social movement discourse, and denotes the dissemination of information for marketing or promotion, whether of a consumer product or a political campaign.

35   Recently, however, predominantly urban activists mobilized against oil extraction in Yasuní National Park.

36   This march took place from March 8 to March 22, 2012, covering 700 kilometers from the Amazon to the capital. Opposition to resource extraction was a pervasive theme.

37   For Correa's plebiscitary style, see Conaghan, "Correa's Plebiscitary Presidency"; De la Torre and Conaghan, "The Hybrid Campaign."

38   For inner and outer edges, see Shapiro and Hacker-Cordón, *Democracy's Edges*.

39   This is an example of what Gordon and Jasper call "grievance extension" (broadening the boundary of "directly affected"). See Gordon and Jasper, "Overcoming the 'NIMBY' label." See also John Vidal, "Yasuni Campaigners Claim Oil Drilling Petition Results Are Being Manipulated," *Guardian*, April 30, 2014 (https://www.theguardian.com/environment/2014/apr/30/yasuni-campaigners-oil-drilling-petition-results-referendum).

40   Correa, *Enlace ciudadano* no. 269.

41   The term *politiquero* is a more negatively inflected version of the term *político*. *Político* means "politician," and in Ecuador and other Latin American countries has a negative connotation, whereas *politiquero* means "corrupt politician" and *politiquería* means "politicking." For more on these terms' broad circulation and ideological malleability, see the discussion of the opposition between *político* and *técnico* in pro-mining discourse in Chapter 5.

42   For the phrase "democratize democracy," see Santos and Avritzer, "Introduction."

43   Correa, *Enlace ciudadano* no. 249, Macas, Ecuador, December 10, 2011.

44   The May 2011 referendum posed questions on media, judicial, and financial policy, a proposal to limit bullfighting, and to prohibit casinos. The "yes" vote won on all questions; Correa declared victory.

45   Correa, *Enlace ciudadano* no. 241.

46   UNAGUA, "Instructions" (*Instructivo*), August 27, 2011, art. 1.

47   "No habrá Consulta Popular por tema minero," *El Ciudadano*, October 26, 2011.

48 Carlos Pérez, interview with the author, November 19, 2011.

49 Correa, *Enlace ciudadano* no. 241.

50 For prospective representation, see Manin, *The Principles of Representative Government*, 161–83.

51 Note that the law has since been reformed to be more investor friendly. For interpretations of the sale, see "Iamgold Bails Out of Ecuador," *Financial Post*, June 21, 2012 (https://business.financialpost.com/commodities/mining /iamgold-bails-out-of-ecuador); "Ecuadorian Communities Welcome Iamgold's Retreat and Warn INV Metals That There's No Social License for Quimsaco-cha," *Marketwire*, June 22, 2012 (http://www.marketwired.com/press-release /ecuadoriancommunities-welcome-iamgolds-retreat-warn-inv-metals-that-theres -no-social-1672687.htm).

52 Rafael Correa, Executive Decree 870, September 5, 2011.

53 As discussed in Chapter 3, on March 17, 2009, CONAIE challenged the constitutionality of the 2009 Mining Law for violating their rights to pre-legislative and prior consultation. The Constitutional Court ruled that the law was "conditionally constitutional" given the "exceptional situation" of a constitutional transition. The quote from Dr. Néstor Arboleda appears in the court's final sentence. See Constitutional Court (*Corte Constitucional*), sentence no. 001-10-SIN-CC, 10, case nos. 008-09-IN and 011-09-IN, March 18, 2010, 13.

54 For the nation and nationalism as constructed through its (textual) representation, see Anderson, *Imagined Communities*. For inner and outer edges, see Shapiro and Hacker-Cordón, *Democracy's Edges*.

55 Monica Chuji, interview with the author, June 27, 2012.

56 Mariuxsi Flores, interview with the author, July 10, 2012.

57 Dussel, *Twenty Theses*, 72–7.

58 Cameron, Hershberg, and Sharpe, "Voice and Consequence"; Fung, "Reinventing Democracy in Latin America"; Santos and Avritzer, "Introduction"; Smulovitz and Peruzzotti, "Societal Accountability in Latin America."

59 Comaroff and Comaroff, "Theory from the South"; Costanza, "Indigenous Peoples' Right to Prior Consultation"; Gustafson and Guzmán Solano, "Mining Movements"; Rodríguez-Garavito, "Ethnicity.Gov"; Sieder, "Legal Cultures in the (Un)Rule of Law"; Svampa, "Commodities Consensus."

60 Gustafson and Guzmán Solano, "Mining Movements," 154.

61 For the term "vernacular statecraft," see Colloredo-Mansfeld, *Fighting Like a Community*.

62 I take the terms "neutralize" and "depoliticize" from Schmitt's critique of liberal constitutionalism and technocracy in *The Concept of the Political*.

Chapter 5: Governing the Future

1 Ferguson, *Anti-Politics Machine*; T. M. Li, "Beyond 'the State' and Failed Schemes"; Mitchell, *Rule of Experts*; O'Donnell, "Toward an Alternative Conceptualization of South American Politics," 255–7, especially the discussion of the importance of a

common technocratic "language" among development experts; Scott, *Seeing Like a State*; Sikkink, *Ideas and Institutions*.

2   Ferguson, *Anti-Politics Machine*.

3   See Hetherington, *Guerrilla Auditors*, for another example of the politicizing effects of claims to expertise; see also Kirsch, *Mining Capitalism*, Chapter 6, for an analysis of what he calls the "politics of time": the battle over perceptions of mining projects that commences well before mineral extraction.

4   For territory as agent, see de la Cadena, "Indigenous Cosmopolitics in the Andes"; F. Li, *Unearthing Conflict*.

5   For "knowledges otherwise," see Escobar, "Worlds and Knowledges Otherwise 1"; de la Cadena, "Indigenous Cosmopolitics."

6   Quoted from the SPMSPC website (http://www.pueblos.gob.ec/?p=2572 /subsecretaria-de-dialogo-social, accessed October 16, 2012).

7   Rosa Cecilia, interview with the author, October 11, 2011.

8   See T. M. Li, "Beyond 'the State'" and *The Will to Improve*.

9   Ferguson, *Anti-Politics Machine*, 186.

10   For the failure of information discourse to depoliticize, see Hetherington, *Guerrilla Auditors*, esp. 1–65. See also F. Li, *Unearthing Conflict*, and T. M. Li, *Will to Improve*, for the point that such critiques of developmentalism may grant too much agency and efficacy to the experts who design and implement projects.

11   This definition of neoliberalism emerged in several interviews, especially with bureaucrats at SENPLADES, the planning ministry (and, at the time, among the most powerful state agencies). The quotes come from four interviews with SENPLADES bureaucrats: María Belen, December 1, 2011; German Guerra, January 23 and January 24, 2012; Eugenio Paladines, May 9, 2012. For a longer discussion of the social movement critique of neoliberalism, see Chapter 1; for more discussion of state officials' conceptions of neoliberalism and post-neoliberalism, see Chapter 2.

12   Secretaría de Pueblos, Movimientos Sociales y Participación Ciudadana (SPM-SPC), "Caracterización de conflictos socio-ambientales," 176. I return to this report later in the chapter.

13   This view also emerged in an interview with Shura Rosero at the Coordinating Ministry of Public Policy. Shura Rosero, interview with the author, September 26, 2011.

14   Walter Garcia, interview with the author, October 24, 2011.

15   In official state parlance, deconcentration is distinguished from decentralization: the former refers to the process of establishing satellite versions of state ministries in every province, although decision-making power is still centralized in the central ministries in the capital. Walter Garcia, interview with the author, October 24, 2011.

16   "Ministra de la Política: hay tergiversación y mentira en el caso Quimsacocha," *Andes*, October 24, 2011 (http://andes.info.ec/2009-2011.php/?p=104806).

17   Francisco Cevallos, interview with the author, April 25, 2012.

18   International Mining Fair (*Feria Minera*), Zamora, Ecuador, October 3–5, 2012.

19 This protest is described in Chapter 3. Shaggly and Cuenca are both located in the southern highland province of Azuay.

20 "Políticos mienten a las comunidades sobre minería," *El Ciudadano*, May 5, 2012.

21 Leonardo Elizade, interview with the author, June 26, 2012. As discussed in Chapter 2, "socialization" refers to publicity or promotional efforts, and is the official term for the processes of state and corporate-led community participation regarding extractive projects.

22 Literally, "regulatory times" or the temporality of regulatory processes.

23 María Clara Herdoíza, interview with the author, August 6, 2012.

24 Carlos Alberto Cordova, interview with the author, June 28, 2012.

25 SPMSPC, "Caracterización de conflictos socio-ambientales," 13.

26 Correa, *Enlace ciudadano* no. 270, Carapungo, Ecuador, May 5, 2012.

27 Auquilla, "Minería responsable en Ecuador," 53.

28 Correa, interview, Gama TV [state-owned TV station], "De Frente" hosted by Jorge Gestoso, June 27, 2012.

29 For other examples of this trope, see Coronil, *The Magical State*, as well as the discussion of resource nationalism (in both its radical and developmentalist variants) in Chapter 1.

30 Mario Ruales, interview with the author, February 14, 2012.

31 Mario Ruales, interview with the author, September 22, 2011.

32 Alicia Hidalgo, interview with the author, July 25, 2012.

33 SPMSPC, "Caracterización de conflictos socio-ambientales," 54.

34 Romulo Heredia, interview with the author, May 29, 2012.

35 Executive Decree 1040 is analyzed in Chapter 3.

36 For a discussion of how competing expert narratives amount to a "labor of confusion" that causes community demobilization in environmentally toxic contexts, see Auyero and Swistun, *Flammable*.

37 Pablo Mera, interview with the author, June 26, 2012.

38 Mario Ruales, interview with the author, September 22, 2011.

39 Monica Chuji, interview with the author, June 27, 2012. As discussed in Chapter 3, Monica Chuji served as Correa's secretary of communication and later as a Constituent Assembly delegate for Correa's party, Alianza País, before leaving the party altogether to return to working as an indigenous activist.

40 This incident occurred on February 28, 2012.

41 Stern and O'Brien, "Politics at the Boundary," 177.

42 T. M. Li, "Beyond 'the State,'" 385.

43 Abrams, "Notes on the Difficulty of Studying the State," 76–7, 79. For ethnographic approaches to the study of the state, see Barragán and Wanderley, "Etnografías del estado en América Latina"; Ferguson and Gupta, "Spatializing States"; Sharma and Gupta, "Introduction."

44 Liliana Guzman, interview with the author, May 14, 2012. There is another layer of uncertainty here, pertaining to the mineral that is the "target" of exploration: the company website says gold, while various news reports, and anti-mining movement communiqués and blog posts, say gold, copper, and silver.

45 Mining Law, 2009, art. 36.

46 Alicia Granda, interview with the author, September 19, 2011.

47 Acosta is a key figure in the debate over extraction. As discussed at length previously, he served as president of the 2007–2008 Constituent Assembly but then resigned from the Correa administration due to disagreements over resource policy. Sacher is a French author with a PhD in Atmospheric Science and Oceanography who now lives in Ecuador, and has written numerous publications on large-scale mining, most notably a volume coauthored with Alain Deneault and Delphine Abide, *Noir Canada: pillage, corruption et criminalité en Afrique,* which resulted in a now-settled lawsuit for defamation by Canadian multinational mining company Barrick Gold.

48 Sacher and Acosta, *La minería a gran escala en Ecuador,* 99–100.

49 The Mirador project in Zamora Chinchipe is the first and only project with a contract for exploitation. The contract was signed just days before the two-week March for Water, Life, and Dignity of Peoples—which Quishpe had a central role in organizing—set off from Pangui, Zamora Chinchipe, on March 8, 2012. The march is discussed at more length in Chapters 1, 2, and 3.

50 Sacher and Acosta, *La minería a gran escala,* 73–4, 99–100.

51 For an official source that defines these terms and categorizes the Ecuadorian reserves accordingly, see Ministerio de Recursos Norenovables, "Plan nacional de desarrollo del sector minero, 2011–2015," 44.

52 Paúl Carrasco was the prefect of Azuay, which, as stated earlier, is a province with two particularly controversial mining projects—Quimsacocha and Vetas Grandes—along with Rio Blanco, a strategic project but less visible in national debate. Carrasco was elected with Correa's support but then emerged as an opposition prefect. Activists worried that his anti-mining stance is a result of political calculus (opposition to Correa and a desire to win electoral support among those skeptical of mining in his province) rather than political commitment to the movement.

53 Alberto Acosta, speaking at the University of Cuenca, May 16, 2011.

54 The public water utility serving the canton of Cuenca, ETAPA is discussed at more length in Chapter 4. Quishpe was the only person I spoke to who was both a bureaucrat and an activist. His anti-mining activity may have been somewhat less risky to his position as he worked in a relatively autonomous (from the central bureaucracy) municipal-level public utility, though he still expressed worry (sometimes seriously, sometimes jokingly) that his activism would have repercussions.

55 Marcelo Quizhpe, interview with the author, November 11, 2011.

56 Francisco Cevallos (Ministry of Nonrenewable Resources), interview with the author, April 25, 2012; María Eulalia (director of Fundación Avina, a "nonpartisan" but effectively pro-mining NGO), interview with the author, May 17, 2012.

57 I am indebted to Anne Norton for this formulation.

58 For use of the term *futuro minero,* see the interview with the minister of non-renewable resources, Wilson Pastor, in "'Consulta previa a la comunidad no es

sinónimo de consulta popular,'" *El Comercio*, April 8, 2012 (http://elcomercio.com
/politica/Consulta-comunidad-sinonimo-consulta-popular_0_677932294.html).

59 María Belen, interview with the author, December 1, 2011.

60 For actor-network theory and nonhuman "actants," see, e.g., Callon, "Some
Elements of a Sociology of Translation," and Latour, *Reassembling the Social.*

61 The phrase is Correa's often-repeated dismissal of anti-mining activists.

62 Federico Auquilla, interview with the author, February 7, 2012.

63 For a longer discussion of this conception of neoliberalism, see Chapter 2.

64 For an analysis of dis/embedding of the economic from the social, see Polanyi,
Great Transformation, Chapter 5. For a discussion of neoliberal technocracy in the
Andean region, see Conaghan, Malloy, and Abugattas, "Business and the 'Boys.'"

65 De la Cadena, "Indigenous Cosmopolitics," 343–5.

66 Scott, *Seeing Like a State*, 318–19. For critical engagement with *Seeing Like a State*,
see T. M. Li "Beyond 'the State.'"

67 De la Cadena, "Indigenous Cosmopolitics," 353.

68 De la Cadena, "Indigenous Cosmopolitics," 356.

69 Polanyi, *Great Transformation*, 136.

Conclusion: The Dilemmas of the Pink Tide

1   For accounts of this conflict, see "La CIDH pide a Ecuador explicaciones por
la muerte de tres líderes indígenas," *El Comercio*, March 17, 2015 (http://www
.elcomercio.com/actualidad/cidh-ecuador-explicaciones-muerte.html); Verónica
Calvopiña, "¿Qué le hemos hecho presidente Correa? Mujeres shuar rompen el
cerco del Estado de excepción en Ecuador," *Des Informemonos*, February 23, 2017
(https://desinformemonos.org/le-hecho-presidente-correa-mujeres-shuar-rompen
-cerco-del-estado-excepcion-ecuador/); Carmen Martínez Novo, "La minería
amenaza a los indígenas shuar en Ecuador," *New York Times*, March 27, 2017
(https://www.nytimes.com/es/2017/03/27/la-mineria-amenaza-a-los-indigenas
-shuar-en-ecuador/).

2   Bebbington and Bury, "Political Ecologies of the Subsoil," 15; Petras and Veltmeyer, "Trade and Development in an Era of Extractive Capitalism," 116.

3   During the years of the boom, Latin America received an average of 26 percent
of global investment in mining. Bebbington and Bury, "Political Ecologies," 15;
de Echave, "La minería peruana y los escenarios de transición," 63; Petras and
Veltmeyer, "Trade and Development," 116.

4   Between 1998 and 2012, 133 mining-related conflicts took place across 21 percent
of all Latin American mining properties (Haslam and Tanimoune, "Determinants
of Social Conflict," 408). The vast majority of these are open-pit mines, which are
particularly disruptive to ecosystems, livelihoods, and indigenous and campesino
territories (Haslam and Tanimoune, "Determinants of Social Conflict"; Conde
and Le Billon, "Why Do Some Communities Resist Mining Projects while Others
Do Not?," 683).

5   Rachel Cox, "New Data Reveals 197 Land and Environmental Defenders Mur-
dered in 2017," Global Witness, February 2, 2018 (https://www.globalwitness.org

/en/blog/new-data-reveals-197-land-and-environmental-defenders-murdered
-2017/); Bill Kyte, "At What Cost?" Global Witness, July 24, 2018 (https://www
.globalwitness.org/en/campaigns/environmental-activists/at-what-cost/).

6   Latorre, Farrell, and Martínez-Alier, "Commodification of Nature," 61.

7   Acosta, "Living Well from an Ecuadorian Perspective," 102; Escobar, "Latin
    America at a Crossroads"; Hollender, "Post-Growth in the Global South"; Munck
    and Delgado Wise, "Introduction"; Svampa, *Debates latinoamericanos*, 367–442.

8   See previous note, and Acosta, "Las dependencias del extractivismo," 1; Gudynas,
    "Extractivism," 62.

9   Compare note 6, and Ramírez Gallegos, "Socialismo del sumak kawsay o bioso-
    cialismo republicano."

10 For the dialectic of the period and the break, see Jameson, *A Singular Modernity*,
    24–9.

11 Webber, "The Retreat of the Pink Tide in Latin America."

12 For an argument along these lines, see Zibechi, *Dispersing Power*. For recent
    discussions and critiques of the argument against engaging and transforming
    the state, see Anria, *When Movements Become Parties*, 1–60; Baiocchi, *We, the
    Sovereign*; Tarlau, *Occupying Schools, Occupying Land*, 1–34. These approaches in
    turn draw on a much longer history of Marxist analyses of state power. See,
    among others, Block, "Ruling Class"; Jessop, *Nicos Poulantzas*, esp. 115–148;
    Miliband, "The Coup in Chile"; Miliband, *The State in Capitalist Society*; Pou-
    lantzas, *State, Power, Socialism*; Therborn, *What Does the Ruling Class Do When It
    Rules?*

13 For this argument, see Rojas, "The Latin American Left's Shifting Tides."

14 Jameson, *A Singular Modernity*, 29; Benjamin, *Illuminations*, 256.

15 It is worth noting that Webber's analysis presents a three-phase periodization of
    the retreat of the Left structured by multiple, dialectically related, causal pro-
    cesses. See Webber, "Retreat of the Pink Tide."

16 Haslam and Heidrich, "From Neoliberalism to Resource Nationalism," 10; Kaup,
    "A Neoliberal Nationalization?"

17 Acosta, "Las dependencias del extractivismo," 1–3; Gudynas, "Natural Resource
    Nationalisms and the Compensatory State in Progressive South America," 104.

18 Acosta, "Las dependencias del extractivismo," 14. For economic coordination
    among Third World governments as a means of decolonization, see Dietrich, *Oil
    Revolution*, 1–25, 158–90; Getachew, *Worldmaking after Empire*, 142–75.

19 Gudynas, "Natural Resource Nationalisms," 105.

20 Lucero, "Locating the 'Indian Problem.'"

21 Dussel, *Twenty Theses*, 75–7.

22 Gudynas, "Natural Resource Nationalisms."

23 These are discussed at more length in the Introduction.

24 Poverty declined from 37.6 percent to 22.5 percent. Income inequality, measured
    by the Gini coefficient, declined from 0.55 to 0.47. See Larrea and Greene, "De la
    lucha contra la probreza a la superación de la codicia"; Ordóñez et al., "Sharing
    the Fruits of Progress"; Weisbrot, Johnston, and Merling, "Decade of Reform";

"The World Bank in Ecuador," World Bank (https://www.worldbank.org/en /country/ecuador, accessed December 19, 2018).

25   For "second incorporation," see Silva and Rossi, *Reshaping the Political Arena in Latin America*, and Spronk and León Trujillo, "Socialism Without Workers?" For the classic text on the first incorporation, see Collier and Collier, *Reshaping the Political Arena*, as well as James, *Resistance and Integration*, esp. 7–40, which is a case study of Argentina under Perón.

26   There is a large, and quite polarized, literature on these participatory institutions in Venezuela. For a range of perspectives, see, for example, Ciccariello-Maher, *Building the Commune*; García-Guadila, "The Incorporation of Popular Sectors and Social Movements in Venezuelan Twenty-First-Century Socialism"; Hetland, "The Crooked Line." For a more general argument that left-populist, Pink Tide governments contributed to the political empowerment of the poor, see Piñeiro, Rhodes-Purdy, and Rosenblatt, "The Engagement Curve."

27   Anria, *When Movements Become Parties*. For a more pessimistic perspective, see Farthing, "An Opportunity Squandered," 9–11.

28   Iturralde, *El negocio invisible de salud*.

29   For a parallel account of alliances of mutual convenience between a leftist government and economic elites in Bolivia, see Farthing, "Opportunity Squandered," 7–11. See also Svampa, *Debates latinoamericanos*, 370. For an explanation of the Odebrecht scandal, in which the region's largest construction conglomerate has been found guilty of bribing politicians in Brazil and across the continent, see "Brazil's Odebrecht corruption scandal explained," *BBC News*, April 17, 2019 (https://www.bbc.com/news/business-39194395).

30   For this dynamic in Bolivia, see Farthing, "The Left in Power."

31   The term "price-taker" refers to having little influence over global prices, compared to "price-makers," that is countries that constitute a much larger share of global oil production, such as Saudi Arabia and, more recently, the United States.

32   For a longer discussion of the resource curse and rentier state theory, see the Introduction.

33   For work on the historic unevenness of the Ecuadorian state, see Bowen, "Rethinking Democratic Governance"; Harbers, "Taxation and the Unequal Reach of the State." For histories of state capacity in the region, see Centeno, "Blood and Debt," and Kurtz, *Latin American State Building in Comparative Perspective*.

34   See Chapter 5.

35   Bowen, "Rethinking Democratic Governance," 97–8.

36   Gudynas, "Natural Resource Nationalisms," 110.

37   Hollender, "Post-Growth," 93.

38   Gudynas, "Natural Resource Nationalisms," 110; Bebbington et al., "Political Settlements."

39   Webber, "Retreat of the Pink Tide."

40   Farthing, "Opportunity Squandered"; Webber, "Retreat of the Pink Tide."

41 Jeffery Webber and Forrest Hylton, "The Eighteenth Brumaire of Macho Camacho," *Verso Books Blog*, November 15, 2019 (https://www.versobooks.com /blogs/4493-the-eighteenth-brumaire-of-macho-camacho-jeffery-r-webber-with -forrest-hylton-on-the-coup-in-bolivia).

42 Riofrancos, "Ecuador after Correa." For developments since Moreno's election, see Becker and Riofrancos, "A Souring Friendship, a Left Divided."

43 Acosta, "Las dependencias del extractivismo"; Gudynas, "Extractivism," 62; Svampa, *Debates latinoamericanos*, 367–75.

44 Acosta, "Las dependencias del extractivismo," 1.

45 For "super-exploitation," see Svampa, *Debates latinoamericanos*, 372.

46 Svampa, *Debates latinoamericanos*, 193–266.

47 Gudynas, *Extractivisms*, 66–7.

48 For a case in point, see the discussion of the 2014 reforms to the Mining Law in the Introduction.

49 Gudynas, *Extractivisms*, 66–7. See also, Baroja, Belmont Guerrón, and Peck, "Deforestación y actividad petrolera en la Amazonia Centro-Sur."

50 Gaudichaud, "The End of a Golden Age?"; Gudynas, *Extractivisms*, 67; Svampa, *Debates latinoamericanos*, 371.

51 Acosta, "Las dependencias del extractivismo," 5.

52 Edgar Lander, quoted in Gaudichaud, "End of a Golden Age?"

53 For the three awards, see Matthew Levine, "ICSID Tribunal Awards Roughly USD380 Million in Compensation for Illegal Expropriation by Ecuador," International Institute for Sustainable Development, September 26, 2017 (https:// www.iisd.org/itn/2017/09/26/icsid-tribunal-awards-roughly-usd380-million -compensation-illegal-expropriation-ecuador-matthew-levine/); "Ecuador-Occidental Arbitration Award Reduced to $1 Billion," *Reuters*, November 2, 2015 (https://www.reuters.com/article/us-ecuador-occidental/ecuador-occidental -arbitration-award-reduced-to-1-billion-idUSKCN0SR24V20151102); "Former Petrobras Subsidiary Wins Claim over Ecuadorean Oil Projects," *Global Arbitration Review*, February 27, 2018 (https://globalarbitrationreview.com/article/1166151 /former-petrobras-subsidiary-wins-claim-over-ecuadorean-oil-projects). For the overturned ruling, see "International Tribunal Rules in Favor of Chevron in Ecuador Case," *Reuters*, September 7, 2018 (https://www.reuters.com/article/us -chevron-ecuador/international-tribunal-rules-in-favor-of-chevron-in-ecuador -case-idUSKCN1LN1WS).

54 For discussion of a "planned decrease," see Acosta, "Las dependencias del extractivismo," 14. For the challenge of the tension "between the social debt and the environmental debt," see Svampa, *Debates latinoamericanos*, 394.

55 See Chapter 2.

56 Jeffery Webber, "Assessing the Pink Tide." Jacobin, April 11, 2017 (https://www .jacobinmag.com/2017/04/lula-correa-rousseff-left-pink-tide).

57 Miriam Lang, in Gaudichaud, "End of a Golden Age?"

58 Gudynas, "Transitions to post-extractivism." See also Hollender, "Post-Growth," 86; Svampa, *Debates latinoamericanos*, 393–5.

59   Hollender, "Post-Growth," 86.

60   Acosta, "Living Well"; Caria and Dominguez, "Ecuador's Buen Vivir"; Hollender, "Post-Growth"; Gudynas, "Value, Growth, Development"; Svampa, *Debates latino-americanos*, 381–8.

61   Acosta, "Living Well," 102–3; Svampa, *Debates latinoamericanos*, 381.

62   The word *kawsay* is also used in Kichwa; as noted in Chapter 1, note 18, Kichwa is a member of the broader Quechua family of languages. Zimmerer, "The Indigenous Andean Concept of Kawsay, the Politics of Knowledge and Development, and the Borderlands of Environmental Sustainability in Latin America," 600.

63   Perreault, "Tendencies in Tension," 24; Svampa, 381–88; Zimmere, 603–4.

64   For an example of official documents, SENPLADES, "Plan nacional de buen vivir."

65   For an example of a high-level bureaucrat under the Correa administration linking *buen vivir* to these sectors, see Ramírez Gallegos, "Socialismo del sumak kawsay," 69.

66   Acosta, "Living Well," 106–8; Hollender, "Post-Growth," 92; Svampa, *Debates latinoamericanos*, 393.

67   Acosta, "Las dependencias del extractivismo," 16–17; Hollender, "Post-Growth," 88–89.

68   For variants of this argument, see Baiocchi, *We, the Sovereign*; Falleti and Riofrancos, "Endogenous Participation"; Peña, "Social Movements, the State, and the Making of Food Sovereignty in Ecuador"; Tarlau, *Occupying Schools, Occupying Land*.

69   Cohen, "The Other Low-Carbon Protagonists."

70   Conde and Le Billon, "Why Do Some Communities Resist Mining Projects?," 682.

71   Conde and Le Billon, "Why Do Some Communities Resist Mining Projects?"; Haslam and Tanimoune, "Determinants of Social Conflict"; Latorre, Farrell, and Martínez-Alier, "Commodification of Nature."

72   Conde and Le Billon, "Why Do Some Communities Resist Mining Projects?"; Haslam and Tanimoune, "Determinants of Social Conflict."

73   Haslam and Tanimoune, "Determinants of Social Conflict."

74   See Chapter 4; Falleti and Riofrancos, "Endogenous Participation"; Riofrancos, "Scaling Democracy."

75   Conde and Le Billon, "Why Do Some Communities Resist Mining Projects?"; Haslam and Tanimoune, "Determinants of Social Conflict"; Riofrancos, "Scaling Democracy."

76   For discussion of this as a more general feature of extractive economies, see Bebbington et al., "Political Settlements," 25.

77   For discussion of this point, see Gudynas, "Natural Resource Nationalisms," 114.

78   "Ecuador moves government out of capital as violent protests rage," *The Guardian*, October 8, 2019 (https://www.theguardian.com/world/2019/oct/08/ecuador-moves-government-out-of-capital-as-violent-protests-rage); "Ecuador's Petroamazonas suspends operations at three oilfields amid protests," *Reuters*, October 7, 2019 (https://www.reuters.com/article/us-ecuador-protests-oil/ecuadors-petroamazonas-suspends-operations-at-three-oilfields-amid-protests-energy

-ministry-idUSKBN1WM2CC); "Ecuador crisis weakens president, strengthens indigenous," *Associated Press*, October 14, 2019 (https://apnews.com/a8cba045f3784 dfe9ffa017ef8af30a1).

79 Riofrancos, "Scaling Democracy." See also Conde and Le Billon, "Why Do Some Communities Resist Mining Projects?" 688; Haarstad and Fløysand, "Globalization and the Power of Rescaled Narratives"; Spalding, "Transnational Activism and National Action"; Urkidi, "The Defence of Community in the Anti-Mining Movement of Guatemala," 575.

80 For a discussion of the social movement scholarship on scale shifting, see McAdam and Boudet, *Putting Social Movements in Their Place*, esp. 132–78. See also Riofrancos, "Scaling Democracy."

81 This paragraph and the next draw on Spalding, "From the Streets to the Chamber"; Spalding, "Transnational Activism."

82 CONAIE, "Proyecto politico."

83 Fawad Maqsood, "Ecuador to Auction 8 Oil Blocks as Government Seeks to Encourage Investment," *Business Recorder,* September 11, 2018 (https://www.brecorder .com/2018/09/12/439697/ecuador-to-auction-8-oil-blocks-as-government-seeks-to -encourage-investment/); "Indigenous Rights 'Invisible' as Ecuador Pushes Mining, Oil Projects: UN," *Reuters,* November 30, 2018 (https://in.reuters.com/article /ecuador-mining-rights/indigenous-rights-invisible-as-ecuador-pushes-mining-oil -projects-un-idINL8N1Y52KR); "Latin American Nations Compete for Capital in Surge of Oil Auctions," *Reuters,* June 28, 2018 (https://www.reuters.com/article/us -latam-oil-reform-analysis/latin-american-nations-compete-for-capital-in-surge -of-oil-auctions-idUSKCN1H90UJ); Alexander Zaitchik, "Rainforest on Fire," *The Intercept,* July 6, 2019.

84 Fawad Maqsood, "Ecuador to Auction 8 Oil Blocks as Government Seeks to Encourage Investment," *Business Recorder,* September 11, 2018; "Indigenous Rights 'Invisible' as Ecuador Pushes Mining, Oil Projects: UN," *Reuters,* November 30, 2018; "Ecuador Announces $700 Mln in Budget Cuts in Austerity Push," *Reuters,* December 18, 2018 (https://www.reuters.com/article/ecuador-economy/ecuador -announces-700-mln-in-budget-cuts-in-austerity-push-idUSL1N1YN1IG). For more context on Moreno's campaign and presidency, see Becker and Riofrancos, "A Souring Friendship"; Riofrancos, "Ecuador after Correa."

85 For evidence that Pink Tide governments (and specifically those labeled as "populist") helped break the cycle of political and economic inequality, see Piñeiro, Rhodes-Purdy, and Rosenblatt, "The Engagement Curve."

86 For the term "fossil capital," and a history of its origins, see Malm, *Fossil Capital.*

BIBLIOGRAPHY

Abrams, Philip. "Notes on the Difficulty of Studying the State." *Journal of Historical Sociology* 1, no. 1 (1988): 58–89.

Acosta, Alberto. "Las dependencias del extractivismo: aporte para un debate incompleto." *Aktuel Marx* 20 (2016): 1–22.

Acosta, Alberto. "Living Well From an Ecuadorian Perspective: Philosophies without Philosophers, Actions without Theories." In *Reframing Latin American Development*, edited by Ronaldo Munck and Raul Delgado Wise, 99–102. London: Routledge, 2018.

Acosta, Alberto. *La maldición de la abundancia*. Quito: Ediciones Abya-Yala, 2009.

Acosta, Alberto, and Esperanza Martínez, eds. *Ecuador post-petrolero*. Quito: Acción Ecológica, 2000.

Agha, Asif. *Language and Social Relations*. Cambridge: Cambridge University Press, 2006.

Akchurin, Maria. "Constructing the Rights of Nature: Constitutional Reform, Mobilization, and Environmental Protection in Ecuador." *Law and Social Inquiry* 40, no. 4 (2015): 937–68.

Albro, Roberto. "The Water Is Ours, Carajo! Deep Citizenship in Bolivia's Water War." In *Social Movements: An Anthropological Reader*, edited by June Nash, 249–71. Malden, MA: Blackwell Publishing, 2005.

Albuja, Verónica, and Pablo Dávalos. "Extractivismo y posneoliberalismo: el caso de Ecuador." *Estudios Críticos del Desarrollo* 3, no. 4 (2013): 83–112.

Alier, Joan Martínez. "El ecologismo popular." *Revista Ecosistemas* 16, no. 3 (2007): 148–51.

Althusser, Louis. *For Marx*. London: Verso, 1969.

Amarante, Verónica, and Martín Brun. "Cash Transfers in Latin America: Effects on Poverty and Redistribution." WIDER Working Paper No. 2016/136. Helsinki: United Nations University World Institute for Development Economics Research, 2016.

Anderson, Benedict. *Imagined Communities: Reflections on the Origin and Spread of Nationalism*, rev. ed. London: Verso Books, 2006.

Andolina, Robert. "The Sovereign and Its Shadow." *Journal of Latin American Studies* 35, no. 4 (2003): 721–50.

Anria, Santiago. *When Movements Become Parties: The Bolivian MAS in Comparative Perspective*. Cambridge: Cambridge University Press, 2018.

Arce, Moisés. *Resource Extraction and Protest in Peru*. Pittsburgh, PA: University of Pittsburgh Press, 2014.

Arditi, Benjamin. "Arguments about the Left Turns in Latin America: A Post-Liberal Politics?" *Latin American Research Review* 43, no. 3 (2008): 59–81.

Arendt, Hannah. *The Human Condition*, 2nd ed. Chicago: University of Chicago Press, 1958.

Auquilla, Federico. "Minería responsable en Ecuador." *Coyuntura* 10 (2011): 66–84.

Austin, J. L. *How to Do Things with Words*, 2nd ed., edited by J. O. Urmson and Marina Sbisá. Cambridge: Harvard University Press, 1962.

Auyero, Javier, and Lauren Joseph. "Introduction: Politics under the Ethnographic Microscope." In *New Perspectives in Political Ethnography*, edited by Lauren Joseph, Matthew Mahler and Javier Auyero, 1–13. New York: Springer, 2006.

Auyero, Javier, and Debora Alejendra Switsun. *Flammable: Environmental Suffering in an Argentine Shantytown*. Oxford: Oxford University Press, 2009.

Baiocchi, Gianpaolo. *We, the Sovereign*. Hoboken, NJ: Wiley, 2018.

Bakhtin, M. M. *The Dialogic Imagination: Four Essays*, edited by Michael Holquist, translated by Caryl Emerson. Austin: University of Texas Press, 1981.

Baroja, Camilo, Philippe Belmont, and Mika Robert Peck. "Deforestación y actividad petrolera en la Amazonia Centro-Sur: escenarios predictivos del uso del suelo." In *¿Está agotado el periodo petrolero en Ecuador?*, edited by Carlos Larrea, 123–60. Quito: Universidad Andina Simón Bolívar, 2017.

Barragán, Rossana, and Fernanda Wanderley. "Etnografías del estado en América Latina." *ICONOS* 34 (2009): 21–5.

Baxsi, Upendra. "'Outline of a Theory of Practice' of Indian Constitutionalism." In *Politics and Ethics of the Indian Constitution*, edited by Rajeev Bhargava, 92–118. Oxford: Oxford University Press, 2009.

Bebbington, Anthony, Abdul-Gafaru Abdulai, Marja Hinfelaar, Denise Humphreys Bebbington, and Cynthia Sanborn. "Political Settlements and the Governance of Extractive Industry: A Comparative Analysis of the Longue Durée in Africa and Latin America." ESID Working Paper No. 81. Manchester: Global Development Institute, University of Manchester, 2017.

Bebbington, Anthony, and Jeffrey Bury. "Political Ecologies of the Subsoil." In *Subterranean Struggles: New Dynamics of Mining, Oil, and Gas in Latin America*, edited by Anthony Bebbington and Jeffrey Bury, 1–26. Austin: University of Texas Press, 2013.

Bebbington, Anthony, and Jeffrey Bury, eds. *Subterranean Struggles: New Dynamics of Mining, Oil, and Gas in Latin America*. Austin: University of Texas Press, 2013.

Bebbington, Anthony, and Denise Humphreys Bebbington. "An Andean Avatar: Post-Neoliberal and Neoliberal Strategies for Promoting Extractive Industries." BWPI Working Paper. Manchester: Brooks World Poverty Institute, 2010.

Bebbington, Anthony, Denise Humphreys Bebbington, Jeannet Lingan, and Jeffrey Bury. "The Glocalization of Environmental Governance: Relations of Scale in Socio-Environmental Movements and the Implications for Rural Territorial Development in Peru and Ecuador." Working Papers on Territory, Conflicts and Development in the Andes. Manchester: University of Manchester, 2007.

Beblawi, Hazem. "The Rentier State in the Arab World." In *The Rentier State*, edited by Hazem Beblawi and Giamcomo Luciani, 49–62. New York: Routledge, 1987.

Becker, Marc. *Indians and Leftists in the Making of Ecuador's Modern Indigenous Movements*. Durham, NC: Duke University Press, 2008.

Becker, Marc, and Thea N. Riofrancos. "A Souring Friendship, a Left Divided." *NACLA Report on the Americas* 50, no. 2 (2018): 124–7.

Benjamin, Walter. *Illuminations*. New York: Penguin Books, 2015.

Bernal, Angélica María. *Beyond Origins: Rethinking Founding in a Time of Constitutional Democracy*. Oxford: Oxford University Press, 2017.

Bernal, Angélica María. "The Meaning and Perils of Presidential Refounding in Latin America." *Constellations: An International Journal of Critical and Democratic Theory* 21, no. 4 (2014): 440–56.

Berrios, Ruben, Andrae Marak, and Scott Morgenstern. "Explaining Hydrocarbon Nationalization in Latin America: Economics and Political Ideology." *Review of International Political Economy* 18, no. 5 (2010): 673–97.

Block, Fred. "The Ruling Class Does Not Rule: Notes on the Marxist Theory of the State." *Socialist Revolution* 33, no. 7 (1977): 6–28.

Boltanski, Luc, and Eve Chiapello. *The New Spirit of Capitalism*. London: Verso, 2006.

Boltanski, Luc, and Laurent Thévenot. *On Justification: Economies of Worth*. Princeton, NJ: Princeton University Press, 2006.

Bourdieu, Pierre. *The Logic of Practice*. Stanford, CA: Stanford University Press, 1992.

Bourdieu, Pierre. "Rethinking the State: Genesis and Structure of the Bureaucratic Field," translated by Loïc J. D. Wacquant and Samar Farage. *Sociological Theory* 12, no. 1 (1994): 1–18.

Bourdieu, Pierre, and Loïc J. D. Wacquant. *An Invitation to Reflexive Sociology*. Chicago: University of Chicago Press, 1992.

Bowen, James D. "Multicultural Market Democracy: Elites and Indigenous Movements in Contemporary Ecuador." *Journal of Latin American Studies* 43, no. 3 (2011): 451–83.

Bowen, James David. "Rethinking Democratic Governance: State Building, Autonomy, and Accountability in Correa's Ecuador." *Journal of Politics in Latin America* 7, no. 1 (2015): 83–110.

Bridge, Gavin. "Contested Terrain: Mining and the Environment." *Annual Review of Environment and Resources* 29, no. 1 (2004): 205–59.

Bridge, Gavin, and Philippe Le Billon. *Oil*. Hoboken, NJ: Wiley, 2017.

Brogan, Christopher. "The Retreat from Oil Nationalism in Ecuador." Latin American Studies Working Papers No. 13. London: University of London Institute, 1984.

Burchardt, Hans-Jürgen, and Kristina Dietz. "(Neo-)Extractivism: A New Challenge for Development Theory from Latin America." *Third World Quarterly* 35, no. 3 (2014): 468–86.

Butler, Judith. *Gender Trouble: Feminism and the Subversion of Identity*. New York: Routledge, 1990.

Butler, Judith. "Performative Acts and Gender Constitution: An Essay in Phenomenology and Feminist Theory." *Theater Journal* 40, no. 4 (1988): 519–31.

Callon, Michel. "Some Elements of a Sociology of Translation." In *Technoscience: The Politics of Interventions*, edited by Kristin Asdal, Brita Brenna and Ingunn Moser, 57–78. Oslo: Unipub, 2007.

Cameron, Maxwell A. "Latin America's Left Turns: Beyond Good and Bad." *Third World Quarterly* 30, no. 2 (2009): 331–48.

Cameron, Maxwell, Eric Hershberg, and Kenneth Sharpe. "Voice and Consequence: Direct Participation and Democracy in Latin America." In *New Institutions for Participatory Democracy in Latin America: Voice and Consequence*, edited by Maxwell Cameron, Eric Hershberg, and Kenneth Sharpe, 1–20. New York: Palgrave Macmillan, 2012.

Cameron, Maxwell A., and Kenneth E. Sharpe. "Andean Left Turns: Constituent Power and Constitution-Making." In *Latin America's Left Turns: Politics, Policies, and Trajectories of Change*, edited by Maxwell A. Cameron and Eric A. Hirschberg, 98–127. Boulder, CO: Lynne Rienner Publishers, 2010.

Camp, Jordan T. *Incarcerating the Crisis: Freedom Struggles and the Rise of the Neoliberal State*. Berkeley: University of California Press, 2016.

Cardoso, Fernando Henrique, and Enzo Faletto. *Dependency and Development in Latin America*, translated by Marjory Mattingly Urquidi. Berkeley: University of California Press, 1979.

Caria, Sara, and Rafael Domínguez. "Ecuador's Buen Vivir: A New Ideology for Development." *Latin American Perspectives* 43, no. 1 (2016): 18–33.

Castañeda, Jorge. "Latin America's Left Turn." *Foreign Affairs* 85, no. 3 (2006): 28–43.

Centeno, Miguel Angel. "Blood and Debt: War and Taxation in Nineteenth-Century Latin America." *American Journal of Sociology* 102, no. 6 (1997): 1565–1605.

CEPAL. "Panorama de la inserción internacional de América Latina y el Caribe, 2009–2010." Comisión Económica para América Latina, 2010. https://repositorio.cepal.org/bitstream/handle/11362/1174/1/S1000783_es.pdf.

Chavez, David. "El estado del debate sobre desarrollo, extractivismo, y acumulación en el Ecuador." Working paper, Centro de Derechos Económicos y Sociales, 2013. http://cdes.org.ec/web/investigacion-el-estado-del-debate-sobre-desarrollo-extractivismo-y-acumulacion-de-capital-en-el-ecuador/.

Chuji, Monica, Mikel Berraondo, and Pablo Dávalos. *Derechos colectivos de los pueblos y nacionalidades: evaluación de una decada 1998–2008*. Quito: IWGIA/CONAIE/Tukui Shimi, 2009.

Ciccariello-Maher, George. *Building the Commune: Radical Democracy in Venezuela*. London: Verso Books, 2016.

Ciccariello-Maher, George. "Constituent Moments, Constitutional Processes: Social Movements and the New Latin American Left." *Latin American Perspectives* 40, no. 3 (2013): 126–45.

Ciplet, David, and J. Timmons Roberts. "Splintering South: Ecologically Unequal Exchange Theory in a Fragmented Global Climate." In *Ecologically Unequal Exchange*, edited by R. Scott Frey, Paul K. Gellert, and Harry Dahms, 273–305. London: Palgrave Macmillan, 2019.

Cisneros, Paúl. *¿Cómo se construye la sustentabilidad ambiental? Experiencias conflictivas de la industria minera en Ecuador*. Quito: Flacso-Sede Ecuador, 2011.

Cisneros, Paúl. "Corporate Social Responsibility and Mining Policy in Ecuador." Paper presented at the annual meeting of the Asociación Latinoamericana de Ciencia Política, Quito, June 12–14, 2012.

Clark, Kim A. "Ecuadorian Indians, the Nation, and Class in Historical Perspective: Rethinking a 'New Social Movement.'" *Anthropologica* 47, no. 1 (2005): 53–65.

Cohen, Daniel Aldana. "The Other Low-Carbon Protagonists: Poor People's Movements and Climate Politics in Sao Paulo." In *The City Is the Factory: New Solidarities and Spatial Strategies in an Urban Age*, edited by Miriam Greenberg and Penny Lewis, 140–57. Ithaca, NY: Cornell University Press, 2017.

Collier, Ruth Berins, and David Collier. *Shaping the Political Arena: Critical Junctures, the Labor Movement, and Regime Dynamics in Latin America.* Notre Dame, IN: University of Notre Dame Press, 2001.

Collins, Jennifer N. "New Left Experiences in Bolivia and Ecuador and the Challenge to Theories of Populism." *Journal of Latin American Studies* 46, no. 1 (2014): 59–86.

Colloredo-Mansfeld, Rudolf Josef. *Fighting Like a Community: Andean Civil Society in an Era of Indian Uprisings.* Chicago: University of Chicago Press, 2009.

Comaroff, Jean, and John Comaroff. "Ethnography on an Awkward Scale: Postcolonial Anthropology and the Violence of Abstraction." *Ethnography* 4, no. 2 (2003): 147–79.

Comaroff, Jean, and John Comaroff. "Theory from the South: Or, How Euro-America Is Evolving toward Africa." *Anthropological Forum* 22, no. 2 (2012): 113–31.

Conaghan, Catherine. "Correa's Plebiscitary Presidency." *Journal of Democracy* 19, no. 2 (2008): 46–60.

Conaghan, Catherine M., James M. Malloy, and Luis A. Abugattas. "Business and the 'Boys': The Politics of Neoliberalism in the Central Andes." *Latin American Research Review* 25, no. 2 (1990): 3–30.

CONAIE. "Proyecto de constitución del estado plurinacional del Ecuador." Quito: Imprenta Nuestra Amazonía, 1997.

CONAIE. "Proyecto político de la CONAIE." Confederación de Nacionalidades Indígenas del Ecuador, 1994. https://www.scribd.com/document/292576751/Proyecto -politico-de-la-CONAIE-1994.

CONAIE. "Resoluciones de la Asamblea Extraordinaria de las Nacionalidades y Pueblos Indígenas del Ecuador." Confederación de Nacionalidades Indígenas del Ecuador, 2008. http://upsidedownworld.org/noticias-en-espa/noticias-en-espa-noticias-en -espa/ecuador-conaie-rompe-relaciones-con-correa/.

Conde, Marta, and Philippe Le Billon. "Why Do Some Communities Resist Mining Projects While Others Do Not?" *Extractive Industries and Society* 4, no. 3 (2017): 681–97.

Coronil, Fernando. *The Magical State: Nature, Money, and Modernity in Venezuela.* Chicago: University of Chicago Press, 1997.

Correa, Rafael. "Ecuador's Path: Interview." *New Left Review* 77 (2012): 88–112.

Costanza, Jennifer N. "Indigenous Peoples' Right to Prior Consultation: Transforming Human Rights From the Grassroots in Guatemala." *Journal of Human Rights* 14, no. 2 (2015): 260–85.

Cypher, James Martín. "South America's Commodities Boom: Developmental Opportunity or Path Dependent Reversion?" *Canadian Journal of Development Studies* 30, nos. 3/4 (2010): 565–638.

Cypher, James M., and Tamar Diana Wilson. "China and Latin America: Processes and Paradoxes." *Latin American Perspectives* 42, no. 6 (November 2015): 5–26.

De, Rohit. *A People's Constitution: The Everyday Life of Law in the Indian Republic*. Princeton: Princeton University Press, 2018.

De Echave, José. "La minería peruana y los escenarios de transición." In *Transiciones: post extractivismo y alternativas al extractivismo en el Perú*, edited by Alejandra Alayza and Eduardo Gudynas, 61–85. Lima: Centro Peruano de Estudios Sociales, 2012.

De la Cadena, Marisol. "Indigenous Cosmopolitics in the Andes: Conceptual Reflections beyond 'Politics.'" *Cultural Anthropology* 25, no. 2 (2010): 334–70.

De la Torre, Carlos and Catherine Conaghan. "The Hybrid Campaign: Tradition and Modernity in Ecuador's 2006 Presidential Election." *International Journal of Press and Politics* 14, no. 3 (2009): 335–52.

Deonandan, Kalowatie, and Michael L. Dougherty, eds. *Mining in Latin America: Critical Approaches to the New Extraction*. New York: Routledge, 2016.

Derrida, Jacques. *Of Grammatology*, translated by Gayatri Chakravorty Spivak. Baltimore: Johns Hopkins University Press, 1998.

Dietrich, Christopher R. W. *Oil Revolution: Anticolonial Elites, Sovereign Rights, and the Economic Culture of Decolonization*. Cambridge: Cambridge University Press, 2017.

Dunning, Thad. *Crude Democracy: Natural Resource Wealth and Political Regimes*. Cambridge: Cambridge University Press, 2008.

Dussel, Enrique. *Twenty Theses on Politics*. Durham, NC: Duke University Press, 2008.

Escobar, Arturo. "Latin America at a Crossroads: Alternative Modernizations, Post-Liberalism, or Post-Development?" *Cultural Studies* 24, no. 1 (2010): 1–65.

Escobar, Arturo. "Worlds and Knowledges Otherwise 1: The Latin American Modernity/Coloniality Research Program." *Cultural Studies* 21, nos. 2/3 (2007): 179–210.

Falleti, Tulia G., and Thea N. Riofrancos. "Endogenous Participation: Prior Consultation in Extractive Economies." *World Politics* 70, no. 1 (2018): 86–121.

Farthing, Linda. "The Left in Power." *Jacobin* 25 (2017): 78–83.

Farthing, Linda. "An Opportunity Squandered? Elites, Social Movements, and the Government of Evo Morales." *Latin American Perspectives* 46, no. 1 (2019): 212–29.

Ferguson, James. *The Anti-Politics Machine: Development, Depoliticization, and Bureaucratic Power in Lesotho*. Minneapolis: University of Minnesota Press, 1994.

Ferguson, James. "The Uses of Neoliberalism." *Antipode* 41, no. 1 (2010): 166–84.

Ferguson, James, and Akhil Gupta. "Spatializing States: Toward an Ethnography of Neoliberal Governmentality." *American Ethnologist* 29, no. 4 (2002): 981–1002.

Flew, Terry. "Six Theories of Neoliberalism." *Thesis Eleven* 122, no. 1 (2014): 49–71.

Fligstein, Neil, and Doug McAdam. "Toward a General Theory of Strategic Action Fields." *Sociological Theory* 29, no. 1 (2011): 1–26.

Flores-Macías, Gustavo A. "Statist vs. Pro-Market: Explaining Leftist Governments' Economic Policies in Latin America." *Comparative Politics* 42, no. 4 (2010): 413–33.

Fontaine, Guillaume. *Petróleo y desarrollo sostenible en Ecuador: reglas del juego*, Vol. 1. Quito: FLACSO/Petroecuador, 2003.

Fontaine, Guillaume. *El precio del petróleo: conflictos socio-ambientales y gobernabilidad en la región Amazónica*. Quito: Abya Yala, 2007.

Foucault, Michel. "Nietzsche, Genealogy, History." In *Language, Counter-Memory, Practice: Selected Essays and Interviews,* edited by D. F. Bouchard, 139–64. Ithaca, NY: Cornell University Press, 1977.

Foucault, Michel. "The Order of Discourse." In *Untying the Text: A Post-Structuralist Reader,* edited by Robert Young, 48–78. New York: Routledge, 1981.

Foucault, Michel. "Politics and the Study of Discourse." In *The Foucault Effect: Studies in Governmentality,* edited by Graham Burchell, Colin Gordon, and Peter Miller, 53–86. Chicago: University of Chicago Press, 1991.

Foucault, Michel. *Security, Territory, Population: Lectures at the College de France, 1977–78,* translated by Graham Burchell. New York: Palgrave Macmillan, 2005.

Frank, Andre Gunder. *Lumpen-Bourgeoisie and Lumpen-Development: Dependency, Class, and Politics in Latin America.* New York: Monthly Review Press, 1972.

Frank, Jason. *Constituent Moments: Enacting the People in Postrevolutionary America.* Durham, NC: Duke University Press, 2010.

Fung, Archon. "Reinventing Democracy in Latin America." *Perspectives on Politics* 9, no. 4 (2011): 857–71.

Gago, Veronica. "Financialization of Popular Life and the Extractive Operations of Capital: A Perspective from Argentina." *South Atlantic Quarterly* 114, no. 1 (2015): 11–28.

Gago, Veronica. *Neoliberalism from Below: Popular Pragmatics and Baroque Economies.* Durham, NC: Duke University Press, 2017.

Gallagher, Kevin, Amos Irwin, and Katherine Koleski. "The New Banks in Town: Chinese Finance in Latin America." *Inter-American Dialogue Report* (March 2012). https://www.thedialogue.org/wp-content/uploads/2012/02/NewBanks _FULLTEXT.pdf.

Garavini, Giuliano. "Completing Decolonization: The 1973 'Oil Shock' and the Struggle for Economic Rights." *International History Review* 33, no. 3 (2011): 473–87.

García-Guadila, María Pilar. "The Incorporation of Popular Sectors and Social Movements in Venezuelan Twenty-First Century Socialism." In *Reshaping the Political Arena in Latin America: From Resisting Neoliberalism to the Second Incorporation,* edited by Eduardo Silva and Federico Rossi, 129–56. Pittsburgh, PA: University of Pittsburgh Press, 2018.

García Linera, Álvaro. "Geopolitics of the Amazon: Landed-Hereditary Power and Capitalist Accumulation," translated by Richard Fidler, 2012. https:// climateandcapitalism.com/wp-content/uploads/2013/01/Geopolitics-of-the -Amazon-8xii.pdf.

Getachew, Adom. *Worldmaking after Empire: The Rise and Fall of Self-Determination.* Princeton, NJ: Princeton University Press, 2019.

Ghandi, Abbas, and C.-Y. Cynthia Lin. "Oil and Gas Service Contracts around the World: A Review." *Energy Strategy Reviews* 3 (2014): 63–71.

Glaeser, Andreas. "An Ontology for the Ethnographic Analysis of Social Processes: Extending the Extended-Case Method." *Social Analysis* 49, no. 3 (2005): 16–45.

Glaeser, Andreas. *Political Epistemics: The Secret Police, the Opposition, and the End of East German Socialism.* Chicago: University of Chicago Press, 2010.

Gledhill, John. "The Persistent Imaginary of 'the People's Oil': Nationalism, Globalisation and the Possibility of Another Country in Brazil, Mexico and Venezuela." In *Crude Domination: An Anthropology of Oil*, edited by Andrea Behrends, Stephen P. Reyna, and Günther Schlee, 165–89. Oxford: Berghahn Books, 2011.

Goffman, Erving. *Forms of Talk*. Philadelphia: University of Pennsylvania Press, 1981.

Golub, Alex. *Leviathans at the Gold Mine: Creating Indigenous and Corporate Actors in Papua New Guinea*. Durham, NC: Duke University Press, 2014.

Gordon, Cynthia, and James M. Jasper. "Overcoming the 'NIMBY' label: Rhetorical and Organizational Links for Local Protestors." *Research in Social Movements, Conflict and Change* 19, no. 2 (1996): 159–81.

Gotkowitz, Laura. "Under the Dominion of the Indian: Rural Mobilization, the Law, and Revolutionary Nationalism in Bolivia in the 1940s." In *Political Cultures in the Andes, 1750–1950*, edited by Nils Jacobsen and Cristóbal Aljovín de Losada, 233–67. Durham, NC: Duke University Press, 2005.

Gramsci, Antonio. *The Prison Notebooks*, 11th ed. New York: International Publishers, 1992.

Green-Barber, Lindsay. "The Ecuadorian State and ICTs." Paper presented at the annual meeting of the Asociación Latinoamericana de Ciencia Política, Quito, June 12–14, 2012.

Gudynas, Eduardo. "Diez tesis urgentes sobre el nuevo extractivismo." In *Extractivismo, política y sociedad*, edited by Centro Andino de Acción Popular, 187–225. Quito: CAAP, 2009.

Gudynas, Eduardo. "Extractivisms: Tendencies and Consequences." In *Reframing Latin American Development*, edited by Ronaldo Munck and Raul Delgado Wise, 61–76. London: Routledge, 2018.

Gudynas, Eduardo. "Natural Resource Nationalisms and the Compensatory State in Progressive South America." In *The Political Economy of Natural Resources and Development: From Neoliberalism to Resource Nationalism*, edited by Paul A. Haslam and Pablo Heidrich, 103–17. New York: Routledge, 2016.

Gudynas, Eduardo. "Si eres tan progresista ¿por qué destruyes la naturaleza? Neoextractivismo, izquierda y alternativas." *Ecuador Debate* 79 (2010): 61–81.

Gudynas, Eduardo. "Transitions to Post-Extractivism: Directions, Options, Areas of Action." In: *Beyond Development. Alternative visions from Latin America*, edited by Miriam Lang and Duani Mokrani, 165–88. Amsterdam: Transnational Institute, 2013.

Gudynas, Eduardo. "Value, Growth, Development: South American Lessons for a New Ecopolitics." *Capitalism, Nature, Socialism* 30, no. 2 (2019): 234–43.

Gustafson, Bret, and Natalia Guzmán Solano. "Mining Movements and Political Horizons in the Andes." In *Mining in Latin America: Critical Approaches to the New Extraction*, edited by Kalowatie Deonandan and Michael L. Dougherty, 143–61. New York: Routledge, 2016.

Haarstad, Håvard, and Arnt Fløysand. "Globalization and the Power of Rescaled Narratives: A Case of Opposition to Mining in Tambogrande, Peru." *Political Geography* 26, no. 3 (2007): 289–308.

Haber, Stephen, and Victor Menaldo. "Do Natural Resources Fuel Authoritarianism? A Reappraisal of the Resource Curse." *American Political Science Review* 105, no. 1 (2011): 1–26.

Harbers, Imke. "Taxation and the Unequal Reach of the State: Mapping State Capacity in Ecuador." *Governance* 28, no. 3 (2015): 373–91.

Harvey, David. *A Brief History of Neoliberalism*. Oxford: Oxford University Press, 2007.

Haslam, Paul A., and Pablo Heidrich. "From Neoliberalism to Resource Nationalism: States, Firms and Development." In *The Political Economy of Natural Resources and Development: From Neoliberalism to Resource Nationalism*, edited by Paul A. Haslam and Pablo Heidrich, 1–32. New York: Routledge, 2016.

Haslam, Paul A., and Pablo Heidrich, eds. *The Political Economy of Natural Resources and Development: From Neoliberalism to Resource Nationalism*. New York: Routledge, 2016.

Haslam, Paul Alexander, and Nasser Ary Tanimoune. "The Determinants of Social Conflict in the Latin American Mining Sector: New Evidence with Quantitative Data." *World Development* 78 (2016): 401–19.

Hetherington, Kregg. *Guerrilla Auditors: The Politics of Transparency in Neoliberal Paraguay*. Durham, NC: Duke University Press, 2011.

Hetland, Gabriel. "The Crooked Line: From Populist Mobilization to Participatory Democracy in Chávez-Era Venezuela." *Qualitative Sociology* 37, no. 4 (2014): 373–401.

Hey, Jeanne, and Thomas Klak. "From Protectionism to Neoliberalism: Ecuador across Four Administrations (1981–1996)." *Studies in Comparative International Development* 34, no. 3 (1999): 66–97.

Hindery, Derrick. *From Enron to Evo: Pipeline Politics, Global Environmentalism, and Indigenous Rights in Bolivia*. Tucson: University of Arizona Press, 2013.

Hogenboom, Barbara. "Depoliticized and Repoliticized Minerals in Latin America." *Journal of Developing Societies* 28, no. 2 (2012): 133–58.

Hollender, Rebecca. "Post-Growth in the Global South: The Emergence of Alternatives to Development in Latin America." *Socialism and Democracy* 29, no. 1 (2015): 73–101.

Huber, Matthew T. *Lifeblood: Oil, Freedom, and the Forces of Capital*. Minneapolis: University of Minnesota Press, 2013.

Humphreys Bebbington, Denise. "Consultation, Compensation and Conflict: Natural Gas Extraction in Weekhayek Territory, Bolivia." *Journal of Latin American Geography* 11, no. 2 (2012): 49–71.

Iturralde, Pablo. *El negocio invisible de la salud: análisis de la acumulación de capital en el sistema de salud Ecuador*. Quito: Centro de Derechos Económicos y Sociales, 2014.

James, Daniel. *Resistance and Integration: Peronism and the Argentine Working Class, 1946–1976*. Cambridge: Cambridge University Press, 1993.

Jameson, Fredric. *A Singular Modernity: Essay on the Ontology of the Present*. London: Verso, 2002.

Jessop, Bob. *Nicos Poulantzas: Marxist Theory and Political Strategy*. London: Macmillan, 1985.

Kalyvas, Andreas. "Popular Sovereignty, Democracy, and the Constituent Power." *Constellations* 12, no. 2 (2005): 223–44.

Karl, Terry Lynn. *The Paradox of Plenty: Oil Booms and Petro-States*. Berkeley: University of California Press, 1997.

Kaup, Brent Z. "A Neoliberal Nationalization? The Constraints on Natural-Gas-Led Development in Bolivia." *Latin American Perspectives* 37, no. 3 (2010): 123-38.

Kirsch, Stuart. *Mining Capitalism: The Relationship between Corporations and Their Critics*. Berkeley: University of California Press, 2014.

Klein, Naomi. *This Changes Everything: Capitalism vs. the Climate*. New York: Simon and Schuster, 2014.

Kohl, Benjamin, and Linda Farthing. "Material Constraints to Popular Imaginaries: The Extractive Economy and Resource Nationalism in Bolivia." *Political Geography* 31 (2012): 225-35.

Kramer, Larry. *The People Themselves: Popular Constitutionalism and Judicial Review*. Oxford: Oxford University Press, 2005.

Kuecker, Glen. "Fighting for the Forests Revisited: Grassroots Resistance to Mining in Northern Ecuador." In *Latin American Social Movements in the Twenty-First Century: Resistance, Power and Democracy*, edited by Richard Stahler-Sholk, Harry E. Vanden, and Glen David Kuecker, 97-112. Lanham, MD: Rowman and Littlefield, 2008.

Kurtz, Marcus J. *Latin American State Building in Comparative Perspective: Social Foundations of Institutional Order*. Cambridge: Cambridge University Press, 2013.

Kurtz, Marcus J. "The Social Foundations of Institutional Order: Reconsidering War and the 'Resource Curse' in Third World State Building." *Politics and Society* 37, no. 4 (2009): 479-520.

Larrea, Carlos, and Natalia Greene. "De la lucha contra la probreza a la superación de la codicia." In *La osadía de lo nuevo: alternativas de política económica*, edited by Miriam Lang, Belén Cevallos, and Claudia López, 11-60. Quito: Abya-Yala, 2015.

Larrea, Carlos, and Liisa North. "Ecuador: Adjustment Policy Impacts on Truncated Development and Democratisation." *Third World Quarterly* 18, no. 5 (1997): 913-34.

Latorre, Sara. "El ecologismo popular en el Ecuador: pasado y presente." Instituto de Estudios Ecuatorianos, 2009. https://www.iee.org.ec/ejes/sociedad-alternativa-2/el-ecologismo-popular-en-el-ecuador-pasado-y-presente.html.

Latorre, Sara, Katharine N. Farrell, and Joan Martínez-Alier. "The Commodification of Nature and Socio-Environmental Resistance in Ecuador: An Inventory of Accumulation by Dispossession Cases, 1980-2013." *Ecological Economics* 116 (2015): 58-69.

Latorre, Sara, and Alejandra Santillana. "Capitalismo estatal o convergencias populares." *Íconos: Revista de Ciencias Sociales* 34 (2009): 13-18.

Latour, Bruno. *Reassembling the Social: An Introduction to Actor-Network-Theory*. Oxford: Oxford University Press, 2007.

Levitsky, Steven, and Kenneth M. Roberts. "Introduction: Latin America's 'Left Turn': A Framework for Analysis." In *The Resurgence of the Latin American Left*, edited by Steven Levitsky and Kenneth M. Roberts, 1-30. Baltimore: Johns Hopkins University Press, 2011.

Li, Fabiana. *Unearthing Conflict: Corporate Mining, Activism, and Expertise in Peru*. Durham, NC: Duke University Press, 2015.

Li, Tania Murray. "Beyond 'the State' and Failed Schemes." *American Anthropologist* 107, no. 3 (2005): 383–94.

Li, Tania Murray. *The Will to Improve: Governmentality, Development, and the Practice of Politics*. Durham, NC: Duke University Press, 2007.

Löwy, Michael. "Marxists and the National Question." *New Left Review* 96 (1976): 81–100.

Lucero, José Antonio. "Locating the 'Indian Problem': Community, Nationality, and Contradiction in Ecuadorian Indigenous Politics." *Latin American Perspectives* 30, no. 1 (2003): 23–48.

Luong, Pauline Jones, and Erika Weinthal. *Oil Is Not a Curse: Ownership Structure and Institutions in Soviet Successor States*. Cambridge: Cambridge University Press, 2010.

Luong, Pauline Jones, and Erika Weinthal. "Rethinking the Resource Curse: Ownership Structure, Institutional Capacity, and Domestic Constraints." *Annual Review of Political Science* 9 (2006): 241–63.

Mahdavy, Hussein. "The Patterns and Problems of Economic Development in Rentier States: The Case of Iran." In *Studies in the Economic History of the Middle East*, edited by M. A. Cook, 428–67. London: Oxford University Press, 1970.

Mähler, Annegret, and Jan Pierskalla. "Indigenous Identity, Natural Resources, and Contentious Politics in Bolivia: A Disaggregated Conflict Analysis, 2000–2011." *Comparative Political Studies* 48, no. 3 (2015): 301–32.

Malm, Andreas. *Fossil Capital: The Rise of Steam Power and the Roots of Global Warming*. London: Verso, 2016.

Manin, Bernard. *The Principles of Representative Government*. Cambridge: Cambridge University Press, 1997.

Martínez Alier, Joan. "El ecologismo popular." *Revista Ecosistemas* 16, no. 3 (2007): 148–51.

Martínez Novo, Carmen. "The Backlash against Indigenous Rights in Ecuador's Citizen's Revolution." In *Latin America's Multicultural Movements: The Struggle between Communitarianism, Autonomy and Human Rights*, edited by Todd A. Eisenstadt, Michael S. Danielson, Moises Jaime Balon Corres, and Carlos Sorroza Polo, 111–32. Oxford: Oxford University Press, 2013.

Martz, John. *Politics and Petroleum in Ecuador*. Piscataway, NJ: Transaction Publishers, 1987.

Marx, Karl. *The German Ideology*. New York: Prometheus Books, 1988 [1846].

Mateo, Juan Pablo, and Santiago García. "El sector petrolero en Ecuador, 2000–2010." *Problemas del Desarrollo* 45, no. 177 (2014): 113–39.

McAdam, Doug, and Hilary Boudet. *Putting Social Movements in Their Place: Explaining Opposition to Energy Projects in the United States, 2000–2005*. Cambridge: Cambridge University Press, 2012.

McGee, Brant. "Community Referendum: Participatory Democracy and the Right to Free, Prior and Informed Consent to Development." *Berkeley Journal of International Law* 27 (2009): 570–635.

Mignolo, Walter. *The Darker Side of Western Modernity: Global Futures, Decolonial Options*. Durham, NC: Duke University Press, 2011.

Mijeski, Kenneth J., and Scott H. Beck. *Pachakutik and the Rise and Decline of the Ecuadorian Indigenous Movement*. Athens: Ohio University Press, 2011.

Miliband, Ralph. "The Coup in Chile." *Socialist Register* 10, no. 10 (1973): 451–74.

Miliband, Ralph. *The State in Capitalist Society*. London: Merlin Press, 2009.

Ministerio de Recursos Norenovables. "Plan nacional de desarrollo del sector minero, 2011–2015." Quito: Ministerio de Recursos Norenovables, 2011.

Mitchell, Timothy. *Carbon Democracy: Political Power in the Age of Oil*. London: Verso, 2011.

Mitchell, Timothy. *Rule of Experts: Egypt, Techno-Politics, Modernity*. Berkeley: University of California Press, 2002.

Moore, Jennifer, and Teresa Velásquez. "Water for Gold: Confronting State and Corporate Mining Discourses in Azuay, Ecuador." In *Subterranean Struggles: New Dynamics of Mining, Oil, and Gas in Latin America*, edited by Anthony Bebbington and Jeffrey Bury, 119–48. Austin: University of Texas Press, 2013.

Mouffe, Chantal. *The Democratic Paradox*. London: Verso, 2000.

Munck, Ronaldo, and Raul Delgado Wise. "Introduction: Framing the Debate." In *Reframing Latin American Development*, edited by Ronaldo Munck and Raul Delgado Wise, 1–7. London: Routledge, 2018.

Munck, Ronaldo, and Raul Delgado Wise, eds. *Reframing Latin American Development*. London: Routledge, 2018.

Nakassis, Constantine V. "Materiality, Materialization." *Hau: Journal of Ethnographic Theory* 3, no. 3 (2013): 399–406.

Nash, June C. *We Eat the Mines and the Mines Eat Us: Dependency and Exploitation in Bolivian Tin Mines*. New York: Columbia University Press, 1979.

Nelson, Maggie. *The Argonauts*. Minneapolis, MN: Graywolf Press, 2015.

Nem Singh, Jewellord T. "Who Owns the Minerals? Repoliticizing Neoliberal Governance in Brazil and Chile." *Journal of Developing Societies* 28, no. 2 (2012): 229–56.

O'Donnell, Guillermo. "Toward an Alternative Conceptualization of South American Politics." In *Promise of Development: Theories of Change in Latin America*, edited by Peter F. Klarén and Thomas J. Bossert, 239–75. Boulder, CO: Westview Press, 1986.

Ordóñez, Andrea, Emma Samman, Chiara Mariotti, and Iván Marcelo Borja Borja. "Sharing the Fruits of Progress: Poverty Reduction in Ecuador." London: Overseas Development Institute, 2015.

Parenti, Christian. *Tropic of Chaos: Climate Change and the New Geography of Violence*. New York: Nation Books, 2011.

Peña, Karla. "Social Movements, the State, and the Making of Food Sovereignty in Ecuador." *Latin American Perspectives* 43, no. 1 (2016): 221–37.

Pérez Ordóñez, Pilar. "El Presidente Rafael Correa y su política de redención." Quito: FLACSO, 2010.

Perreault, Tom. "Assessing the Limits of Neoliberal Environmental Governance in Bolivia." In *Beyond Neoliberalism in Latin America? Societies and Politics at the Crossroads*, edited by John Burdick, Philip Oxhorn, and Kenneth M. Roberts, 135–56. New York: Palgrave Macmillan, 2009.

Perreault, Tom. "Political Contradictions of Extractive Development." Paper presented at the annual meeting of the Latin American Studies Association, Barcelona, May 25, 2018.

Perreault, Tom. "Tendencies in Tension: Resource Governance and Social Contradictions in Contemporary Bolivia." In *Governance in the Extractive Industries*, edited by Lori Leonard and Siba N. Grovogui, 17–38. London: Routledge, 2017.

Perreault, Tom, and Gabriela Valdivia. "Hydrocarbons, Popular Protest and National Imaginaries: Ecuador and Bolivia in Comparative Context." *Geoforum* 41, no. 5 (2010): 689–99.

Petras, James, and Henry Veltmeyer. "Trade and Development in an Era of Extractive Imperialism." In *Extractive Imperialism in the Americas*, edited by James Petras and Henry Veltmeyer, 101–27. Leiden: Brill, 2014.

Piñeiro, Rafael, Matthew Rhodes-Purdy, and Fernando Rosenblatt. "The Engagement Curve: Populism and Political Engagement in Latin America." *Latin American Research Review* 51, no. 4 (2016): 3–23.

Polanyi, Karl. *The Great Transformation: The Political and Economic Origins of Our Time.* Boston: Beacon Press, 1944.

Ponce, Juan, and Rob Vos. "Redistribution without Structural Change in Ecuador: Rising and Falling Income Inequality in the 1990s and 2000s." Working Paper, United Nations University World Institute for Development Economics Research, 2012. https://www.wider.unu.edu/publication/redistribution-without-structural-change-ecuador.

Poulantzas, Nicos. *State, Power, Socialism*. London: Verso, 2000.

Prebisch, Raúl. "Crecimiento desequilibrio y disparidades: interpretación del proceso de desarrollo económico." *Estudio Económico de América Latina* 164, no. 1 (1950): 3–89.

Ramírez Gallegos, Franklin. "Fragmentación, reflujo y desconcierto: movimientos sociales y cambio político en el Ecuador (2000–2010)." *Observatorio Social de América Latina* 6, no. 28 (2010): 18–47.

Ramírez Gallegos, René. "Socialismo del Sumak Kawsay o biosocialismo republicano." In *Socialismo y Sumak Kawsay: los nuevos retos de América Latina,* edited by SENPLADES, 55–76. Quito: SENPLADES, 2010.

Rancière, Jacques. *Disagreement: Politics and Philosophy*. Minneapolis: University of Minnesota Press, 2004.

Rancière, Jacques. "Who Is the Subject of the Rights of Man?" *South Atlantic Quarterly* 103, nos. 2/3 (2004): 297–310.

Riofrancos, Thea. "Discursive Institutionalization: Theory and Method." Paper presented at the annual meeting of the American Political Science Association, Philadelphia, September 1, 2016.

Riofrancos, Thea. "Ecuador after Correa." *n+1* no. 29 (2017). https://nplusonemag.com/issue-29/politics/ecuador-after-correa-2/.

Riofrancos, Thea. "Scaling Democracy: Participation and Resource Extraction in Latin America." *Perspectives on Politics* 15, no. 3 (2017): 678–96.

Rodríguez-Garavito, César A. "Ethnicity.Gov: Global Governance, Indigenous Peoples, and the Right to Prior Consultation in Social Minefields." *Indiana Journal of Global Legal Studies* 18, no. 1 (2011): 263–305.

Rojas, Rene. "The Latin American Left's Shifting Tides." *Catalyst* 2, no. 2 (2018): 7–71.

Rosales, Antulio. "Going Underground: The Political Economy of the 'Left Turn' in South America." *Third World Quarterly* 34, no. 8 (2013): 1443–57.

Roseberry, William. "Hegemony and the Language of Contention." In *Everyday Forms of State Formation: Revolution and the Negotiation of Rule in Modern Mexico*, edited by Gilbert M. Joseph and Daniel Nugent, 355–66. Durham, NC: Duke University Press, 1994.

Ross, Michael. "Does Oil Hinder Democracy?" *World Politics* 53 (2001): 325–61.

Ross, Michael. *The Oil Curse: How Petroleum Wealth Shapes the Development of Nations.* Princeton, NJ: Princeton University Press, 2012.

Ruiz Acosta, Miguel, and Pablo Iturralde. *La alquimía de la riqueza: estado, petroleo y patrón de acumulación en Ecuador*. Quito: Centro de Derechos Económicos y Sociales, 2013.

Sacher, William, and Alberto Acosta. *La minería a gran escala en Ecuador: análisis y datos estadísticos sobre la minería industrial en el Ecuador*. Quito: Abya Yala, 2012.

Santos, Boaventura de Sousa, and Leonardo Avritzer. "Introduction: Opening up the Canon of Democracy." In *Democratizing Democracy: Beyond the Liberal Democratic Canon*, edited by Boaventura de Sousa Santos, vii–xxxiii. London: Verso, 2005.

Sarat, Austin, and Thomas Kearns. "Beyond the Great Divide: Forms of Legal Scholarship and Everyday Life." In *Law in Everyday Life*, edited by Austin Sarat and Thomas Kearns, 21–61. Ann Arbor: University of Michigan Press, 1993.

Sawyer, Suzana. *Crude Chronicles: Indigenous Politics, Multinational Oil, and Neoliberalism in Ecuador*. Durham, NC: Duke University Press, 2004.

Schatz, Edward, ed. *Political Ethnography: What Immersion Contributes to the Study of Power*. Chicago: University of Chicago Press, 2009.

Scheppele, Kim L. "Constitutional Ethnography: An Introduction." *Law and Society Review* 38, no. 3 (2004): 389–406.

Schmidt, Vivien A. "Discursive Institutionalism: The Explanatory Power of Ideas and Discourse." *Annual Review of Political Science* 11 (2008): 303–26.

Schmitt, Carl. *The Concept of the Political*. Chicago: University of Chicago Press, 2007.

Scott, James C. *Seeing Like a State: How Certain Schemes to Improve the Human Condition Have Failed*. New Haven, CT: Yale University Press, 1999.

Searle, John R. *Speech Acts: An Essay in the Philosophy of Language*. Cambridge: Cambridge University Press, 1969.

SENPLADES. "El plan nacional de buen vivir 2009–2013." Secretaría Técnica Planifica Ecuador, 2009. http://www.planificacion.gob.ec/plan-nacional-para-el-buen-vivir -2009-2013/.

Shapiro, Ian, and Casiano Hacker-Cordón, eds. *Democracy's Edges*. Cambridge: Cambridge University Press, 1999.

Sharma, Aradhana, and Akhil Gupta. "Introduction: Rethinking Theories of the State in an Age of Globalization." In *The Anthropology of the State: A Reader*, edited by Aradhana Sharma and Akhil Gupta, 1–41. Malden, MA: Blackwell Publishing, 2006.

Shever, Elana. *Resources for Reform: Oil and Neoliberalism in Argentina*. Stanford, CA: Stanford University Press, 2012.

Sieder, Rachel. "Legal Cultures in the (Un)Rule of Law: Indigenous Rights and Juridification in Guatemala." *Cultures of Legality: Judicialization and Political Activism in Latin America*, edited by Javier Couso, Alexander Huneeus, and Rachel Sieder, 161–81. New York: Cambridge University Press, 2010.

Sikkink, Kathryn. *Ideas and Institutions: Developmentalism in Brazil and Argentina*. Ithaca, NY: Cornell University Press, 1991.

Silva, Eduardo. *Challenging Neoliberalism in Latin America*. New York: Cambridge University Press, 2009.

Silva, Eduardo. "Exchange Rising? Karl Polanyi and Contentious Politics in Contemporary Latin America." *Latin American Politics and Society* 54, no. 3 (2012): 1–32.

Silva, Eduardo, and Federico Rossi, eds. *Reshaping the Political Arena in Latin America: From Resisting Neoliberalism to the Second Incorporation*. Pittsburgh, PA: University of Pittsburgh Press, 2018.

Silverstein, Michael. "Metapragmatic Discourse and Metapragmatic Function." In *Reflexive Language: Reported Speech and Metapragmatics*, edited by John A. Lucy, 33–58. Cambridge: Cambridge University Press, 1993.

Sinnot, Emily, John Nash, and Augusto de la Torre. "Natural Resources in Latin America and the Caribbean: Beyond Booms and Busts?" World Bank Latin American and Caribbean Studies. Washington, DC: World Bank, 2010.

Slack, Keith. "Digging Out from Neoliberalism: Responses to Environmental (Mis)Governance of the Mining Sector in Latin America." In *Beyond Neoliberalism in Latin America? Societies and Politics at the Crossroads*, edited by John Burdick, Philip Oxhorn, and Kenneth M. Roberts, 117–33. New York: Palgrave Macmillan, 2009.

Slobodian, Quinn. *Globalists: The End of Empire and the Birth of Neoliberalism*. Cambridge, MA: Harvard University Press, 2018.

Smith, Benjamin. *Hard Times in the Lands of Plenty: Oil Politics in Iran and Indonesia*. Ithaca, NY: Cornell University Press, 2007.

Smith, Benjamin. "Resource Wealth and Political Regimes: How Solid a Link after Forty Years of Research?" *APSA Comparative Democratization Newsletter* 11, no. 2 (2004): 17–20.

Smulovitz, Catalina, and Enrique Peruzzotti. "Societal Accountability in Latin America." *Journal of Democracy* 11, no. 4 (2000): 147–58.

Spalding, Rose J. "From the Streets to the Chamber: Social Movements and the Mining Ban in El Salvador." *European Review of Latin American and Caribbean Studies* 106 (2018): 47–74.

Spalding, Rose J. "Transnational Networks and National Action: El Salvador's Antimining Movement." In *Transnational Activism and National Movements in Latin America*, edited by Eduardo Silva, 39–71. London: Routledge, 2013.

SPMSPC. "Caracterización de conflictos socio-ambientales: proyectos estratégicos." Quito: Secretaría de Pueblos, Movimientos Sociales y Participación Ciudadana, 2010.

Spronk, Susan, and Jorge León Trujillo. "Socialism without Workers? Trade Unions and the New Left in Bolivia and Ecuador." In *Reshaping the Political Arena in Latin America: From Resisting Neoliberalism to the Second Incorporation*, edited by Eduardo Silva and Federico Rossi, 129–56. Pittsburgh, PA: University of Pittsburgh Press, 2018.

Steinberg, Marc W. "The Talk and Back Talk of Collective Action: A Dialogic Analysis of Repertoires of Discourse among Nineteenth-Century English Cotton Spinners." *American Journal of Sociology* 105, no. 3 (1999): 736–80.

Stern, Rachel E., and Kevin J. O'Brien. "Politics at the Boundary: Mixed Signals and the Chinese State." *Modern China* 38, no. 2 (2012): 174–98.

Stern, Steve J. "Feudalism, Capitalism, and the World-System in the Perspective of Latin America and the Caribbean." *American Historical Review* 93, no. 4 (1988): 829–72.

Svampa, Maristella. "Commodities Consensus: Neoextractivism and Enclosure of the Commons in Latin America." *South Atlantic Quarterly* 114, no. 1 (2015): 65–82.

Svampa, Maristella. *Debates Latinoamericanos: indianismo, desarrollo, dependencia, populismo*. Cochabamba: Centro de Documentación e Información Bolivia, 2016.

Tarlau, Rebecca. *Occupying Schools, Occupying Land: How the Landless Workers Movement Transformed Brazilian Education*. Oxford: Oxford University Press, 2019.

Therborn, Goran. *What Does the Ruling Class Do When It Rules?* London: Verso, 1978.

Tockman, Jason, and John Cameron. "Indigenous Autonomy and the Contradictions of Plurinationalism in Bolivia." *Latin American Politics and Society* 56, no. 3 (2014): 46–69.

Unger, Roberto Mangabeira. *Democracy Realized: The Progressive Alternative*. London: Verso, 1998.

Urkidi, Leire. "The Defence of Community in the Anti-Mining Movement of Guatemala." *Journal of Agrarian Change* 11, no. 4 (2011): 556–80.

Valdivia, Gabriela. "Governing Relations between People and Things: Citizenship, Territory and the Political Economy of Petroleum in Ecuador." *Political Geography* 27, no. 4 (2008): 456–77.

Van Cott, Donna. "Ecuador Ratifies ILO Convention 169." *Native Americas* 2, no. 11 (June 30, 1998).

Veltmeyer, Henry. "The Political Economy of Natural Resource Extraction: A New Model or Extractive Imperialism?" *Canadian Journal of Development Studies* 34, no. 1 (2013): 79–95.

Veltmeyer, Henry, and James Petras, eds. *The New Extractivism: A Post-Neoliberal Development Model of Imperialism of the Twenty-First Century?* London: Zed Books, 2014.

Wacquant, Loïc. *Punishing the Poor: The Neoliberal Government of Social Insecurity*. Durham, NC: Duke University Press, 2009.

Walter, Mariana, and Leire Urkidi. "Community Mining Consultations in Latin America (2002–2012): The Contested Emergence of a Hybrid Institution for Participation." *Geoforum* 84 (2017): 265–79.

Warner, Michael. *Publics and Counterpublics*. New York: Zone Books, 2005.

Watts, Michael. "Resource Curse? Governmentality, Oil and Power in the Niger Delta, Nigeria." *Geopolitics* 9, no. 1 (2004): 50–80.

Watts, Michael. "Righteous Oil? Human Rights, the Oil Complex, and Corporate Social Responsibility." *Annual Review of Environmental Resources* 30 (2005): 373–407.

Webber, Jeffery R. "The Retreat of the Pink Tide in Latin America." *International Socialist Review* 110 (2018). https://isreview.org/issue/110/retreat-pink-tide-latin -america.

Webber, Jeffery R. "Revolution against 'Progress': Neo-Extractivism, the Compensatory State, and the TIPNIS Conflict in Bolivia." In *Crisis and Contradiction: Marxist Perspectives on Latin America in the Global Political Economy*, edited by Susan Spronk and Jeffery R. Webber, 302–34. Leiden: Brill, 2014.

Wedeen, Lisa. *Ambiguities of Domination: Politics, Rhetoric, and Symbols in Contemporary Syria*. Chicago: University of Chicago Press, 1999.

Wedeen, Lisa. *Peripheral Visions: Publics, Power, and Performance in Yemen*. Chicago: University of Chicago Press, 2008.

Wedeen, Lisa. "Reflections on Ethnographic Work in Political Science." *Annual Review of Political Science* 13 (2010): 255–72.

Weisbrot, Mark, Jake Johnston, and Lara Merling. "Decade of Reform: Ecuador's Macroeconomic Policies, Institutional Changes, and Results." Washington, DC: Center for Economic and Policy Research, 2017.

Welzer, Harald. *Climate Wars: What People Will Be Killed for in the Twenty-First Century*. Hoboken, NJ: Wiley, 2015.

Weyland, Kurt. "The Rise of Latin America's Two Lefts: Insights from Rentier State Theory." *Comparative Politics* 41, no. 2 (2009): 145–64.

Widener, Patricia. "Global Links and Environmental Flows: Oil Disputes in Ecuador." *Global Environmental Politics* 9, no. 1 (2009): 31–57.

Wolff, Jonas. "Towards Post-Liberal Democracy in Latin America? A Conceptual Framework Applied to Bolivia." *Journal of Latin American Studies* 45, no. 1 (2013): 31–59.

Wolin, Sheldon. "Fugitive Democracy." *Constellations* 1, no. 1 (1994): 11–25.

Woo-Cumings, Meredith, ed. *The Developmental State*. Ithaca, NY: Cornell University Press, 1999.

Wuthnow, Robert. *Communities of Discourse: Ideology and Social Structure in the Reformation, the Enlightenment, and European Socialism*. Cambridge, MA: Harvard University Press, 1993.

Yashar, Deborah. *Contesting Citizenship in Latin America: The Rise of Indigenous Movements and the Postliberal Challenge*. Cambridge: Cambridge University Press, 2005.

Zaiden Benvindo, Juliano. "The Seeds of Change: Popular Protest as Constitutional Moments." *Marquette Law Review* 99, no. 2 (2015): 363–426.

Zeisberg, Mariah. *War Powers: The Politics of Constitutional Authority*. Princeton, NJ: Princeton University Press, 2013.

Zibechi, Raúl. *Dispersing Power: Social Movements as Anti-State Forces*. Chico, CA: AK Press, 2010.

Zimmerer, Karl S. "The Indigenous Andean Concept of Kawsay, the Politics of Knowledge and Development, and the Borderlands of Environmental Sustainability in Latin America." *PMLA* 127, no. 3 (2012): 600–606.

INDEX

Italicized pages locate illustrations

CONFENIAE (Confederación de Nacionalidades Indígenas de la Amazonía
Ecuatoriana), 35–38, 43, 47, 58–61
Consortium of Social Organizations of
El Pangui, 103–4
Constituent Assembly (1997–98), 44, 85
Constituent Assembly (2007–8): origin
of, 80–82; and prior consultation, 96,
213n3; and resource extraction, 51–54,
74, 77–78, 113
Constituent Mandate Number Six
(2008), 52–54. *See also* Mining Mandate
(2008)
constituent politics, 78–81, 87, 109, 113
constituent power, 78–81, 95, 99, 109, 113,
118–26, 137, 205n3
Constitution (1998), 44, 82–86, 98, 115,
210n66
Constitution (2008): and *buen vivir*, 87,
178; contradictory nature of, 77–79,
88–96, 113, 169; and prior consultation, 95–96, 98, 105, 115; and resource
extraction, 27, 51–54
Constitutional Court, 101–2
consultations. *See* prior consultation
Contento, Luis, 91
"Conversation: Mining in Ecuador"
(Cuenca, 2012), 142–44
Coordinating Ministry of Patrimony, 66
Cordero, Fernando, 100–101
CORDES (Corporación de Estudios para
el Desarrollo), 44
Cordova, Carlos Alberto, 146–47,
204n38
Cornerstone Capital Resources, 108–10,
142–45, 153–54, 157–58
Correa, Rafael, 45; and anti-extractive
opposition, 26–27, 54, 71–73, 148,
164, 169; and Constituent Assembly
(2007–8), 80; election of (2006), 50–51,
74; on information, 149–50, 161; and
prior consultation, 84, 112, 115, 126–35;
and resource extraction, 1–2, 27, 30,
50–51, 69–73, 82–83; and social debt,

10; and socialism, 2, 182; and social
spending, 170–72
Correa administration: and anti-
extractivist opposition, 11–12, 26–27,
39, 62–73; and grassroots empowerment, 170; and infrastructure spending, 171–72; and neoliberalism, 39, 66;
and prior consultation, 84, 96–102;
and resource extraction, 9, 11–12, 15, 39,
58; and resource nationalism, 15, 39,
189n62; and social spending, 170–72
Cunambi, Enrique, 47

debt peonage, 33
de la Cadena, Marisol, 163
dependency theory, 54, 67, 165, 174–75
Derrida, Jacques, 210n65
developmentalism: and Correa government, 4, 6, 8–12, 16, 82, 95, 175, 217n10;
and Pink Tide governments, 165, 169;
and Rodríguez Lara government, 17,
39, 57, 67, 73, 169; and Western civilization, 57, 61
día de resistencia de los pueblos, El (2005),
48–49
Dietz, Kristina, 190n67
dollars, 60, 171
Dunning, Thad, 23
Durán-Ballén, Sixto, 41–42
Dussel, Enrique, 117

ecological debt, 76
ecológismo popular. See environmental
movements
ECORAE (Instituto para el Ecodesarrollo
Regional Amazónico), 68, 135
ecotourism, 47, 75
ECSA (Ecuacorrientes S.A.), 12, 68, 102–3,
145
Ecuador Estratégico, 134
"Ecuador's Path" (Correa), 1
Ecuarunari (Ecuador Runacana-pac
Riccharimui), 18–19, 34–38, 50, 54–56,
89, 118

Hetherington, Kregg, 80
Hidalgo, Alicia, 111, 114, 150
historical institutionalist theory, 192n94
huasipungo system, 33–34
Hurtado, Osvaldo, 39–40, 44
Hydrocarbons Law (1971), 8, 42
Hydrocarbons Law (1982), 40

Iamgold mining company, 118, 134, 157, 159
ICSID (International Center for Settlement of Investment Disputes), 199n100
ILO Convention 169 (Indigenous and Tribal Peoples Convention, 1989), 83, 94, 96, 102, 115, 120, 124, 207n30, 209n51, 211n90. *See also* prior consultation
IMF (International Monetary Fund), 40, 46, 180
"In defense of sovereignty, natural resources, and national dignity" protest (2006), 49
Indigenous and Tribal Peoples Convention (1989). *See* ILO Convention 169
Indigenous-Campesino Alliance of Pastaza Province, 43
information, 18–19, 102, 105–12, 128–29, 138–63, 210n71, 215n34
Inter-American Court of Human Rights, 128, 201n132, 207n32
INV Metals, 118
Isch, Edgar, 49, 202n2
Iturralde, Pablo, 29–30

Jacombe, Lorena, 65–66
Jameson, Fredric, 166
Junín Mine (Intag Valley), 188n39

Kalyvas, Andreas, 205n3
Kichwa: emergence of organizations among, 34–36, 41; language of, 78, 195n18, 214n16, 224n62; and resource extraction, 47, 157, 207n32
Kimsacocha, 214n16. *See also* Quimsacocha gold mine

Kinross, 11, 59, 146
Kipu (annual publication), 25
Kohl, Benjamin, 14

land redistribution, 33, 36, 42, 80
Lasso, Guillermo, 173
Latour, Bruno, 57
Law of Environmental Management (1999), 210n66
levantamientos (1990, 1992, 1994, 1997–98), 36–38, 82, 94
Ley de organización y regimen de comunas (1937), 33–34
Ley de reforma agraria y colonización (1964), 33
López Obrador, Andrés Manuel, 166, 183
Lowell Mineral Exploration Ecuador S.A., 146, 204n38
Lucero, José Antonio, 36

Macas, Luis, 50
Macri, Mauricio, 165
Mahler, Garland, 185n11
Mahuad, Jamil, 44
Marak, Andrae, 188n40
March for Water, Life, and the Dignity of Peoples (2012), 18–19, 25, 54–56, 60–62, 61–62, 88–93, 89–93, 129–30
Martínez, Esperanza, 200n107, 207n22
Martínez Alier, Joan, 186n19
Marx, Karl, 191n81
Marxism, 61, 195n30. *See also* socialism
"Meeting of Social Movements for Democracy and Life" (Quito, 2011), 1–2
Mejia, Oscar, 104, 111–12
Melo, Mario, 55–56
Mera, Alexis, 101
mestizaje assimilationism, 36
middle-class identity, 171
Minería Muerte, 60–61
minga, 124
mining: Iamgold mining company, 118, 134, 157, 159; Junín Mine (Intag Valley), 188n39; Kinross, 11, 59, 146; Mirador

"Plan nacional de desarrollo del sector minero" (Ministry of Nonrenewable Resources), 70
"Plan nacional para el buen vivir" (SENPLADES), 67, 70
Plan of Life (Sarayaku Association), 47
plurinational state: Constituent Assembly (2007–8) and, 49, 78, 85; Constitution (2008) and, 81–82, 88, 169; Correa administration and, 66, 104; popular movements and, 35–37, 39, 41–44, 54, 60, 75, 82, 92; and prior consultation, 96, 117, 122
Polanyi, Karl, 41, 220n64
político, 120, 148, 215n41
Ponce, Juan, 10, 188n46
Popular Democratic Party, 40
popular sectors, 42, 46, 75, 167, 169–71, 179–81, 186n21
post-extractive society, 12–16, 30, 66–67, 75, 176–78. *See also* anti-extractivism
post-neoliberalism. *See* neoliberalism
price cycles, 3, 171
prior consultation: and Constituent Assembly (1997–98), 85; and Constituent Assembly (2007–8), 78, 83–87, 96, 213n3; and Constitution (1998), 83–84, 115, 210n66; and Constitution (2008), 95–96, 105, 115; and Correa administration, 84–87, 96–102, 104–8, 110–14, 128–35; ILO Convention 169 (Indigenous and Tribal Peoples Convention, 1989), 83, 94, 96, 102, 115, 120, 124, 209n51, 211n90; and Law of Environmental Management (1999), 210n66; throughout Latin America, 115–18, 179–80, 182, 213n1; and Mirador copper mine, 102–4, 106–8, 112; and national interests, 84–87, 128–35, 211n86; and prior consent, 83–86, 96, 213n3; and Quimsacocha gold mine, 27, 115, 117–37, *121*, *123*, *125*; and Water Law, 93–95
problematic, 19, 22, 191n84
pueblos and *naciones*, 36–38, 54, 99, 154

Quimsacocha gold mine, 27, 75, 115, 117–37, 142
Quishpe, Salvador, 68, 88, 90, 94–95, 134, 155, 157
Quizhpe, Marcelo, 156

recession (2015), 10
RED (Red Ética y Democracia), 53
Renner, Karl, 196n30
rentier states, 3, 23–24, 171–72
resource curse, 23–24, 172
resource dependency, 3–5, 23, 28, 65, 70, 203n34. *See also* commodity boom
resource governance, 6–16, 21–22, 40, 51, 73, 134
resource nationalism: and Correa government, 9–12, 15, 18, 74, 169–70, 189n62; and neoliberalism, 38–50, 73; and Pink Tide governments, 10–12, 175; and popular movements, 5–6, 73–74, 168–70; radical resource nationalism, 3, 6, 13–18, 21–22, 26, 31–32, 38–54, 74–75; and Rodríguez Lara government, 9, 17, 73; and Velasco Ibarra government, 8
resource radicalisms: concept of, 3–6, 13; confrontation of, 52, 73–76; and leftist electoral successes, 12–16; origin of, 18, 21, 26. *See also* anti-extractivism; resource nationalism
rights of nature, 1, 25, 78, 81, 88, 104
Rodríguez Lara, Guillermo, 8–9, 17, 33–34, 73, 187n28, 194n14
Roldós, Jaime, 196n44
Roldós, Martha, 53
Román, Marcelo, 46
Rousseff, Dilma, 165
Ruales, Mario, 150

Sacher, William, 155–56, 219n47
Salesian Catholic missionaries, 35. *See also* Catholic Church
San Carlos copper mining project, 9, 73, 164